Taste of Home

Make it!

TAKE IT

TASTE OF HOME BOOKS • RDA ENTHUSIAST BRANDS, LLC • MILWAUKEE, WI

PAGE 50

PAGE 83

PAGE 119

PAGE 16

CONTENTS

PAGE 146

PAGE 201

PAGE 191

PAGE 252

Visit us at **tasteofhome.com** for other
Taste of Home books and products.

Executive Editor: Mark Hagen
Senior Art Director: Raeann Thompson
Editor: Christine Rukavena
Art Director: Maggie Conners
Designer: Arielle Jardine
Senior Editor, Copy Desk: Dulcie Shoener
Contributing Copy Editor: Deb Warlaumont Mulvey

Cover:
Photographer: Mark Derse
Set Stylist: Melissa Franco
Food Stylist: Shannon Roum

Pictured on front cover:
Strawberry Pretzel Dessert, p. 208

Pictured on title page:
Polenta Chili Casserole, p. 78

Pictured on back cover:
Grandmother's Orange Salad, p. 117
Chicken Sliders with Sesame Slaw, p. 180
Spinach-Orzo Salad with Chickpeas, p. 102
Stuffing & Turkey Casserole, p. 80

International Standard Book Numbers:
D 978-1-61765-984-3
U 978-1-61765-985-0
International Standard Serial Number:
2166-0522
Component Numbers:
D 118100100H
U 118100102H

Printed in Malaysia
1 3 5 7 9 10 8 6 4 2

More ways to connect with us:

Good cooks know that memorable get-togethers don't just happen. They're the result of thorough planning, choosing the dishes folks love, and many hands chipping in to make light work and great fun for all.

This edition of *Make It, Take It* is brimming with awesome dishes, planning tips and entertaining ideas.

Make the most of your reunions, potlucks, office parties and more with the sage advice and incomparable recipes of *Taste of Home*.

Here you'll find 261 crowd-pleasing recipes. And watch for these useful features throughout the book.

EASIER THAN EVER: The No-Cook Recipe Rescue chapter offers dozens of last-minute dishes ready in a flash, no cooking required.

MAKE AHEAD dishes let you do most of the work ahead and pop the dish in the fridge or freezer for simple serving on a moment's notice. Aren't you smart?

BRING IT
Watch for these tips throughout the book. Find great insights for organizing the buffet, keeping foods hot or cold, and making sure your dish is the star of the get-together.

PACK LIKE A PRO
These tips and tricks will have you hitting the road with confidence.

1 **Build a DIY Multi-Level Tote**
If you have more dishes than hands, reach for a cooling rack with folding legs. Fold out the legs and use the rack to create sturdy, stable levels inside a carrying tote without crushing what's below. Get creative. You can also build layers by propping up a sheet pan with ring molds or cans.

2 **Ensure a No-Slip Trip**
Place grippy drawer liners or silicone baking mats in the car before loading your food. The lining will keep dishes from sliding and contain any errant spills. An old yoga mat works well for this, too.

3 **Keep a Lid on It**
Use a bungee cord, painter's tape or thick ribbon to keep the lid for your slow cooker or Dutch oven in place. Secure the cord around the handles and over the top. Now you're ready to transport without risk of a mess.

4 **Bring a Salad**
Yes, you can serve a crisp, freshly tossed salad when you're far from home. Just bring the fixings in a serving bowl, along with the utensils. Toss the salad at your destination. Voila! Remember to bring a grocery bag to corral the leftovers and dirties.

5 **Frosting Is Good Glue**
If you're transporting cake to a special event, make it easier to tote with this little tip. Secure the cake (or cardboard cake circle, if you're using one) onto the presentation plate with a dab of frosting. This makes the cake less likely to slide around, even if you have to brake suddenly. And you're the only one who'll know the frosting is there!

6 **Pack a Touch-Up Kit**
Make a little touch-up kit of decorations and frosting (just in case) to bring with your decorated cake. Pack the items with a clean dish towel and offset spatula. Bring the frosting in its pastry bag if you used one.

7 **Tailgate Grill Skills**
Place the grill on a solid surface, away from any activities so no one bumps into it. Don't set the grill near shrubs, grass, overhangs or fences. Keep coolers away from the grill. Set the cooler out of direct sunlight and replenish the ice if possible.

8 **Tailgate Kit**
Store all your tailgate needs (such as linens, serveware, games and sunblock) in a plastic bin inside a cooler. You'll be ready to go at a moment's notice.

Sweet Sausage Rolls
page 9

Appetizers & Dips

Everyone loves a good party…and this chapter has the perfect bites for your next celebration. From hot, creamy dips to cool cucumber canapes, you'll find it all here.

WATERMELON CUPS

This lovely appetizer is almost too pretty to eat! Sweet watermelon cubes hold a refreshing topping that showcases cucumber, red onion and fresh herbs.
—*Taste of Home* Test Kitchen

Takes: 25 min. • **Makes:** 16 appetizers

16	seedless watermelon cubes (1 in.)
⅓	cup finely chopped cucumber
5	tsp. finely chopped red onion
2	tsp. minced fresh mint
2	tsp. minced fresh cilantro
½	to 1 tsp. lime juice

1. Using a small melon baller or measuring spoon, scoop out the center of each watermelon cube, leaving a ¼-in. shell (save pulp for another use).
2. In a small bowl, combine the remaining ingredients; spoon into watermelon cubes.
1 piece: 7 cal., 0 fat (0 sat. fat), 0 chol., 1mg sod., 2g carb. (2g sugars, 0 fiber), 0 pro.

SWEET SAUSAGE ROLLS

Refrigerated dough makes these appetizers a snap to prepare, smoked sausage gives them a smoky heat, and honey and brown sugar give them an appealing sweetness. Add it all up, and you have savory finger food that is downright addicting!
—Lori Cabuno, Canfield, OH

- -

Prep: 25 min. • **Bake:** 15 min.
Makes: 2 dozen

1 tube (8 oz.) refrigerated
   crescent rolls
24 miniature smoked sausage links
½ cup butter, melted
½ cup chopped nuts
3 Tbsp. honey
3 Tbsp. brown sugar

1. Unroll crescent dough and separate into triangles; cut each lengthwise into 3 triangles. Place sausages on wide end of triangles; roll up tightly.
2. Combine the remaining ingredients in an 11x7-in. baking dish. Arrange sausage rolls, seam side down, in butter mixture. Bake, uncovered, at 400° for 15-20 minutes or until golden brown.

1 appetizer: 128 cal., 10g fat (4g sat. fat), 16mg chol., 194mg sod., 8g carb. (5g sugars, 0 fiber), 2g pro.

MARINATED CHEESE

This special appetizer always makes it to our neighborhood parties and is the first to disappear at the buffet table. It's attractive, delicious—and so easy!
—Laurie Casper, Coraopolis, PA

Prep: 30 min. + marinating
Makes: about 2 lbs.

- 2 blocks (8 oz. each) white cheddar cheese
- 2 pkg. (8 oz. each) cream cheese
- ¾ cup chopped roasted sweet red peppers
- ½ cup olive oil
- ¼ cup white wine vinegar
- ¼ cup balsamic vinegar
- 3 Tbsp. chopped green onions
- 3 Tbsp. minced fresh parsley
- 2 Tbsp. minced fresh basil
- 1 Tbsp. sugar
- 3 garlic cloves, minced
- ½ tsp. salt
- ½ tsp. pepper
  Assorted crackers or toasted sliced French bread

1. Slice each block of cheddar cheese into twenty ¼-in. slices. Cut each block of cream cheese into 18 slices. Create four 6-in.-long blocks of stacked cheeses, sandwiching 9 cream cheese slices between 10 cheddar slices for each stack. Place in a 13x9-in. dish.
2. In a small bowl, combine the roasted peppers, oil, vinegars, onions, herbs, sugar, garlic, salt and pepper; pour over cheese stacks.
3. Cover and refrigerate overnight, turning cheese blocks once. Drain excess marinade. Serve with crackers or toasted bread.
1 oz.: 121 cal., 11g fat (6g sat. fat), 30mg chol., 153mg sod., 1g carb. (0 sugars, 0 fiber), 5g pro.

APRICOT KIELBASA SLICES

These satisfying sausage bites are coated in a thick, zesty sauce with just the right amount of sweetness. You'll love 'em!
—Barbara McCalley, Allison Park, PA

Takes: 15 min. • **Makes:** 12 servings

- 1 lb. fully cooked kielbasa or Polish sausage, cut into ¼-in. slices
- 1 jar (12 oz.) apricot preserves
- 2 Tbsp. lemon juice
- 2 tsp. Dijon mustard
- ¼ tsp. ground ginger

1. In a large cast-iron or other heavy skillet, cook and stir sausage until browned. Remove from pan; discard drippings.
2. Add remaining ingredients to skillet; cook and stir over low heat until heated through, 2-3 minutes. Stir in sausage; heat through.
4 slices: 47 cal., 3g fat (1g sat. fat), 6mg chol., 110mg sod., 5g carb. (4g sugars, 0 fiber), 1g pro.

CHICKEN BACON TRIANGLES

We host an annual Christmas party, and I whip up a new menu item every year. These golden hors d'oeuvres were an absolute hit.
—Annette Fecht, Sorrento, BC

Prep: 60 min. + chilling • **Bake:** 15 min.
Makes: 4 dozen

½	lb. bacon strips, chopped
¾	lb. boneless skinless chicken breasts, cubed
½	cup condensed cream of mushroom soup, undiluted
4	oz. cream cheese, cubed
2	garlic cloves, minced
1½	tsp. dried minced onion
⅛	tsp. pepper
1	cup shredded part-skim mozzarella cheese
½	cup shredded Parmesan cheese
24	sheets phyllo dough, 14x9 in.
¼	cup butter, melted Ranch dip, optional

1. In a large skillet, cook bacon over medium heat until crisp. Remove to paper towels with a slotted spoon; drain, reserving drippings. Saute chicken in drippings until no longer pink; drain.

2. Add the soup, cream cheese, garlic, onion, pepper and bacon to skillet; cook and stir until blended. Remove from the heat. Stir in mozzarella and Parmesan cheeses; cool slightly. Cover and refrigerate for at least 2 hours.

3. Lightly brush 1 sheet of phyllo dough with butter; place another sheet of phyllo on top and brush with butter. (Keep the remaining phyllo covered with a damp towel to prevent it from drying out.) Cut into four 14x2¼-in. strips.

4. Place a scant Tbsp. of filling on lower corner of each strip. Fold dough over filling, forming a triangle. Fold triangle up, then fold triangle over, forming another triangle. Continue folding, like a flag, until you come to the end of the strip. Brush end of dough with butter and press onto triangle to seal. Repeat with remaining strips of dough and with remaining sheets of phyllo.

5. Place triangles on a greased baking sheet. Bake at 375° for 15-17 minutes or until golden brown. If desired, serve with ranch.

Freeze option: Freeze unbaked triangles on baking sheets. When frozen, transfer to resealable freezer containers. Bake frozen triangles for 18-22 minutes or until golden brown.

1 appetizer: 70 cal., 5 g fat (2 g sat. fat), 13mg chol., 121mg sod., 4g carb., trace fiber, 3g pro.

TOUCHDOWN BRAT SLIDERS

It's game time when these minis make an appearance. Two things my husband loves—beer and brats—get stepped up a notch with these cute sandwiches.
—Kirsten Shabaz, Lakeville, MN

Takes: 50 min. • **Makes:** 16 sliders

- 5 thick-sliced bacon strips, chopped
- 1 lb. uncooked bratwurst links, casings removed
- 1 large onion, finely chopped
- 2 garlic cloves, minced
- 1 pkg. (8 oz.) cream cheese, cubed
- 1 cup dark beer or nonalcoholic beer
- 1 Tbsp. Dijon mustard
- ¼ tsp. pepper
- 16 dinner rolls, split and toasted
- 2 cups cheddar and sour cream potato chips, crushed

1. In a large cast-iron or other heavy skillet, cook bacon over medium heat until crisp. Remove to paper towels with a slotted spoon; drain, reserving drippings. Cook bratwurst and onion in drippings over medium heat, breaking into crumbles until meat is no longer pink. Add garlic; cook 1 minute longer. Drain well.

2. Stir in the cream cheese, beer, mustard and pepper. Bring to a boil. Reduce heat; simmer, uncovered, until thickened, for 15-20 minutes, stirring occasionally. Stir in bacon. Spoon ¼ cup onto each roll; sprinkle with chips. Replace tops.

1 slider: 354 cal., 24g fat (10g sat. fat), 62mg chol., 617mg sod., 23g carb. (2g sugars, 2g fiber), 10g pro.

SPINACH-ARTICHOKE STUFFED MUSHROOMS

Guests will think you fussed over these rich, creamy stuffed mushrooms, but they go together so easily. The flavorful artichoke filling makes this party appetizer something special.
—Amy Gaisford, Salt Lake City, UT

- -

Prep: 20 min. • **Bake:** 20 min.
Makes: about 2½ dozen

- 3 oz. cream cheese, softened
- ½ cup mayonnaise
- ½ cup sour cream
- ¾ tsp. garlic salt
- 1 can (14 oz.) water-packed artichoke hearts, rinsed, drained and chopped
- 1 pkg. (10 oz.) frozen chopped spinach, thawed and squeezed dry
- ⅓ cup shredded part-skim mozzarella cheese
- 3 Tbsp. shredded Parmesan cheese
- 30 to 35 large fresh mushrooms, stems removed
  Additional shredded Parmesan cheese

1. Preheat oven to 400°. Mix the first 4 ingredients. Stir in artichoke hearts, spinach, mozzarella cheese and 3 Tbsp. Parmesan cheese.

2. Place mushrooms on foil-lined baking sheets, stem side up. Spoon about 1 Tbsp. filling into each. If desired, top with additional Parmesan cheese. Bake until mushrooms are tender, 16-20 minutes.

1 stuffed mushroom: 51 cal., s 4g fat (1g sat. fat), 4mg chol., 116mg sod., 2g carb. (0 sugars, 0 fiber), 2g pro.

So Easy Stuffed Mushrooms: Omit first 8 ingredients. Mix 1 pkg. (6½ oz.) garlic-herb spreadable cheese and 2 Tbsp. Parmesan cheese. Fill mushroom caps; sprinkle tops with 1 Tbsp. Parmesan cheese. Reduce baking time to 10-12 minutes.

Sausage-Stuffed Mushrooms: Omit first 8 ingredients. Finely chop mushroom stems. Cook ½ lb. bulk sausage and the chopped mushrooms over medium heat until meat is no longer pink; drain. Remove from heat; stir in ½ cup shredded mozzarella cheese and ¼ cup seasoned bread crumbs. Fill and bake as recipe directs.

Canadian Bacon-Stuffed Mushrooms: Omit first 8 ingredients. Finely chop mushroom stems. Cook mushrooms, ¼ lb. diced Canadian bacon, ⅓ cup chopped sweet red pepper, ¼ cup chopped red onion, ½ tsp. salt and ½ tsp. pepper in 2 Tbsp. canola oil until vegetables are crisp-tender. Add 1 minced garlic clove; cook 1 minute. Remove from heat; stir in ½ cup crumbled goat or feta cheese and ½ cup shredded cheddar cheese. Fill mushrooms and bake as recipe directs.

TZATZIKI SHRIMP CUCUMBER ROUNDS

I created this recipe with what I had on hand one night, and now it's one of my husband's favorites! The bacon-wrapped shrimp, garlicky sauce and burst of cool cuke flavor make these irresistible.
—Shannon Trelease, East Hampton, NY

Prep: 25 min. • **Cook:** 10 min./batch
Makes: 2 dozen

- ¼ cup reduced-fat plain yogurt
- 2 Tbsp. finely chopped peeled cucumber
- ⅛ tsp. garlic salt
- ⅛ tsp. dill weed
- 6 bacon strips
- 24 uncooked shrimp (31-40 per lb.), peeled and deveined
- 1 to 2 Tbsp. canola oil
- 2 medium cucumbers, cut into ¼-in. slices

1. In a small bowl, combine the yogurt, chopped cucumber, garlic salt and dill weed; set aside.
2. Cut each bacon strip in half widthwise and then lengthwise. Wrap a piece of bacon around each shrimp. Secure bacon with toothpicks.
3. In a large nonstick skillet, heat oil over medium heat; cook shrimp in batches for 3-4 minutes on each side or until bacon is crisp.
4. Spoon a rounded ½ tsp. yogurt sauce onto each cucumber slice; top with shrimp.
1 appetizer: 30 cal., 2g fat (0 sat. fat), 18mg chol., 64mg sod., 1g carb. (0 sugars, 0 fiber), 3g pro.

PEPPER MANGO SALSA

The idea for a homemade mango salsa hit me after I saw a chef on TV make something similar. It sounded so good, and it wasn't something I could find in a store at the time. The salsa is especially tasty served with artisan chips—the black bean and roasted garlic ones are my favorite. When strawberries are in season, I add them to the mix, too. Whenever I take this to a party, I come home with an empty bowl.
—Wendy Rusch, Cameron, WI

Prep: 15 min. + chilling • **Makes:** 6 cups

- 3 Tbsp. lime juice
- 3 Tbsp. honey
- 1 tsp. olive oil
  Dash salt
  Dash coarsely ground pepper
- 3 medium mangoes, peeled and finely chopped
- 2 cups finely chopped fresh pineapple
- 1 large sweet red pepper, finely chopped
- 1 Anaheim or poblano pepper, seeded and finely chopped
- ½ cup finely chopped red onion
- ¼ cup chopped fresh cilantro
  Tortilla chips

1. Whisk together first 5 ingredients. In a large bowl, combine fruit, peppers, onion and cilantro; toss with lime juice mixture.
2. Refrigerate, covered, 1 hour to allow flavors to blend. Stir before serving. Serve with chips.
¼ cup: 47 cal., 0 fat (0 sat. fat), 0 chol., 63mg sod., 11g carb. (10g sugars, 1g fiber), 1g pro.
Diabetic exchanges: ½ starch.

SPANAKOPITA PINWHEELS

I'm enthralled with spanakopita, and this spinach and feta pinwheel recipe was a quick and easy way to enjoy it. I have used the recipe for teacher get-togethers and family events.
—Ryan Palmer, Windham, ME

Prep: 30 min. + cooling • **Bake:** 20 min.
Makes: 2 dozen

- 1 medium onion, finely chopped
- 2 Tbsp. olive oil
- 1 tsp. dried oregano
- 1 garlic clove, minced
- 2 pkg. (10 oz. each) frozen chopped spinach, thawed and squeezed dry
- 2 cups (8 oz.) crumbled feta cheese
- 2 large eggs, lightly beaten
- 1 pkg. (17.3 oz.) frozen puff pastry, thawed

1. In a small skillet, saute onion in oil until tender. Add oregano and garlic; cook 1 minute longer. Add spinach; cook 3 minutes longer or until the liquid is evaporated. Transfer to a large bowl; cool.
2. Add feta cheese and eggs to spinach mixture; mix well. Unfold puff pastry. Spread each sheet with half the spinach mixture to within ½ in. of edges. Roll up jelly-roll style. Cut each into twelve ¾-in. slices. Place cut side down on greased baking sheets.
3. Bake at 400° for 18-22 minutes or until golden brown. Serve warm.
1 piece: 197 cal., 13g fat (5g sat. fat), 39mg chol., 392mg sod., 14g carb. (1g sugars, 3g fiber), 7g pro.

GINGER PORK LETTUCE WRAPS

When I make Asian-spiced lettuce wraps with lean ground pork, I remind my family they're meant to be an appetizer—but maybe I should just call it supper.
—Mary Kisinger, Medicine Hat, AB

Takes: 30 min. • **Makes:** 2 dozen

- 1   lb. lean ground pork
- 1   medium onion, chopped
- ¼   cup hoisin sauce
- 4   garlic cloves, minced
- 1   Tbsp. minced fresh gingerroot
- 1   Tbsp. red wine vinegar
- 1   Tbsp. reduced-sodium soy sauce
- 2   tsp. Thai chili sauce
- 1   can (8 oz.) sliced water chestnuts, drained and finely chopped
- 4   green onions, chopped
- 1   Tbsp. sesame oil
- 24 Bibb or Boston lettuce leaves

1. In a large skillet, cook pork and onion over medium heat 6-8 minutes or until the pork is no longer pink and onion is tender, breaking up pork into crumbles.

2. Stir in hoisin sauce, garlic, ginger, vinegar, soy sauce and chili sauce until blended. Add water chestnuts, green onions and oil; heat through. To serve, place pork mixture in lettuce leaves; fold lettuce over filling.

Freeze option: Freeze cooled meat mixture in freezer containers. To use, partially thaw in refrigerator overnight. Heat through in a saucepan, stirring occasionally and adding a little water if necessary.

1 filled lettuce wrap: 54 cal., 3g fat (1g sat. fat), 11mg chol., 87mg sod., 4g carb. (2g sugars, 1g fiber), 4g pro.

BEEF FLAUTAS

This traditional Mexican dish is one of my family's favorites. The spices and onion give the meat so much flavor!
—Maria Goclan, Katy, TX

- -

Prep: 1 hour 20 min. • **Cook:** 5 min./batch.
Makes: 20 flautas

2½ tsp. canola oil
2 lbs. fresh beef brisket
2 medium onions, chopped
2 medium green peppers, chopped
2 cups water
1 tsp. salt
1 tsp. dried oregano
1 tsp. dried marjoram
1 tsp. pepper
20 corn tortillas (6 in.), warmed
Oil for deep-fat frying

1. In a Dutch oven, heat oil over medium heat. Brown brisket on all sides. Add onions, peppers, water and seasonings. Bring to a boil. Reduce heat; simmer, covered, 1-1½ hours or until meat is tender.
2. Remove meat; cool slightly. Shred meat with 2 forks. Drain onion mixture; add to meat. Spoon ¼ cup beef mixture down the center of each tortilla. Roll up and secure with toothpicks. In a cast-iron or electric skillet, heat oil to 375°. Fry flautas, in batches, for 1 minute on each side or until golden brown.
3. Drain on paper towels. Remove and discard toothpicks.
1 flauta: 162 cal., 8g fat (1g sat. fat), 19mg chol., 145mg sod., 12g carb. (1g sugars, 2g fiber), 11g pro.

CURRIED CRAB SPREAD

At holiday time, I always have cream cheese and crabmeat on hand. In case of drop-ins, I just mix up an easy spread by adding mango chutney and spices.
—Jennifer Phillips, Goffstown, NH

- -

Takes: 30 min. • **Makes:** 24 servings

1 pkg. (8 oz.) cream cheese, softened
1 tsp. grated lemon zest
¾ tsp. curry powder
¼ tsp. salt
1 to 2 tsp. Sriracha chili sauce, optional
1 can (6 oz.) lump crabmeat, drained
1 Tbsp. canola oil
½ cup panko bread crumbs
¾ cup mango chutney
1 Tbsp. minced fresh cilantro or chives
Assorted crackers

1. In a small bowl, beat cream cheese, lemon zest, curry powder, salt and, if desired, chili sauce; gently fold in crab. Shape mixture into a disk; wrap in plastic. Refrigerate 15 minutes.
2. Meanwhile, in a large skillet, heat oil over medium heat. Add bread crumbs; cook and stir for 2-3 minutes or until golden brown. Transfer bread crumbs to a shallow bowl.
3. Unwrap disk and press all sides into bread crumbs; place on a serving plate. Spoon chutney over top; sprinkle with cilantro. Serve with crackers.
1 serving: 78 cal., 4g fat (2g sat. fat), 17mg chol., 188mg sod., 8g carb. (5g sugars, 0 fiber), 2g pro.

TEST KITCHEN TIP
Oregano comes in two types. The sweet Mediterranean one is often simply labeled oregano. It belongs to the mint family. Mexican oregano, a member of the verbena family, has a more intense flavor and citrusy notes.

CASHEW CHEESE

Spread this vegan cashew cheese on crackers or over a toasted bagel, or serve with fresh vegetables. It also makes a great sandwich topper!
—*Taste of Home* Test Kitchen

Prep: 1 hour + chilling • **Makes:** ¾ cup

- 1 **cup raw cashews**
- ⅓ **cup water**
- 2 **Tbsp. nutritional yeast**
- 2 **tsp. lemon juice**
- ½ **tsp. salt**
- ⅛ **tsp. garlic powder**

1. Place cashews in a small bowl. Add enough warm water to cover completely. Soak cashews for 1-2 hours; drain and discard water.
2. Add cashews and remaining ingredients to food processor. Cover and process until smooth, 1-2 minutes, scraping down sides occasionally. Transfer to serving dish. Cover and refrigerate cheese for at least 1 hour before serving.

1 Tbsp.: 56 cal., 4g fat (1g sat. fat), 0 chol., 101mg sod., 3g carb. (1g sugars, 0 fiber), 2g pro. **Diabetic exchanges:** 1 fat.

TEST KITCHEN TIP
Soaking the cashews is an important step to create a smooth and creamy texture. Add your favorite herbs and spices to create different flavors.

HONEY-GARLIC GLAZED MEATBALLS

My husband and I raise cattle on our farm here in southwestern Ontario, so it's no surprise that we enjoy hearty dishes like these saucy meatballs. I know your family will like them, too.
—Marion Foster, Kirkton, ON

Prep: 25 min. • **Bake:** 15 min.
Makes: 5½ dozen

- 2 **large eggs**
- ¾ **cup 2% milk**
- 1 **cup dry bread crumbs**
- ½ **cup finely chopped onion**
- 2 **tsp. salt**
- 2 **lbs. ground beef**
- 4 **garlic cloves, minced**
- 1 **Tbsp. butter**
- ¾ **cup ketchup**
- ½ **cup honey**
- 3 **Tbsp. soy sauce**

1. In a large bowl, combine eggs and milk. Add the bread crumbs, onion and salt. Crumble beef over mixture and mix well. Shape into 1-in. balls. Place on greased racks in shallow baking pans. Bake, uncovered, at 400° for 12-15 minutes or until meat is no longer pink.
2. Meanwhile, in a large saucepan, saute garlic in butter until tender. Stir in the ketchup, honey and soy sauce. Bring to a boil. Reduce heat; cover and simmer for 5 minutes. Drain meatballs; add to sauce. Carefully stir to coat. Cook mixture 5-10 minutes longer.

1 meatball: 48 cal., 2g fat (1g sat. fat), 15mg chol., 172mg sod., 4g carb. (3g sugars, 0 fiber), 3g pro.

SAUSAGE DIP

My warm sausage dip is a family favorite on cool fall days. Anyone with a hearty appetite will love digging into this country-style appetizer.
—Susie Wingert, Panama, IA

Takes: 30 min. • **Makes:** 6 cups

- 1½ lbs. bulk pork sausage
- 2½ cups chopped fresh mushrooms
- 2 medium green peppers, chopped
- 1 large tomato, seeded and chopped
- 1 medium red onion, chopped
- 1½ tsp. salt
- 1 tsp. pepper
- 1 tsp. garlic powder
- ½ tsp. onion powder
- 2 pkg. (8 oz. each) cream cheese, cubed
- 1 cup sour cream
  Tortilla chips

1. In a large skillet over medium heat, cook the sausage until no longer pink; drain. Add the next 8 ingredients; cook until the vegetables are tender.
2. Reduce heat to low; add cream cheese and sour cream. Cook and stir until cheese is melted and well blended (do not boil). Serve warm with tortilla chips.

2 Tbsp.: 59 cal., 5g fat (3g sat. fat), 13mg chol., 149mg sod., 1g carb. (1g sugars, 0 fiber), 2g pro.

BRING IT
Always bring your own serving utensils, even if the gathering is in someone's home. This is considerate because you're not assuming they will have something you might need. And it's less mess for your host. Also pack a plastic bag to tote home your dirty dishes.

MARINATED SHRIMP

My husband's aunt shared this recipe with me ages ago. Not only is it a Christmas Eve tradition in my home, but in the homes of our grown children as well.
—Delores Hill, Helena, MT

Prep: 10 min. + marinating • **Cook:** 10 min.
Makes: about 3 dozen

- 2 lbs. uncooked jumbo shrimp, peeled and deveined
- 1 cup olive oil
- 2 garlic cloves, minced
- 4 tsp. dried rosemary, crushed
- 2 tsp. dried oregano
- 2 bay leaves
- 1 cup dry white wine or chicken broth
- ¾ tsp. salt
- ⅛ tsp. pepper

1. In a bowl, combine the shrimp, oil, garlic, rosemary, oregano and bay leaves. Cover and refrigerate for 2-4 hours.
2. Pour shrimp and marinade into a large deep skillet. Add wine or broth, salt and pepper. Cover and cook over medium-low heat for 10-15 minutes or until shrimp turn pink, stirring occasionally. Discard bay leaves. Transfer with a slotted spoon to a serving dish.

1 piece: 40 cal., 2g fat (0 sat. fat), 31mg chol., 42mg sod., 0 carb. (0 sugars, 0 fiber), 4g pro.

HERB-ROASTED OLIVES & TOMATOES

Eat these roasted veggies with a crunchy baguette or a couple of cheeses. You can also double or triple the amounts and have leftovers to toss with spaghetti the next day.
—Anndrea Bailey, Huntington Beach, CA

- -

Takes: 25 min. • **Makes:** 4 cups

- 2 cups cherry tomatoes
- 1 cup garlic-stuffed olives
- 1 cup Greek olives
- 1 cup pitted ripe olives
- 8 garlic cloves, peeled
- 3 Tbsp. olive oil
- 1 Tbsp. herbes de Provence
- ¼ tsp. pepper

Preheat oven to 425°. Combine the first 5 ingredients on a greased 15x10x1-in. baking pan. Add oil and seasonings; toss to coat. Roast until tomatoes are softened, 15-20 minutes, stirring occasionally.

¼ cup: 71 cal., 7g fat (1g sat. fat), 0 chol., 380mg sod., 3g carb. (1g sugars, 1g fiber), 0 pro.

PUMPKIN HUMMUS

Traditional hummus gets an update for autumn with the addition of canned pumpkin. Hot pepper sauce lends just the right amount of heat.
—*Taste of Home* Test Kitchen

Takes: 15 min. • **Makes:** 4 cups

- 2 cans (15 oz. each) garbanzo beans or chickpeas, rinsed and drained
- 1 can (15 oz.) solid-pack pumpkin
- ½ cup olive oil
- ⅓ cup tahini
- 5 Tbsp. lemon juice
- 2 tsp. hot pepper sauce
- 2 garlic cloves, minced
- 1 tsp. salt
  Baked pita chips
  Assorted fresh vegetables, optional

Place the first 8 ingredients in a food processor; cover and process until blended. Serve with chips and, if desired, vegetables.
¼ cup: 173 cal., 13g fat (2g sat. fat), 0 chol., 243mg sod., 12g carb. (2g sugars, 4g fiber), 5g pro.

BAKED POT STICKERS WITH DIPPING SAUCE

Twisting these wontons like little candy wrappers makes them a snap to assemble, and the dipping sauce is packed with sweet heat.
—Taylor Marsh, Algona, IA

Prep: 30 min. • **Bake:** 15 min./batch
Makes: 4 dozen (¾ cup sauce)

- 2   cups finely chopped
      cooked chicken breast
- 1   can (8 oz.) water chestnuts,
      drained and chopped
- 4   green onions, thinly sliced
- ¼   cup shredded carrots
- ¼   cup reduced-fat mayonnaise
- 1   large egg white
- 1   Tbsp. reduced-sodium soy sauce
- 1   garlic clove, minced
- 1   tsp. grated fresh gingerroot
- 48 wonton wrappers
      Cooking spray

SAUCE
- ½   cup jalapeno pepper jelly
- ¼   cup rice vinegar
- 2   Tbsp. reduced-sodium soy sauce

1. Preheat oven to 425°. In a large bowl, combine the first 9 ingredients. Place 2 tsp. of filling in center of a wonton wrapper. (Cover rest of wrappers with a damp paper towel until ready to use.)
2. Moisten wrapper edges with water. Fold edge over filling and roll to form a log; twist ends to seal. Repeat with the remaining wrappers and filling.
3. Place pot stickers on a baking sheet coated with cooking spray; spritz each with cooking spray. Bake 12-15 minutes or until edges are golden brown.
4. Meanwhile, place pepper jelly in a small microwave-safe bowl; microwave, covered, on high until melted. Stir in vinegar and soy sauce. Serve sauce with pot stickers.
1 pot sticker with ¾ tsp. sauce: 52 cal., 1g fat (0 sat. fat), 6mg chol., 101mg sod., 8g carb. (2g sugars, 0 fiber), 3g pro.
Diabetic exchanges: ½ starch.

CHILI CHEESE SNACKS

I've been gathering recipes for more than 20 years and have accumulated quite a collection. These hand-held morsels are perfect for parties because they're easy to eat while walking around and mingling.
—Carol Nelson, Cool, CA

Takes: 30 min. • **Makes:** 80 appetizers

- 6 **oz. cream cheese, softened**
- 1 **cup shredded cheddar cheese**
- ¼ **cup chopped green chiles**
- ¼ **cup chopped ripe olives, drained**
- 2 **tsp. dried minced onion**
- ¼ **tsp. hot pepper sauce**
- 2 **tubes (8 oz. each) refrigerated crescent rolls**

1. In a small bowl, beat cream cheese. Add the cheddar cheese, chiles, olives, onion and hot pepper sauce. Separate each tube of crescent dough into 4 rectangles; press perforations to seal.

2. Spread cheese mixture over dough. Roll up jelly-roll style, starting with a long side. Cut each roll into 10 slices; place on greased baking sheets. Bake at 400° until golden brown, 8-10 minutes.

1 piece: 34 cal., 2g fat (1g sat. fat), 4mg chol., 63mg sod., 3g carb. (1g sugars, 0 fiber), 1g pro.

GREEN BEAN CASSEROLE STUFFED MUSHROOMS

Green bean casserole is a constant go-to for us, but it needed some updating. This bite-sized version gets fun reactions every time.
—Kaytie Pickett, Jackson, MS

- -

Prep: 20 min. • **Bake:** 20 min.
Makes: 2½ dozen

- 3 turkey bacon strips, diced
- 1½ tsp. minced garlic
- 1 can (14½ oz.) french-style green beans, drained
- ¾ cup grated Parmesan cheese, divided
- ¼ cup condensed cream of onion soup, undiluted
- ¼ cup water
- ⅛ tsp. ground nutmeg
- ⅛ tsp. pepper
- 1 cup dry bread crumbs
- 30 whole baby portobello mushrooms
  Cooking spray
- 1 can (2.8 oz.) french-fried onions

1. In a small skillet, cook bacon over medium heat until crisp. Add garlic; cook 1 minute longer. Place the green beans, ½ cup cheese, soup, water, nutmeg, pepper and bacon mixture in a food processor; process until blended. Transfer to a small bowl; fold in bread crumbs.

2. Remove stems from mushrooms; discard the stems or save for another use. Spritz mushroom caps with cooking spray; place in an ungreased 15x10x1-in. baking pan, stem side down. Bake at 425° for 10 minutes, turning once.

3. Drain liquid from caps; fill with green bean mixture. Top with remaining cheese and fried onions. Bake 8-10 minutes longer or until mushrooms are tender and filling is heated through.

Freeze option: After baking mushroom caps, drain and stuff mushrooms. Cool. Freeze on waxed paper-lined baking sheets until firm. Transfer to freezer containers; return to freezer. To use, bake mushrooms as directed, increasing time as necessary to heat through.

1 stuffed mushroom: 52 cal., 3g fat (1g sat. fat), 3mg chol., 157mg sod., 5g carb. (1g sugars, 1g fiber), 2g pro.

Lemon Pound
Cake Muffins
page 49

Breakfast for a Bunch

When these amazing dishes are on the menu, it's impossible not to rise and shine. Whether you're prepping for a brunch, fundraiser or shower, here are the foods you need.

PRESSURE-COOKER CARROT CAKE OATMEAL

This warm breakfast cereal made in the pressure cooker is a great way to get your veggies in the morning and keep a healthy diet! For extra crunch, I garnish individual servings with ground walnuts or pecans.
—Debbie Kain, Colorado Springs, CO

- -

Prep: 10 min. • **Cook:** 10 min. + releasing
Makes: 8 servings

- 4½ cups water
- 1 can (20 oz.) crushed pineapple, undrained
- 2 cups shredded carrots
- 1 cup steel-cut oats
- 1 cup raisins
- 2 tsp. ground cinnamon
- 1 tsp. pumpkin pie spice
  Brown sugar, optional

In a 6-qt. electric pressure cooker coated with cooking spray, combine the first 7 ingredients. Lock lid; make sure vent is closed. Select manual setting; adjust pressure to high, and set time for 10 minutes. When finished cooking, allow pressure to naturally release for 10 minutes, then quick-release any remaining pressure. If desired, sprinkle with brown sugar.

1 serving: 197 cal., 2g fat (0 sat. fat), 0 chol., 46mg sod., 46g carb. (26g sugars, 4g fiber), 4g pro.

SPARKLING PEACH BELLINIS

You will savor the subtle peach flavor in this elegant brunch beverage.
—*Taste of Home* Test Kitchen

- -

Prep: 35 min. + cooling • **Makes:** 12 servings

- 3 medium peaches, halved
- 1 Tbsp. honey
- 1 can (11.3 oz.) peach nectar, chilled
- 2 bottles (750 ml each) champagne or sparkling grape juice, chilled

1. Line a baking sheet with a large piece of heavy-duty foil (about 18x12 in.). Place peach halves, cut sides up, on foil; drizzle with honey. Fold foil over peaches and seal.
2. Bake at 375° for 25-30 minutes or until tender. Cool completely; remove and discard peels. In a food processor, process peaches until smooth.
3. Transfer peach puree to a pitcher. Add the nectar and 1 bottle of champagne; stir until combined. Pour into 12 champagne flutes or wine glasses; top with remaining champagne. Serve immediately.

¾ cup: 74 cal., 0 fat (0 sat. fat), 0 chol., 2mg sod., 9g carb. (7g sugars, 1g fiber), 0 pro.

★ ★ ★ ★ ★ **READER REVIEW**

"Great recipe. Used moscato d'Asti. It added more peach flavor with a hint of apple. Total brunch drink."

BRANDON TASTEOFHOME.COM

BRUNCH ENCHILADAS

If you want something a little different for brunch, try this recipe—folks love it!
—Linda Braun, Park Ridge, IL

Takes: 30 min. • **Makes:** 8 servings

- 8 hard-boiled large eggs, chopped
- 1 can (8¼ oz.) cream-style corn
- ⅔ cup shredded cheddar cheese
- 1 can (4 oz.) chopped green chiles
- 2 tsp. taco seasoning
- ¼ tsp. salt
- 8 corn tortillas, warmed
- 1 bottle (8 oz.) mild taco sauce
  Sour cream, optional

1. Combine the first 6 ingredients; spoon ½ cup down the center of each tortilla. Roll up tightly. Place, seam side down, in a greased 13x9-in. baking dish. Top tortillas with taco sauce.
2. Bake, uncovered, at 350° for 15 minutes or until heated through. Serve with sour cream if desired.
1 enchilada: 208 cal., 9g fat (4g sat. fat), 222mg chol., 600mg sod., 22g carb. (3g sugars, 2g fiber), 11g pro. **Diabetic exchanges:** 1½ starch, 1 medium-fat meat.

HEAVENLY CHEESE DANISH

This tempting cheese Danish is baked to flaky perfection, with a simple egg wash gloss adding shine. It tastes just as decadent as any breakfast pastry you'd find in a bakery or coffee shop.
—Josephine Triton, Lakewood, OH

Prep: 50 min. + chilling • **Bake:** 15 min.
Makes: 16 rolls

- 2 pkg. (¼ oz. each) active dry yeast
- ½ cup warm water (110° to 115°)
- 4 cups all-purpose flour
- ⅓ cup sugar
- 2 tsp. salt
- 1 cup cold butter, cubed
- 1 cup 2% milk
- 4 large egg yolks, room temperature

ASSEMBLY
- 3 tsp. ground cinnamon, divided
- 12 oz. cream cheese, softened
- ⅓ cup sugar
- 1 large egg, room temperature, separated
- 1 Tbsp. water
- 2 Tbsp. maple syrup

1. Dissolve yeast in warm water. In another bowl, mix flour, sugar and salt; cut in butter until crumbly. Add milk, egg yolks and yeast mixture; stir to form a soft dough (dough will be sticky). Cover and refrigerate for 8-24 hours.
2. To assemble, punch down dough; divide into 4 portions. On a lightly floured surface, pat each portion into a 9x4-in. rectangle; sprinkle each with ¾ tsp. cinnamon. Cut each rectangle lengthwise into four 9x1-in. strips. Twist each strip, then loosely wrap strip around itself to form a coil; tuck under end and pinch to seal. Place 3 in. apart on greased baking sheets.
3. Beat cream cheese, sugar and egg yolk until smooth. Press an indentation in center of each roll; fill with 1 rounded Tbsp. cream cheese mixture. Cover with greased plastic wrap; let rise in a warm place until doubled, about 45 minutes. Preheat oven to 350°.
4. Whisk egg white with water; brush over rolls. Bake until golden brown, 15-20 minutes. Remove to wire racks; brush with syrup. Serve warm. Refrigerate leftovers.
1 roll: 359 cal., 21g fat (12g sat. fat), 111mg chol., 468mg sod., 37g carb. (12g sugars, 1g fiber), 7g pro.

SAGE TURKEY SAUSAGE PATTIES

Turkey sausage is a good option when you want to cut fat and saturated fat. You'll love the aroma of this recipe when it's sizzling in the pan.
—Sharman Schubert, Seattle, WA

Takes: 30 min. • **Makes:** 12 servings

- ¼ cup grated Parmesan cheese
- 3 Tbsp. minced fresh parsley or 1 Tbsp. dried parsley flakes
- 2 Tbsp. fresh sage or 2 tsp. dried sage leaves
- 2 garlic cloves, minced
- 1 tsp. fennel seed, crushed
- ¾ tsp. salt
- ½ tsp. pepper
- 1½ lbs. lean ground turkey
- 1 Tbsp. olive oil

1. In a large bowl, combine the first 7 ingredients. Crumble turkey over mixture and mix well. Shape into twelve 3-in. patties.
2. In a large skillet, cook patties in oil in batches over medium heat for 3-5 minutes on each side or until meat is no longer pink. Drain on paper towels if necessary.
Freeze option: Wrap each patty in plastic wrap; transfer to a resealable freezer container. To use, unwrap patties and place on a baking sheet coated with cooking spray. Bake in a preheated 350° oven 15 minutes on each side or until heated through.
1 patty: 104 cal., 6g fat (2g sat. fat), 46mg chol., 227mg sod., 0 carb. (0 sugars, 0 fiber), 11g pro. **Diabetic exchanges:** 1 lean meat, 1 fat.

HAM & SWISS EGG CASSEROLE

The buttery crunch of croissants goes perfectly with the rich, tangy Swiss cheese and tender eggs. Breakfast for a crew doesn't get much easier than this!
—Kathy Harding, Richmond, MO

Prep: 20 min. • **Bake:** 35 min.
Makes: 12 servings

16 large eggs
2 cups 2% milk
½ tsp. salt
¼ tsp. ground nutmeg
4 cups shredded Swiss cheese
8 oz. sliced deli ham, chopped
4 croissants, torn into 1½-in. pieces
1 Tbsp. minced chives

1. Preheat oven to 350°. Whisk together eggs, milk, salt and nutmeg. Sprinkle cheese and ham into a greased 13x9-in. baking dish or pan; pour in egg mixture. Sprinkle croissant pieces over top.
2. Bake, uncovered, until puffed and golden brown, 35-40 minutes. Sprinkle with chives. Let stand 5-10 minutes before serving.
To make ahead: Refrigerate unbaked casserole, covered, several hours or overnight. To use, preheat oven to 350°. Remove casserole from refrigerator while oven heats. Bake as directed.
1 piece: 354 cal., 23g fat (11g sat. fat), 306mg chol., 545mg sod., 12g carb. (5g sugars, 1g fiber), 24g pro.

AMISH BREAKFAST CASSEROLE

We enjoyed hearty breakfast casseroles during a visit to an Amish inn. When I asked for the recipe, one of the women told me the ingredients right off the top of her head. I modified it to create this version, which my family loves. Also try breakfast sausage in place of bacon.
—Beth Notaro, Kokomo, IN

- -

Prep: 15 min. • **Bake:** 35 min. + standing
Makes: 12 servings

1	lb. sliced bacon, diced
1	medium sweet onion, chopped
6	large eggs, lightly beaten
4	cups frozen shredded hash brown potatoes, thawed
2	cups shredded cheddar cheese
1½	cups 4% cottage cheese
1¼	cups shredded Swiss cheese

1. Preheat oven to 350°. In a large skillet, cook bacon and onion over medium heat until bacon is crisp; drain. In a large bowl, combine remaining ingredients; stir in bacon mixture. Transfer to a greased 13x9-in. baking dish.

2. Bake, uncovered, until a knife inserted in the center comes out clean, 35-40 minutes. Let stand 10 minutes before cutting.

1 piece: 273 cal., 18g fat (10g sat. fat), 153mg chol., 477mg sod., 8g carb. (3g sugars, 1g fiber), 18g pro.

STRAWBERRY RHUBARB COFFEE CAKE

Although my coffee cake makes a large pan, it never lasts very long! It's great for a Sunday brunch after church and nice to bring to family reunions, too.
—Dorothy Morehouse, Massena, NY

Prep: 45 min. • **Bake:** 40 min. + cooling
Makes: 20 servings

FILLING
- 3 cups sliced fresh or frozen rhubarb (1-in. pieces)
- 1 qt. fresh strawberries, mashed
- 2 Tbsp. lemon juice
- 1 cup sugar
- ⅓ cup cornstarch

CAKE
- 3 cups all-purpose flour
- 1 cup sugar
- 1 tsp. baking powder
- 1 tsp. baking soda
- ½ tsp. salt
- 1 cup butter, cut into pieces
- 1½ cups buttermilk
- 2 large eggs, room temperature
- 1 tsp. vanilla extract

TOPPING
- ¼ cup butter
- ¾ cup all-purpose flour
- ¾ cup sugar

1. In a large saucepan, combine rhubarb, strawberries and lemon juice. Cover and cook over medium heat about 5 minutes. Combine sugar and cornstarch; stir into saucepan. Bring to a boil; cook and stir 2 minutes or until thickened. Remove from heat and set aside.

2. Preheat oven to 350°. In a large bowl, combine flour, sugar, baking powder, baking soda and salt. Cut in butter until mixture resembles coarse crumbs. Beat buttermilk, eggs and vanilla; stir into crumb mixture.

3. Spread half of the batter evenly into a greased 13x9-in. baking dish. Carefully spread filling on top. Drop remaining batter by tablespoonfuls over filling.

4. For topping, melt butter in a saucepan over low heat. Remove from heat; stir in flour and sugar until mixture resembles coarse crumbs. Sprinkle over batter. Lay aluminum foil on lower oven rack to catch any juice spillovers.

5. Place coffee cake on middle rack; bake 40-45 minutes. Cool on a wire rack.

1 piece: 328 cal., 12g fat (7g sat. fat), 53mg chol., 285mg sod., 51g carb. (30g sugars, 2g fiber), 4g pro.

SOUTHWESTERN EGG CASSEROLE

The more time I spend in the kitchen, the happier I am! These baked eggs with a true southwestern flavor are perfect to serve overnight guests.
—Sandra Greaves, Yuma, AZ

- -

Prep: 15 min. • **Bake:** 35 min.
Makes: 12 servings

- 10 large eggs
- ½ cups all-purpose flour
- 1 tsp. baking powder
- ⅛ tsp. salt
- 4 cups shredded Monterey Jack cheese
- 2 cups (16 oz.) 4% cottage cheese
- ½ cup butter, melted
- 2 cans (4 oz. each) chopped green chiles

In a large bowl, beat eggs. Combine flour, baking powder and salt; stir into eggs (batter will be lumpy). Add cheeses, butter and chiles. Pour into a greased 13x9-in. baking dish. Bake, uncovered, at 350° for 30-40 minutes or until a knife inserted in the center comes out clean. Let stand 5 minutes before cutting.
1 piece: 330 cal., 25g fat (14g sat. fat), 239mg chol., 560mg sod., 7g carb. (2g sugars, 0 fiber), 19g pro.

HOW TO
To melt butter without spattering all over the microwave, repurpose that butter wrapper you'd have otherwise tossed out. Cover the cup or bowl with the wrapper before melting a stick of butter.

PUMPKIN-CRANBERRY BREAKFAST BAKE

I love trying new ways to use pumpkin. This bread pudding was a hit with my family for a weekend breakfast.
—Terri Crandall, Gardnerville, NV

- -

Prep: 15 min. + chilling • **Bake:** 30 min.
Makes: 12 servings

- 1 loaf (1 lb.) brioche, cut into 1-in. cubes
- ½ cup dried cranberries
- ½ cup chopped walnuts, toasted
- 2 cups 2% milk
- 1 cup canned pumpkin
- ¾ cup packed brown sugar
- 4 large eggs
- ½ tsp. grated lemon zest
- 2 Tbsp. butter, melted
- 1 tsp. vanilla extract
- 1 tsp. ground cinnamon
- ¼ tsp. ground nutmeg
- ¼ tsp. ground ginger
- ⅛ tsp. ground cloves
- Maple syrup

1. Place bread cubes in a greased 13x9-in. baking dish; sprinkle with cranberries and walnuts. Whisk together next 11 ingredients until blended; pour over bread. Refrigerate, covered, overnight.
2. Preheat oven to 350°. Remove casserole from refrigerator while oven heats. Bake, uncovered, until puffed and golden, and a knife inserted in the center comes out clean, 30-35 minutes. Let stand 5-10 minutes before serving. Serve with syrup.
1 piece: 303 cal., 12g fat (6g sat. fat), 101mg chol., 230mg sod., 43g carb. (26g sugars, 2g fiber), 7g pro.

RAISIN BUTTERMILK COFFEE CAKE

Folks will be lining up in your kitchen while this coffee cake is baking, then they'll come back for more once they've tasted it! Along with awesome aroma and flavor, this fruity treat is light and tender—and sure to be a hit whenever you serve it.
—Lauren D. Heyn, Oak Creek, WI

Prep: 15 min. • **Bake:** 35 min.
Makes: 15 servings

- 1 cup packed brown sugar
- 1 cup chopped nuts
- ⅓ cup butter, melted
- 2 Tbsp. all-purpose flour
- 4 tsp. ground cinnamon

BATTER
- ½ cup butter, softened
- 1½ cups sugar
- 2 large eggs, room temperature
- 3 cups all-purpose flour
- 4 tsp. baking powder
- ½ tsp. salt
- 2 cups buttermilk
- 1 cup raisins

1. In a bowl, combine the first 5 ingredients until the mixture resembles coarse crumbs; set aside.
2. In another bowl, cream butter and sugar. Add eggs, 1 at a time, beating well after each addition.
3. Combine the dry ingredients; add to the creamed mixture alternately with buttermilk. Stir in raisins. Spread half of the batter into a greased 13x9-in. baking pan. Sprinkle with half of the crumb mixture. Carefully spread with remaining batter and sprinkle with remaining crumb mixture.
4. Bake at 350° until a toothpick inserted in the center comes out clean, 35-40 minutes.
1 piece: 421 cal., 16g fat (7g sat. fat), 57mg chol., 339mg sod., 65g carb. (42g sugars, 2g fiber), 7g pro.

RICHARD'S BREAKFAST BARS

My homemade fiber bars are so delicious they're addictive. For clean slices, spray a pizza cutter or knife with cooking spray.
—Richard Cole, Richmond, TX

Prep: 10 min. • **Bake:** 25 min. + cooling
Makes: 2 dozen

- 1 can (14 oz.) sweetened condensed milk
- 2 large eggs, room temperature, beaten
- 2 cups Fiber One bran cereal
- 2 cups quick-cooking oats
- 1½ cups chopped pecans
- 1 cup miniature semisweet chocolate chips
- 1 cup golden raisins
- 1 cup sweetened shredded coconut
- 1 can (8 oz.) unsweetened crushed pineapple, undrained

1. Preheat oven to 350°. Whisk together condensed milk and eggs; mix in remaining ingredients. Firmly press mixture evenly into a greased 13x9-in. baking dish.
2. Bake, uncovered, until edges are golden brown, 25-30 minutes. Cool completely in dish on a wire rack. Chill 1 hour; cut into bars. Store refrigerated in an airtight container.
1 bar: 219 cal., 11g fat (4g sat. fat), 21mg chol., 57mg sod., 31g carb. (20g sugars, 5g fiber), 4g pro.

PEPPERONI & SAUSAGE DEEP-DISH PIZZA QUICHE

Try this savory pizza quiche for a hearty change-of-pace breakfast. Needless to say, it makes a wonderful lunch and dinner, too.
—Donna Chesney, Naples, FL

Prep: 20 min. • **Cook:** 40 min.
Makes: 8 servings

- 2 cups shredded mozzarella cheese, divided
- 1 cup shredded sharp cheddar cheese
- 4 large eggs
- 4 oz. cream cheese, softened
- ⅓ cup 2% milk
- ¼ cup grated Parmesan cheese
- ½ tsp. garlic powder
- ½ tsp. Italian seasoning
- ½ lb. bulk Italian sausage
- ½ cup pizza sauce
- 1 cup chopped pepperoni
  Fresh basil, optional

1. Preheat oven to 350°. Sprinkle 1 cup mozzarella and cheddar cheese in a greased 13x9-in. baking dish. In a small bowl, beat eggs, cream cheese, milk, Parmesan, garlic powder and Italian seasoning; pour into dish. Bake 30 minutes.
2. Meanwhile, in a small skillet, cook sausage over medium heat until no longer pink, 5-6 minutes, breaking into crumbles; drain. Spread pizza sauce over egg mixture; top with sausage, pepperoni and remaining 1 cup mozzarella cheese. Bake until golden brown and bubbly, 10-15 minutes longer. Let stand 5 minutes before serving. Top with fresh basil if desired.
1 piece: 409 cal., 34g fat (16g sat. fat), 177mg chol., 971mg sod., 5g carb. (2g sugars, 0 fiber), 21g pro.

PISTACHIO GRANOLA

After a search for the perfect granola, I found this recipe and tweaked it just a little for my taste. Enjoy it as a crunchy topping on your yogurt or give it away as a thoughtful homemade gift.
—Candy Summerhill, Alexander, AR

Prep: 10 min. • **Cook:** 15 min. + cooling
Makes: 6 cups

- 2 cups old-fashioned oats
- ⅔ cup packed brown sugar
- ¼ cup apple cider or unsweetened apple juice
- ½ tsp. ground cinnamon
- ¼ tsp. salt
- ⅔ cup Cheerios
- ⅔ cup pistachios, chopped
- ⅔ cup dried cherries
- ½ cup dried apples, chopped
- ½ cup dried blueberries
- ½ cup sunflower kernels

1. In a large cast-iron or other heavy skillet, toast oats over medium heat until golden brown. Remove and set aside. In the same skillet, cook and stir brown sugar and apple cider over medium-low heat until brown sugar is dissolved, 1-2 minutes. Add the cinnamon and salt; stir to combine.
2. Stir in the cereal, pistachios, fruits, sunflower kernels and reserved oats until coated. Cool. Store in an airtight container.
½ cup: 233 cal., 7g fat (1g sat. fat), 0 chol., 122mg sod., 39g carb. (22g sugars, 4g fiber), 5g pro.

LATKES WITH LOX

Lox, a salty smoked salmon, is a year-round delicacy. This recipe, inspired by one from the Jewish Journal, *uses lox as a topping.*
—*Taste of Home* Test Kitchen

Prep: 20 min. • **Cook:** 5 min./batch
Makes: 3 dozen

- 2 **cups finely chopped onion**
- ¼ **cup all-purpose flour**
- 6 **garlic cloves, minced**
- 2 **tsp. salt**
- 1 **tsp. coarsely ground pepper**
- 4 **large eggs, lightly beaten**
- 4 **lbs. russet potatoes,
    peeled and shredded**
- ¾ **cup canola oil**

TOPPINGS
- 4 **oz. lox**
   **Optional: Sour cream and minced
   fresh chives**

1. In a large bowl, combine the first 5 ingredients. Stir in eggs until blended. Add potatoes; toss to coat.
2. Heat 2 Tbsp. oil in a large nonstick skillet over medium heat. Drop batter by ¼ cupfuls into oil; press lightly to flatten. Fry in batches until golden brown on both sides, using remaining oil as needed.
3. Drain on paper towels. Serve with lox; top with sour cream and chives if desired.
3 latkes with ⅓ oz. lox: 270 cal., 16g fat (2g sat. fat), 73mg chol., 610mg sod., 26g carb. (3g sugars, 2g fiber), 6g pro.

HAM & CHEESE OMELET ROLL

This brunch dish has wonderful ingredients and an impressive look all rolled into one. I love hosting, and this is one of my very favorite things to share. A platter of these swirled slices disappears in no time.
—Nancy Daugherty, Cortland, OH

- -

Prep: 15 min. • **Bake:** 35 min.
Makes: 12 servings

```
 4    oz. cream cheese, softened
 ¾    cup 2% milk
 2    Tbsp. all-purpose flour
 ¼    tsp. salt
12    large eggs
 2    Tbsp. Dijon mustard
2¼    cups shredded cheddar
      cheese, divided
 2    cups finely chopped fully cooked ham
 ½    cup thinly sliced green onions
```

1. Line the bottom and sides of a greased 15x10x1-in. baking pan with parchment; grease the paper and set aside.

2. In a small bowl, beat cream cheese and milk until smooth. Add flour and salt; mix until combined. In a large bowl, whisk eggs until blended. Add cream cheese mixture; mix well. Pour into prepared pan.

3. Bake at 375° until eggs are puffed and set, 30-35 minutes. Remove from the oven. Immediately spread with mustard and sprinkle with 1 cup cheese. Sprinkle with ham, onions and 1 cup cheese.

4. Roll up from a short side, peeling parchment away while rolling. Sprinkle top of roll with the remaining cheese; bake until cheese is melted, 3-4 minutes longer.

1 slice: 239 cal., 17g fat (9g sat. fat), 260mg chol., 637mg sod., 4g carb. (2g sugars, 0 fiber), 17g pro.

TEST KITCHEN TIP
Grease the parchment well and be patient when you're rolling the cooked egg and peeling off the paper. You'll be left with a great-looking pinwheel.

GRITS & SAUSAGE CASSEROLE

You could call this the "so good" casserole, because that's what people say when they try it. It's a southern specialty. It can even be assembled, covered and refrigerated overnight.
—Marie Poppenhager, Old Town, FL

Prep: 30 min. • **Bake:** 1¼ hours
Makes: 12 servings

- 3 cups water
- 1 cup quick-cooking grits
- ¾ tsp. salt, divided
- 2 lbs. bulk pork sausage, cooked and drained
- 2 cups shredded cheddar cheese, divided
- 3 large eggs
- 1½ cups whole milk
- 2 Tbsp. butter, melted
  Pepper to taste

1. In a saucepan, bring water to a boil. Slowly whisk in the grits and ½ tsp. salt. Reduce heat; cover and simmer for 5 minutes, stirring occasionally.
2. In a large bowl, combine grits, sausage and 1½ cups cheese. Beat the eggs and milk; stir into grits mixture. Add the butter, pepper and remaining salt.
3. Transfer to a greased 13x9-in. baking dish. Bake, uncovered, at 350° until a knife inserted in the center comes out clean, about 1 hour. Sprinkle with remaining cheese; bake 15 minutes longer or until cheese is melted. Let stand for 5 minutes before cutting.
Note: This casserole can be covered and refrigerated overnight. Remove from the refrigerator 30 minutes before baking. Bake as directed.
1 cup: 316 cal., 24g fat (11g sat. fat), 110mg chol., 621mg sod., 13g carb. (3g sugars, 1g fiber), 13g pro.

LEMON POUND CAKE MUFFINS

I make these lemony muffins for all kinds of occasions. My family is always asking for them. They have a rich cakelike taste and a sweet, tangy flavor. All I can say is: They're so unbelievably good!
—Lola Baxter, Winnebago, MN

- -

Prep: 15 min. • **Bake:** 20 min.
Makes: 1 dozen

- ½ cup butter, softened
- 1 cup sugar
- 2 large eggs, room temperature
- ½ cup sour cream
- 1 tsp. vanilla extract
- ½ tsp. lemon extract
- 1¾ cups all-purpose flour
- ½ tsp. salt
- ¼ tsp. baking soda

GLAZE
- 2 cups confectioners' sugar
- 3 Tbsp. lemon juice

1. In a large bowl, cream the butter and sugar until light and fluffy, 5-7 minutes. Add eggs, 1 at a time, beating well after each addition. Beat in sour cream and extracts. Combine the flour, salt and baking soda; add to the creamed mixture just until moistened.

2. Fill 12 greased or paper-lined muffin cups three-fourths full. Bake at 400° until a toothpick inserted in the center comes out clean, 18-20 minutes. Cool for 5 minutes before removing from pan to a wire rack.

3. Combine the glaze ingredients; drizzle over muffins. Serve warm.

1 muffin: 311 cal., 10g fat (6g sat. fat), 63mg chol., 218mg sod., 51g carb. (36g sugars, 1g fiber), 3g pro.

COASTAL CAROLINA MUFFIN-TIN FRITTATAS

Incorporating the flavors of a low country South Carolina crab boil, these tasty frittatas are easy to make and fun to eat. If you have leftover cooked potatoes (roasted or boiled), try dicing them and substituting them for the refrigerated shredded potatoes in this recipe.
—Shannon Kohn, Summerville, SC

Prep: 30 min. • **Bake:** 30 min.
Makes: 1 dozen

- ½ cup mayonnaise
- 1 Tbsp. lemon juice
- 2 tsp. sugar
- 1 tsp. seafood seasoning
- 2 cups refrigerated shredded hash brown potatoes
- 1½ cups chopped smoked sausage
- 1 can (8 oz.) jumbo lump crabmeat, drained
- ¼ cup chopped roasted sweet red peppers
- 7 large eggs
- ¾ cup heavy whipping cream
- 1 Tbsp. Louisiana-style hot sauce
- ½ tsp. salt
- 12 bacon strips, cooked and crumbled
- ¼ cup thinly sliced green onions

1. Preheat oven to 350°. In a small bowl, combine mayonnaise, lemon juice, sugar and seafood seasoning. Refrigerate sauce until serving.

2. Meanwhile, in a large bowl, combine potatoes, sausage, crab and red peppers. Divide among 12 greased jumbo muffin cups. In another large bowl, whisk the eggs, cream, hot sauce and salt. Pour over potato mixture. Top with bacon.

3. Bake until a knife inserted in the center comes out clean, 30-35 minutes. Serve with sauce and green onions.

1 frittata: 292 cal., 23g fat (8g sat. fat), 164mg chol., 768mg sod., 7g carb. (2g sugars, 1g fiber), 13g pro.

RASPBERRY CHEESE BLINTZ BAKE

For a special breakfast, try this twist on traditional blintzes. It puffs during baking and will fall a bit while standing, making the perfect bed for a vibrant berry sauce.
—Kristi Twohig, Waterloo, WI

- -

Prep: 25 min. • **Bake:** 40 min. + standing
Makes: 12 servings

- ½ cup orange juice
- 6 large eggs
- 2 large egg whites
- 1½ cups sour cream
- 1 cup all-purpose flour
- ½ cup sugar
- ¼ cup butter, softened
- 2 tsp. baking powder
- 1 tsp. grated orange zest
- 1 tsp. vanilla extract
  Dash salt

FILLING
- 2 large egg yolks
- 1 tsp. vanilla extract
- 2 cups 4% cottage cheese
- 1 pkg. (8 oz.) cream cheese, softened
- ¼ cup sugar

TOPPING
- 1 pkg. (12 oz.) frozen unsweetened raspberries, thawed
- 2 Tbsp. cornstarch
- ¾ cup orange juice
  Mandarin oranges, optional

1. Combine the first 11 ingredients in a blender. Cover and process until smooth. Set aside 2 cups batter; pour remaining batter into a greased 13x9-in. baking dish.
2. For filling, combine the egg yolks, vanilla, cottage cheese, cream cheese and sugar in a blender. Cover and process until smooth. Spoon filling over batter; cut through with a knife to swirl. Top with reserved batter. Bake, uncovered, at 350° until center is just set (mixture will jiggle), 40-45 minutes. Let stand for 10 minutes before cutting.
3. For topping, press raspberries through a strainer; discard seeds and pulp. In a small saucepan, combine cornstarch and orange juice until smooth; stir in raspberry puree. Bring to a boil. Cook and stir until thickened, about 2 minutes. Serve with blintz bake. Top with mandarin oranges if desired.
1 serving: 364 cal., 20g fat (12g sat. fat), 199mg chol., 365mg sod., 31g carb. (19g sugars, 1g fiber), 12g pro.

BLUEBERRY-SAUSAGE BREAKFAST CAKE

I fix this breakfast cake for my co-workers often. The blueberries and sausage are such a nice sweet-salty flavor combo.
—Peggy Frazier, Indianapolis, IN

Prep: 25 min. • **Bake:** 35 min.
Makes: 12 servings

- ½   cup butter, softened
- ¾   cup sugar
- ¼   cup packed brown sugar
- 2   large eggs, room temperature
- 2   cups all-purpose flour
- 1   tsp. baking powder
- ½   tsp. baking soda
- 1   cup sour cream
- 1   lb. bulk pork sausage,
      cooked and drained
- 1   cup fresh or frozen blueberries
- ½   cup chopped pecans

BLUEBERRY SAUCE
- ½   cup sugar
- 2   Tbsp. cornstarch
- ½   cup water
- 2   cups fresh or frozen blueberries

1. In a bowl, cream butter and sugars. Add eggs, 1 at a time, beating well after each addition. Combine flour, baking powder and baking soda; add alternately with sour cream to creamed mixture, beating well after each addition. Fold in pork sausage and blueberries.
2. Pour into a greased 13x9-in. baking pan. Sprinkle with pecans. Bake at 350° for 35-40 minutes or until cake tests done.
3. For sauce, combine sugar and cornstarch in a saucepan. Add water and blueberries. Cook and stir until thick and bubbly. Spoon over individual servings. Refrigerate any leftover cake and sauce.
1 piece: 429 cal., 23g fat (10g sat. fat), 83mg chol., 341mg sod., 50g carb. (30g sugars, 2g fiber), 7g pro.

MAKE AHEAD
CINNAMON FRENCH TOAST

Any day is special when Mom makes this do-ahead baked French toast.
—Jill Baughman, New York, NY

Prep: 20 min. + chilling
Bake: 40 min. + standing • **Makes:** 8 servings

- 8   oz. day-old French bread, unsliced
- 4   large eggs
- 2   Tbsp. sugar
- 1   Tbsp. brown sugar
- 2   tsp. vanilla extract
- 1   tsp. maple extract
- ¼   tsp. kosher salt
- 2   cups whole milk
- ½   cup heavy whipping cream

TOPPING
- ¼   cup all-purpose flour
- 3   Tbsp. brown sugar
- 3   Tbsp. unsalted butter,
      cut into ¼-in. cubes
- 1   tsp. ground cinnamon
      Freshly grated nutmeg, optional
      Fresh blueberries or raspberries
      Confectioners' sugar

1. Cut bread into 1-in.-thick slices. Arrange in a single layer in a greased 13x9-in. baking dish. Lightly beat next 6 ingredients; stir in milk and cream. Pour egg mixture over bread, turning once to coat. Refrigerate, covered, overnight.
2. Preheat oven to 375°. Turn bread again to coat. For topping, combine flour, brown sugar, butter, cinnamon and, if desired, nutmeg. Sprinkle flour mixture over bread.
3. Bake, uncovered, until a knife inserted in center comes out clean and topping is golden brown, 40-45 minutes. Let stand 10 minutes before cutting. Top with the blueberries or raspberries; sprinkle with confectioners' sugar.
1 serving: 297 cal., 15g fat (8g sat. fat), 128mg chol., 299mg sod., 32g carb. (15g sugars, 1g fiber), 9g pro.

BACON & EGG LASAGNA

My sister-in-law served this special dish for Easter breakfast one year, and our whole family loved the mix of bacon, eggs, noodles and cheese. Now I sometimes assemble it the night before and bake it in the morning for a terrific hassle-free brunch entree.
—Dianne Meyer, Graniteville, VT

- -

Prep: 45 min. • **Bake:** 35 min. + standing
Makes: 12 servings

- 1 lb. bacon strips, diced
- 1 large onion, chopped
- ⅓ cup all-purpose flour
- ½ to 1 tsp. salt
- ¼ tsp. pepper
- 4 cups 2% milk
- 12 lasagna noodles, cooked and drained
- 12 hard-boiled large eggs, sliced
- 2 cups shredded Swiss cheese
- ⅓ cup grated Parmesan cheese
- 2 Tbsp. minced fresh parsley, optional

1. In a large skillet, cook bacon until crisp. Remove with a slotted spoon to paper towels. Drain, reserving ⅓ cup drippings. In the drippings, saute onion until tender. Stir in the flour, salt and pepper until blended. Gradually stir in milk. Bring to a boil; cook and stir for 2 minutes or until thickened. Remove from the heat.
2. Spread ½ cup sauce in a greased 13x9-in. baking dish. Layer with 4 noodles, a third of the eggs and bacon, Swiss cheese and white sauce. Repeat layers twice. Sprinkle with Parmesan cheese.
3. Bake, uncovered, at 350° until bubbly, 35-40 minutes. If desired, sprinkle with fresh parsley. Let stand for 15 minutes before cutting.
1 piece: 386 cal., 20g fat (9g sat. fat), 252mg chol., 489mg sod., 28g carb. (7g sugars, 1g fiber), 23g pro.

BLUEBERRY SOUR CREAM COFFEE CAKE

At our house, special breakfasts would not be the same without this delicious coffee cake. Folks rave about the treat when I bring it to special occasions.
—Susan Walschlager, Anderson, IN

- -

Prep: 25 min. • **Bake:** 55 min. + cooling
Makes: 12 servings

- ¾ cup butter, softened
- 1½ cups sugar
- 4 large eggs, room temperature
- 1 tsp. vanilla extract
- 3 cups all-purpose flour
- 1½ tsp. baking powder
- ¾ tsp. baking soda
- ¼ tsp. salt
- 1 cup sour cream

FILLING
- ¼ cup packed brown sugar
- 1 Tbsp. all-purpose flour
- ½ tsp. ground cinnamon
- 2 cups fresh or frozen blueberries

GLAZE
- 1 cup confectioners' sugar
- 2 to 3 Tbsp. 2% milk

1. Preheat oven to 350°. In a large bowl, cream butter and sugar until light and fluffy, 5-7 minutes. Add eggs, 1 at a time, beating well after each addition. Beat in vanilla. Combine the flour, baking powder, baking soda and salt; add to creamed mixture alternately with sour cream, beating well after each addition.
2. Spoon a third of the batter into a greased and floured 10-in. fluted tube pan. Combine brown sugar, flour and cinnamon; sprinkle half over batter. Top with half of the berries. Repeat layers. Top with remaining batter.
3. Bake 55-65 minutes or until a toothpick inserted in the center comes out clean. Cool 10 minutes before removing from pan to a wire rack to cool completely. Combine glaze ingredients; drizzle over coffee cake.
1 piece: 448 cal., 17g fat (10g sat. fat), 114mg chol., 328mg sod., 68g carb. (42g sugars, 1g fiber), 6g pro.

OLD-FASHIONED BUTTERMILK DOUGHNUTS

Guests will have a touch of nostalgia when they bite into one of these old-fashioned doughnuts. Accents of nutmeg and cinnamon, along with a subtle burst of lemon, make them hard to resist.
—June Jones, Harveyville, KS

- -

Prep: 20 min. • **Cook:** 5 min./batch
Makes: 2½ dozen

2	cups mashed potatoes (without added milk and butter)
2	large eggs, room temperature
1¼	cups sugar
⅔	cup buttermilk
¼	cup butter, melted
1	Tbsp. grated lemon zest
4	cups all-purpose flour
3	tsp. baking powder
2	tsp. salt
2	tsp. ground nutmeg
¼	tsp. baking soda
	Oil for deep-fat frying

TOPPING
½	cup sugar
1½	tsp. ground cinnamon

1. In a large bowl, beat the potatoes, eggs, sugar, buttermilk, butter and lemon zest until blended. Combine the flour, baking powder, salt, nutmeg and baking soda; gradually beat into the potato mixture and mix well.

2. Turn onto a lightly floured surface; roll to ½-in. thickness. Cut with a floured 2½-in. doughnut cutter. In a deep cast-iron or electric skillet, heat oil to 375°. Fry doughnuts, a few at a time, until golden brown on both sides. Drain on paper towels. Combine sugar and cinnamon; roll warm doughnuts in mixture.

1 doughnut with 1 doughnut hole: 184 cal., 7g fat (2g sat. fat), 18mg chol., 232mg sod., 27g carb. (12g sugars, 1g fiber), 3g pro.

BROCCOLI HAM QUICHE

My signature quiche is featured in a family cookbook I put together. My husband's love of this dish is proof that quiche can satisfy even a very healthy appetite.
—Marilyn Day, North Fort Myers, FL

- -

Prep: 20 min. • **Bake:** 55 min. + standing
Makes: 8 servings

- 1 unbaked deep-dish pie crust (9 in.)
- 1 cup shredded Swiss cheese
- 1 cup shredded part-skim mozzarella cheese
- 2 Tbsp. all-purpose flour
- 4 large eggs, lightly beaten
- 1½ cups whole milk
- 2 Tbsp. chopped green onion
- ¼ tsp. salt
- ⅛ tsp. pepper
- ⅛ tsp. dried thyme
- ⅛ tsp. dried rosemary, crushed
- ½ cup diced fully cooked ham
- ½ cup chopped fresh broccoli

1. Line unpricked pie crust with a double thickness of heavy-duty foil. Bake at 450° for 8 minutes. Remove foil; bake 5 minutes longer. Cool on a wire rack while preparing the filling.

2. Toss cheeses with flour; set aside. In a large bowl, combine the eggs, milk, onion and seasonings. Stir in ham, broccoli and cheese mixture. Pour into prepared crust.

3. Bake at 350° for 55-60 minutes or until set. Let stand 10 minutes before cutting.

1 slice: 269 cal., 17g fat (7g sat. fat), 140mg chol., 408mg sod., 16g carb. (3g sugars, 0 fiber), 14g pro.

RICH CHOCOLATE CHIP COFFEE CAKE

When I was a teacher, this recipe was recommended by one of my student's parents. I've made it so many times, I can't imagine hosting a brunch without it. Chocolate chips add sweet bursts of flavor to the rich and tender coffee cake.
—Michelle Krzmarzick, Torrance, CA

Prep: 15 min. • **Bake:** 50 min. + cooling
Makes: 12 servings

- 1 cup butter, softened
- 1 pkg. (8 oz.) cream cheese, softened
- 1½ cups sugar, divided
- 2 large eggs, room temperature
- 1 tsp. vanilla extract
- 2 cups all-purpose flour
- 1 tsp. baking powder
- ½ tsp. baking soda
- ¼ tsp. salt
- ¼ cup 2% milk
- 1 cup (6 oz.) semisweet chocolate chips
- ¼ cup chopped pecans
- 1 tsp. ground cinnamon

1. Cream the butter, cream cheese and 1¼ cups of sugar until light and fluffy, 5-7 minutes. Beat in eggs and vanilla. Combine the flour, baking powder, baking soda and salt; add to creamed mixture alternately with milk and mix well. Stir in chocolate chips.

2. Pour into a greased 9-in. springform pan. Combine the pecans, cinnamon and remaining sugar; sprinkle over batter.

3. Bake uncovered at 350° for 30 minutes; cover and bake 30-40 minutes longer or until a toothpick inserted in the center comes out clean. Cool for 15 minutes. Carefully run a knife around edge of pan to loosen. Cool completely before cutting.

1 slice: 474 cal., 29g fat (17g sat. fat), 98mg chol., 360mg sod., 51g carb. (33g sugars, 2g fiber), 6g pro.

CHILES RELLENOS BREAKFAST BAKE

My family loves anything with a southwestern flavor, so I turned classic chiles rellenos into a breakfast casserole and they became fans in an instant.
—Joan Hallford, North Richland Hills, TX

Prep: 10 min. • **Bake:** 35 min. + standing
Makes: 15 servings

- 1 pkg. (20 oz.) refrigerated shredded hash brown potatoes
- 1 can (27 to 28 oz.) whole green chiles
- 1 cup chunky salsa
- 1 lb. bulk pork sausage or fresh chorizo, cooked, drained and crumbled
- 2 cups shredded Mexican cheese blend
- 6 large eggs
- ½ cup 2% milk
- ¼ tsp. ground cumin
  Salt and pepper to taste
  Optional ingredients: Warm flour tortillas (8 in.), sour cream and salsa

1. Preheat oven to 350°. In a greased 13x9-in. baking dish, layer half the potatoes; all the chiles, opened flat; all the salsa; half the sausage; and half the cheese. Cover with remaining potatoes, sausage and cheese.

2. Beat eggs and milk; add cumin, salt and pepper. Pour over potato mixture.

3. Bake, uncovered, until eggs are set in center, 35-40 minutes. Let stand for 15 minutes. If desired, serve with warm tortillas, sour cream and additional salsa.

1 piece: 210 cal., 13g fat (5g sat. fat), 105mg chol., 440mg sod., 11g carb. (3g sugars, 1g fiber), 10g pro.

MINI HAM & CHEESE FRITTATAS

I found this recipe a few years ago and made some little changes to it. I'm diabetic, and it fits into my low-carb and low-fat diet. Every time I serve a brunch, the frittatas are the first to disappear, and nobody knows they are low in fat!
—Susan Watt, Basking Ridge, NJ

Prep: 15 min. • **Bake:** 25 min.
Makes: 3 servings

- 6 large eggs
- 4 large egg whites
- 2 Tbsp. fat-free milk
- ¼ tsp. salt
- ¼ tsp. pepper
- 3 Tbsp. minced fresh chives
- ¾ cup cubed fully cooked ham (about 4 oz.)
- 1 cup shredded fat-free cheddar cheese

1. Preheat oven to 375°. In a bowl, whisk the first 5 ingredients until blended; stir in chives. Divide ham and cheese among 8 muffin cups coated with cooking spray. Top with egg mixture, filling cups three-fourths full.
2. Bake until a knife inserted in the center comes out clean, 22-25 minutes Carefully run a knife around sides to loosen.
1 mini frittata: 106 cal., 4g fat (1g sat. fat), 167mg chol., 428mg sod., 2g carb. (1g sugars, 0 fiber), 14g pro. **Diabetic exchanges:** 2 medium-fat meat.

BAKED FRENCH TOAST WITH STRAWBERRIES

French toast is a crowd-pleaser, but it's hard to make and serve to a big group all at once. This overnight recipe with fresh strawberries and a pecan topping fixes everything.
—David Stelzl, Waxhaw, NC

Prep: 20 min. + chilling
Bake: 40 min. + standing
Makes: 12 servings

- 12 slices day-old French bread (1 in. thick)
- 6 large eggs
- 1½ cups 2% milk
- 1 cup half-and-half cream
- 2 Tbsp. maple syrup
- 1 tsp. vanilla extract
- ½ tsp. ground cinnamon
- ¼ tsp. ground nutmeg

TOPPING
- 1 cup packed brown sugar
- ½ cup butter, melted
- 2 Tbsp. maple syrup
- 1 cup chopped pecans
- 4 cups chopped fresh strawberries
  Additional maple syrup

1. Place bread in a single layer in a greased 13x9-in. baking dish. In a large bowl, whisk eggs, milk, cream, syrup, vanilla, cinnamon and nutmeg; pour over bread. For topping, in a small bowl, mix brown sugar, butter and syrup; stir in pecans. Spread over bread. Refrigerate, covered, overnight.
2. Preheat oven to 350°. Remove French toast from refrigerator while oven heats. Bake, uncovered, 40-50 minutes or until a knife inserted in the center comes out clean. Let stand 10 minutes before serving. Serve with strawberries and additional maple syrup.
1 piece: 377 cal., 20g fat (8g sat. fat), 126mg chol., 266mg sod., 42g carb. (27g sugars, 3g fiber), 8g pro.

SAVORY APPLE-CHICKEN SAUSAGE

These easy, healthy sausages taste incredible, and they make an elegant brunch dish. The recipe is also very versatile. It can be doubled or tripled for a crowd, and the sausage freezes well either cooked or raw.
—Angela Buchanan, Longmont, CO

- -

Takes: 25 min. • **Makes:** 8 patties

1	**large tart apple, peeled and diced**
2	**tsp. poultry seasoning**
1	**tsp. salt**
¼	**tsp. pepper**
1	**lb. ground chicken**

1. In a large bowl, combine the first 4 ingredients. Crumble chicken over the mixture and mix well. Shape into eight 3-in. patties.

2. In a large, greased cast-iron or other heavy skillet, cook patties over medium heat until no longer pink, 5-6 minutes on each side. Drain if necessary.

1 sausage patty: 92 cal., 5g fat (1g sat. fat), 38mg chol., 328mg sod., 4g carb. (3g sugars, 1g fiber), 9g pro. **Diabetic exchanges:** 1 medium-fat meat.

BRING IT
To keep these sausages hot on a buffet, layer them with paper towels in a slow cooker set on low or warm.

BROCCOLI-MUSHROOM BUBBLE BAKE

 I got bored with the same old breakfast casseroles served at our monthly moms' meeting, so I decided to come up with something new. Judging by the reactions of the other moms, this one's a keeper.
—Shannon Koene, Blacksburg, VA

Prep: 20 min. • **Bake:** 25 min.
Makes: 12 servings

- 1 tsp. canola oil
- ½ lb. fresh mushrooms, finely chopped
- 1 medium onion, finely chopped
- 1 tube (16.3 oz.) large refrigerated flaky biscuits
- 1 pkg. (10 oz.) frozen broccoli with cheese sauce
- 3 large eggs
- 1 can (5 oz.) evaporated milk
- 1 tsp. Italian seasoning
- ½ tsp. garlic powder
- ½ tsp. salt
- ¼ tsp. pepper
- 1½ cups shredded Colby-Monterey Jack cheese

1. Preheat oven to 350°. In a large skillet, heat oil over medium-high heat. Add mushrooms and onion; cook and stir until tender, 4-6 minutes.
2. Cut each biscuit into 8 pieces; place in a greased 13x9-in. baking dish. Top with mushroom mixture.
3. Cook broccoli with cheese sauce according to package directions. Spoon over mushroom mixture.
4. In a large bowl, whisk the eggs, milk and seasonings; pour over top. Sprinkle with cheese. Bake until golden brown, 25-30 minutes.

1 serving: 233 cal., 13g fat (6g sat. fat), 64mg chol., 648mg sod., 21g carb. (6g sugars, 1g fiber), 9g pro.

Creamy Turkey
Casserole
page 83

Main Dishes

When you're in charge of bringing the main attraction, look here for a guaranteed crowd-pleaser. These recipes will make your gathering great.

ROASTED LIME CHICKEN

The hints of lime that infuse this moist, juicy chicken make it the most requested dish for our family dinners.
—Kathy Lewis-Martinez, Spring Valley, CA

Prep: 20 min. + marinating
Bake: 2 hours + standing
Makes: 10 servings

- ½ cup Dijon mustard
- ¼ cup lime juice
- ¼ cup soy sauce
- 2 Tbsp. minced fresh parsley or 2 tsp. dried parsley flakes
- 2 Tbsp. minced fresh rosemary or 2 tsp. dried rosemary, crushed
- 2 Tbsp. minced fresh sage or 2 tsp. rubbed sage
- 2 Tbsp. minced fresh thyme or 2 tsp. dried thyme
- 1 tsp. white pepper
- 1 tsp. ground nutmeg
- 1 roasting chicken (6 to 7 lbs.)
- 4 medium limes, cut into wedges

1. Combine the first 9 ingredients in a small bowl. Cover and refrigerate ¼ cup marinade; pour remaining marinade into a large shallow bowl. Add the chicken; turn to coat. Refrigerate for at least 4 hours.

2. Drain chicken and discard marinade. Place lime wedges inside the cavity. Tuck the wings under chicken; tie drumsticks together. Place chicken breast side up on a rack in a shallow roasting pan. Brush reserved marinade over chicken.

3. Bake at 350° 2-2½ hours or until a thermometer inserted in thigh reads 165°. Cover loosely with foil if chicken browns too quickly. Let stand for 15 minutes before carving.

5 oz. cooked chicken: 341 cal., 19g fat (5g sat. fat), 108mg chol., 629mg sod., 4g carb. (1g sugars, 1g fiber), 35g pro.

MEDITERRANEAN BULGUR SALAD

Whether it's health or taste you're after, it doesn't get any better than this. Bulgur, beans, tomatoes, pine nuts and olive oil team up beautifully in this vegetarian main dish salad.
—*Taste of Home* Test Kitchen

Prep: 15 min. • **Cook:** 20 min. + cooling
Makes: 9 servings

- 3 cups vegetable broth
- 1½ cups uncooked bulgur
- 6 Tbsp. olive oil
- 2 Tbsp. lemon juice
- 2 Tbsp. minced fresh parsley
- ½ tsp. salt
- ¼ tsp. pepper
- 1 can (15 oz.) garbanzo beans or chickpeas, rinsed and drained
- 2 cups halved cherry tomatoes
- 1 cup chopped cucumber
- 8 green onions, sliced
- 1 pkg. (4 oz.) crumbled feta cheese
- ½ cup pine nuts, toasted

1. In a large saucepan, bring the broth and bulgur to a boil over high heat. Reduce heat; cover and simmer for 20 minutes or until bulgur is tender and broth is almost absorbed. Remove from heat; let stand at room temperature, uncovered, until the broth is absorbed.
2. In a small bowl, whisk the oil, lemon juice, parsley, salt and pepper.
3. In a large serving bowl, combine the bulgur, beans, tomatoes, cucumber and onions. Drizzle with dressing; toss to coat. Sprinkle with cheese and pine nuts.
1 cup: 298 cal., 17g fat (3g sat. fat), 7mg chol., 657mg sod., 31g carb. (4g sugars, 8g fiber), 10g pro.

MEATLESS CHILI MAC

I came across this recipe in a newspaper years ago. It's been a hit at our house ever since. It's fast and flavorful, and it appeals to all ages.
—Cindy Ragan, North Huntingdon, PA

- -

Prep: 15 min. • **Cook:** 25 min.
Makes: 8 servings

- 1   large onion, chopped
- 1   medium green pepper, chopped
- 1   Tbsp. olive oil
- 1   garlic clove, minced
- 2   cups water
- 1½ cups uncooked elbow macaroni
- 1   can (16 oz.) mild chili beans, undrained
- 1   can (15½ oz.) great northern beans, rinsed and drained
- 1   can (14½ oz.) diced tomatoes, undrained
- 1   can (8 oz.) tomato sauce
- 4   tsp. chili powder
- 1   tsp. ground cumin
- ½   tsp. salt
- ½   cup fat-free sour cream

1. In a Dutch oven, saute onion and green pepper in oil until tender. Add garlic; cook 1 minute longer. Stir in the water, macaroni, beans, tomatoes, tomato sauce, chili powder, cumin and salt.
2. Bring to a boil. Reduce heat; cover and simmer for 15-20 minutes or until macaroni is tender. Top each serving with 1 Tbsp. sour cream.

1¼ cups: 206 cal., 3g fat (1g sat. fat), 1mg chol., 651mg sod., 37g carb. (6g sugars, 9g fiber), 10g pro. **Diabetic exchanges:** 2 starch, 1 lean meat, 1 vegetable.

MAKE AHEAD
ITALIAN SAUSAGE CALZONE

My teenage daughter and I have been experimenting in the kitchen to re-create some old-time family dishes. This calzone with spinach and sausage is definitely a favorite. Since it uses refrigerated pizza crust, it's a cinch to prepare.
—Terri Gallagher, King George, VA

- -

Prep: 20 min. • **Bake:** 30 min. + standing
Makes: 8 servings

- 1   tube (13.8 oz.) refrigerated pizza crust
- 1   can (8 oz.) pizza sauce
- 1   pkg. (10 oz.) frozen chopped spinach, thawed and squeezed dry
- 1   lb. bulk Italian sausage, cooked and drained
- 1   jar (4½ oz.) sliced mushrooms, drained
- 2   cups shredded part-skim mozzarella cheese

1. Unroll pizza dough onto an ungreased baking sheet; pat into a 14x11-in. rectangle. Spread pizza sauce over 1 long side of dough to within ½ in. of edges.
2. Layer the spinach, sausage, mushrooms and cheese over sauce. Fold dough over filling; pinch seams to seal.
3. Bake at 400° for 30-35 minutes or until golden brown. Let stand for 10-15 minutes before slicing.

Freeze option: Freeze cooled unsliced calzone in a freezer container. To use, place calzone on an ungreased baking sheet, cover with aluminum foil and reheat in a preheated 375° oven 10 minutes. Uncover; bake until heated through.

1 slice: 322 cal., 15g fat (6g sat. fat), 44mg chol., 870mg sod., 28g carb. (4g sugars, 3g fiber), 17g pro.

HEARTY CHICKEN SPAGHETTI CASSEROLE

This creamy, cheesy casserole is so homey, second helpings are a must!
—Lynne German, Buford, GA

Prep: 25 min. • **Bake:** 25 min.
Makes: 6 servings

- 8 oz. uncooked spaghetti, broken into 3-in. pieces
- 3 cups cubed cooked chicken
- 1 can (10¾ oz.) condensed cream of chicken soup, undiluted
- 1 medium onion, chopped
- 1 cup 2% milk
- 1 cup shredded sharp cheddar cheese, divided
- 1 cup shredded Swiss cheese, divided
- 1 can (4 oz.) mushroom stems and pieces, drained
- ½ cup chopped roasted sweet red peppers
- 3 Tbsp. mayonnaise
- 1½ tsp. steak seasoning
- ½ tsp. dried basil

1. Cook spaghetti according to package directions. Meanwhile, in a large bowl, combine the chicken, soup, onion, milk, ½ cup cheddar cheese, ½ cup Swiss cheese, mushrooms, peppers, mayonnaise, steak seasoning and basil.

2. Drain spaghetti. Add to chicken mixture; toss to coat. Transfer to a greased 13x9-in. baking dish. Cover and bake at 350° for 20 minutes. Uncover; sprinkle with remaining cheeses. Bake until heated through and cheese is melted, 5-10 minutes longer.

Freeze option: Cover and freeze unbaked casserole. To use, partially thaw dish in refrigerator overnight. Remove from refrigerator 30 minutes before baking. Bake as directed, increasing time as needed to heat through.

1⅓ cups: 549 cal., 25g fat (11g sat. fat), 109mg chol., 957mg sod., 40g carb. (6g sugars, 2g fiber), 38g pro.

UPPER PENINSULA PASTIES

I grew up in Michigan's Upper Peninsula, where pasties—traditional meat pies often eaten by hand—are popular. There's a debate on whether they should be served with gravy or ketchup, but no matter what you dunk them in, they're super comforting.
—Carole Derifield, Valdez, AK

- -

Prep: 35 min. + chilling • **Bake:** 1 hour
Makes: 12 servings

  2 **cups shortening**
  2 **cups boiling water**
5½ **to 6 cups all-purpose flour**
  2 **tsp. salt**
FILLING
  6 **medium red potatoes**
     (about 3 lbs.), peeled
  2 **small rutabagas (about**
     1½ lbs.), peeled
  1 **lb. ground beef**
  ½ **lb. ground pork**
  2 **medium onions, chopped**
     into ¼-in. pieces
  3 **tsp. salt**
  2 **tsp. pepper**
  2 **tsp. garlic powder**
  ¼ **cup butter**

Half-and-half cream or a lightly beaten large egg, optional

1. In a large bowl, stir shortening and water until shortening is melted. Gradually stir in flour and salt until a very soft dough is formed; cover and refrigerate for 1½ hours.
2. Cut potatoes and rutabagas into ⅛- or ¼-in. cubes; do not make cubes too large or they will not cook properly. Gently combine ground beef and pork; break into small crumbles. In a large bowl, combine the potatoes, rutabagas, onions, meat mixture and seasonings.
3. Divide dough into 12 equal portions. On a floured surface, roll out 1 portion at a time into a 8-in. circle. Mound 1½-2 cups filling on half of each circle; dot with 1 tsp. butter. Moisten edges with water; carefully fold dough over filling and press edges with a fork to seal.
4. Place on ungreased baking sheets. Cut several slits in top of pasties. If desired, brush with cream or beaten egg. Bake at 350° until golden brown, about 1 hour. Cool on wire racks. Serve hot or cold. Store in the refrigerator.
1 pasty: 757 cal., 44g fat (13g sat. fat), 46mg chol., 1060mg sod., 69g carb. (5g sugars, 5g fiber), 19g pro.

LOBSTER ROLLS

Mayonnaise infused with dill and lemon lends refreshing flavor to these super sandwiches. Try pan-toasting the buns in butter for something special.
—*Taste of Home* Test Kitchen

Takes: 30 min. • **Makes:** 8 sandwiches

1 cup chopped celery
⅓ cup mayonnaise
2 Tbsp. lemon juice
½ tsp. dill weed
5 cups cubed cooked lobster meat (about 4 small lobsters)
8 hoagie rolls, split and toasted

In a large bowl, combine the celery, mayonnaise, lemon juice and dill weed. Gently stir in lobster. Serve on rolls.

1 sandwich: 354 cal., 12g fat (2g sat. fat), 133mg chol., 887mg sod., 36g carb. (5g sugars, 1g fiber), 25g pro.

IRISH BEEF STEW

Rich and hearty, this stew is my husband's favorite. The beef is incredibly tender. Served with crusty bread, it's an ideal cool-weather meal and perfect for any Irish holiday.
—Carrie Karleen, St. Nicolas, QC

- -

Prep: 40 min. • **Cook:** 3¼ hours
Makes: 15 servings (3¾ qt.)

- 8 bacon strips, diced
- ⅓ cup all-purpose flour
- 1 tsp. salt
- ½ tsp. pepper
- 3 lbs. beef stew meat, cut into 1-in. cubes
- 1 lb. whole fresh mushrooms, quartered
- 3 medium leeks (white portion only), chopped
- 2 medium carrots, chopped
- ¼ cup chopped celery
- 1 Tbsp. canola oil
- 4 garlic cloves, minced
- 1 Tbsp. tomato paste
- 4 cups reduced-sodium beef broth
- 1 cup dark stout beer or additional reduced-sodium beef broth
- 2 bay leaves
- 1 tsp. dried thyme
- 1 tsp. dried parsley flakes
- 1 tsp. dried rosemary, crushed
- 2 lbs. Yukon Gold potatoes, cut into 1-in. cubes
- 2 Tbsp. cornstarch
- 2 Tbsp. cold water
- 1 cup frozen peas

1. In a stockpot, cook bacon over medium heat until crisp. Using a slotted spoon, remove to paper towels. In a large shallow dish, combine flour, salt and pepper. Add beef, a few pieces at a time, and turn to coat. Brown beef in the bacon drippings. Remove and set aside.
2. In the same pan, saute the mushrooms, leeks, carrots and celery in oil until tender. Add garlic; cook 1 minute longer. Stir in tomato paste until blended. Add the broth, beer, bay leaves, thyme, parsley and rosemary. Return beef and bacon to pan. Bring to a boil. Reduce heat; cover and simmer for 2 hours or until beef is tender.
3. Add potatoes. Return to a boil. Reduce heat; cover and simmer 1 hour longer or until the potatoes are tender. Combine cornstarch and water until smooth; stir into stew. Bring to a boil; cook and stir for 2 minutes or until thickened. Add peas; heat through. Discard bay leaves.

1 cup: 301 cal., 13g fat (4g sat. fat), 66mg chol., 441mg sod., 21g carb. (3g sugars, 2g fiber), 23g pro.
Beef Stew with Barley: Prepare stew as directed, stirring in whole grain mustard and quick-cooking barley 1 hour before serving.
Asian Beef Stew: Prepare stew as directed, adding hoisin sauce, fish sauce and chopped bok choy. Serve over jasmine rice.
Cola Beef Stew: Prepare stew as directed, substituting cola for the beer.

GRILLED HULI HULI CHICKEN

I got this grilled chicken recipe from a friend while living in Hawaii. It sizzles with the flavors of brown sugar, ginger and soy sauce. Huli means "turn" in Hawaiian. The sweet and savory glaze is fantastic on pork chops, too.
—Sharon Boling, San Diego, CA

Prep: 15 min. + marinating • **Grill:** 15 min.
Makes: 12 servings

- 1 cup packed brown sugar
- ¾ cup ketchup
- ¾ cup reduced-sodium soy sauce
- ⅓ cup sherry or chicken broth
- 2½ tsp. minced fresh gingerroot
- 1½ tsp. minced garlic
- 24 boneless skinless chicken thighs (about 6 lbs.)

1. In a small bowl, mix first 6 ingredients. Reserve 1⅓ cups for basting; cover and refrigerate. Divide remaining marinade between 2 large shallow dishes. Add 12 chicken thighs to each; turn to coat. Refrigerate, covered, 8 hours or overnight.
2. Drain chicken, discarding marinade. Grill, covered, on an oiled rack over medium heat for 6-8 minutes on each side or until a thermometer reads 170°; baste chicken occasionally with the reserved marinade during the last 5 minutes.
2 chicken thighs: 391 cal., 16g fat (5g sat. fat), 151mg chol., 651mg sod., 15g carb. (14g sugars, 0 fiber), 43g pro.

> **TEST KITCHEN TIP**
> For grilling, we love the moistness of chicken thighs, and they're economical, too. But use any cut of chicken you like. This sweet and savory glaze is also fantastic on pork chops.

HAM & SWISS CASSEROLE

When I prepare this noodle casserole for church gatherings, it's always a hit. It can easily be doubled or tripled for a crowd.
—Doris Barb, El Dorado, KS

Prep: 15 min. • **Bake:** 40 min.
Makes: 8 servings

- 1 pkg. (8 oz.) egg noodles, cooked and drained
- 2 cups cubed fully cooked ham
- 2 cups shredded Swiss cheese
- 1 can (10¾ oz.) condensed cream of celery soup, undiluted
- 1 cup sour cream
- ½ cup chopped green pepper
- ½ cup chopped onion

1. In a greased 13x9-in. baking dish, layer half of the noodles, ham and cheese.
2. In a large bowl, combine the soup, sour cream, green pepper and onion; spread half over the top. Repeat all layers. Bake casserole, uncovered, at 350° for 40-45 minutes or until heated through.
1 serving: 360 cal., 18g fat (10g sat. fat), 92mg chol., 815mg sod., 27g carb. (4g sugars, 1g fiber), 20g pro.

EASY MARINATED GRILLED FLANK STEAK

Friends shared this three-ingredient marinade years ago, and it's been a favorite ever since. Serve the steak with salad and grilled potatoes for an excellent meal.
—Beverly Dietz, Surprise, AZ

- -

Prep: 5 min. + marinating • **Grill:** 15 min.
Makes: 8 servings

1 cup barbecue sauce
½ cup burgundy wine or beef broth
¼ cup lemon juice
1 beef flank steak (2 lbs.)

1. Whisk barbecue sauce, wine and lemon juice until blended. Pour 1 cup marinade into a shallow dish. Add beef; turn to coat. Cover; refrigerate 4 hours or overnight. Chill remaining marinade.

2. Drain beef, discarding marinade. Grill steak, covered, over medium heat until meat reaches desired doneness (for medium-rare, a thermometer should read 135°; medium, 140°; medium-well, 145°), 6-8 minutes on each side. Let stand for 5 minutes before thinly slicing across the grain. Serve with reserved marinade.

3 oz. cooked steak with 1½ Tbsp. reserved marinade: 195 cal., 9g fat (4g sat. fat), 54mg chol., 271mg sod., 4g carb. (3g sugars, 0 fiber), 22g pro. **Diabetic exchanges:** 3 lean meat, 1 fat.

BRING IT

Marinated beef is a great choice to pack and grill on-site at your gathering. Since it's widely considered safe cooked to a range of temperatures, and it doesn't carry as much risk for cross-contamination as chicken, turkey or pork.

HOT BROWN TURKEY CASSEROLE

If you've ever tried the Hot Brown sandwich at the Brown Hotel in Louisville, Kentucky, you'll love this version. It can be assembled ahead and refrigerated; just adjust baking time accordingly if cold.
—Diane Halferty, Corpus Christi, TX

Prep: 40 min. • **Bake:** 20 min.
Makes: 12 servings

¼ cup butter
¼ cup all-purpose flour
4 cups 2% milk
1 large egg
⅔ cup grated Parmesan cheese, divided
¼ tsp. salt
¼ tsp. pepper
12 slices bread, toasted and divided
2 lbs. thinly sliced cooked turkey or chicken
¼ tsp. paprika
6 bacon strips, cooked and crumbled
1 cup tomatoes, chopped and seeded
1 tsp. minced fresh parsley

1. Preheat oven to 350°. In a large saucepan, melt butter over medium heat. Stir in flour until smooth; gradually whisk in milk. Bring to a boil, stirring constantly; cook until slightly thickened, 6-8 minutes. Remove from heat.
2. In a small bowl, lightly beat egg. Gradually whisk in ½ cup sauce. Slowly return all to the pan, whisking constantly. Add ½ cup Parmesan cheese, salt and pepper. Cook and stir until thickened. (Do not allow to boil.)
3. In a greased 13x9-in. baking dish, layer 6 toast slices and turkey; pour sauce over top. Sprinkle with paprika, bacon and remaining Parmesan cheese.
4. Bake until heated through, 20-25 minutes. Top with tomatoes and parsley. Cut remaining toast in half diagonally; serve on the side.

1 piece: 316 cal., 13g fat (6g sat. fat), 117mg chol., 472mg sod., 19g carb. (6g sugars, 1g fiber), 30g pro.

POLENTA CHILI CASSEROLE

This delicious vegetarian bake combines spicy chili, mixed veggies and homemade polenta. It's so hearty that no one seems to miss the meat.
—Dan Kelmenson, West Bloomfield, MI

- -

Prep: 20 min. • **Bake:** 35 min. + standing
Makes: 8 servings

- 4 cups water
- ½ tsp. salt
- 1¼ cups yellow cornmeal
- 2 cups shredded cheddar cheese, divided
- 3 cans (15 oz. each) vegetarian chili with beans
- 1 pkg. (16 oz.) frozen mixed vegetables, thawed and well drained

1. Preheat oven to 350°. In a large heavy saucepan, bring water and salt to a boil. Reduce heat to a gentle boil; slowly whisk in cornmeal. Cook and stir with a wooden spoon 15-20 minutes or until polenta is thickened and pulls away cleanly from sides of pan.
2. Remove from heat. Stir in ¼ cup cheddar cheese until melted.
3. Spread into a 13x9-in. baking dish coated with cooking spray. Bake, uncovered, for 20 minutes. Meanwhile, heat chili according to package directions.
4. Spread mixed vegetables over polenta; top with chili. Sprinkle with remaining cheese. Bake 12-15 minutes longer or until cheese is melted. Let stand 10 minutes before serving.
1 piece: 297 cal., 7g fat (4g sat. fat), 20mg chol., 556mg sod., 43g carb. (7g sugars, 12g fiber), 19g pro.

SAUSAGE RATATOUILLE

You'll feel like Ratatouille's great chef, Remy, when you serve this veggie-packed dish party guests will rave about. Don't let the ingredient list fool you: Pantry staples and an easy-cook method make this one a cinch.
—Janine Freeman, Blaine, WA

- -

Prep: 20 min. • **Cook:** 25 min.
Makes: 10 servings

- 2 lbs. sweet Italian sausage links
- ½ lb. fresh green beans, trimmed and cut into 2-in. pieces
- 2 medium green peppers, julienned
- 1 large onion, chopped
- 5 shallots, chopped
- 2 garlic cloves, minced
- 2 Tbsp. butter
- 2 Tbsp. olive oil
- 4 medium zucchini, quartered and sliced
- 5 plum tomatoes, chopped
- ½ tsp. sugar
- ½ tsp. salt
- ¼ tsp. pepper
- ¼ tsp. crushed red pepper flakes
- ⅛ tsp. ground allspice
- ¼ cup minced fresh parsley
- ⅓ cup grated Parmesan cheese
  Hot cooked rice

1. In a large skillet, cook sausage over medium heat until no longer pink; drain. Remove and cut into ½-in. slices.
2. In the same skillet, cook the beans, green peppers, onion, shallots and garlic in butter and oil in batches over medium heat until tender. Stir in the zucchini, tomatoes, sugar, salt, pepper, pepper flakes and allspice. Cook and stir for 6-8 minutes or until vegetables are tender.
3. Stir in sausage and parsley; heat through. Sprinkle with cheese. Serve with rice.
1¼ cups: 337 cal., 26g fat (8g sat. fat), 57mg chol., 752mg sod., 15g carb. (6g sugars, 3g fiber), 14g pro.

FRENCH MARKET SANDWICHES

I first tasted this warm ham and cheese sandwich at a luncheon, and it quickly became a favorite in our house. I keep some in the freezer for fast meals. My bridge club enjoys them with soup and fresh fruit.
—Florence McNulty, Montebello, CA

Takes: 25 min. • **Makes:** 10 servings

- ½ cup butter, softened
- ½ cup Dijon mustard
- 2 Tbsp. chopped green onions
- ½ tsp. poppy seeds
- ¼ tsp. curry powder
- 10 croissants, split
- 1¼ lbs. thinly sliced deli ham
- 10 slices Swiss cheese

1. Preheat oven to 325°. In a small bowl, combine butter, mustard, onions, poppy seeds and curry powder. Spread over cut sides of croissants. Place ham and Swiss cheese on croissants; replace tops. Wrap individually in foil.
2. Bake 15-20 minutes or until heated through. Serve immediately.
1 serving: 476 cal., 30g fat (18g sat. fat), 108mg chol., 1303mg sod., 31g carb. (6g sugars, 2g fiber), 21g pro.

NINE-LAYER SALAD

Layered salads rank among the classics in the potluck hall of fame. In this one, the combination of ham, cheese, egg and bacon is like a deconstructed sandwich, making it hearty enough to serve for a main course.
—Stacy Huggins, Valley Center, CA

Takes: 30 min. • **Makes:** 12 servings

- 2 cups mayonnaise
- 1 cup sour cream
- ½ tsp. sugar
- ⅛ tsp. salt
- ⅛ tsp. pepper
- 8 cups fresh baby spinach (about 6 oz.)
- 6 hard-boiled large eggs, chopped
- ½ lb. sliced fully cooked ham, cut into strips
- 4 cups torn iceberg lettuce
- 2½ cups frozen petite peas (about 10 oz.), thawed, optional
- 1 small red onion, halved and thinly sliced
- 8 oz. sliced Swiss cheese, cut into strips
- ½ lb. bacon strips, cooked and crumbled

For dressing, mix first 5 ingredients. In a 3-qt. or larger glass bowl, layer spinach, eggs, ham, lettuce, peas, if desired, and onion. Spread with dressing. Sprinkle with cheese and bacon. Refrigerate, covered, until serving.
1 cup: 501 cal., 43g fat (12g sat. fat), 137mg chol., 665mg sod., 11g carb. (5g sugars, 3g fiber), 19g pro.

STUFFING & TURKEY CASSEROLE

This is a plate full of love, comfort and hearty goodness.
—Debbie Fabre, Fort Myers, FL

Prep: 15 min. • **Bake:** 45 min. + standing
Makes: 12 servings

- 4 cups leftover stuffing
- 1 cup dried cranberries
- 1 cup chopped pecans
- ¾ cup chicken broth
- 1 large egg, lightly beaten
- 2 cups shredded part-skim mozzarella cheese
- 1 cup whole-milk ricotta cheese
- 4 cups cubed cooked turkey, divided
- 1 cup shredded cheddar cheese

1. Preheat oven to 350°. Place stuffing, cranberries and pecans in a large bowl; stir in broth. In a small bowl, mix egg and mozzarella and ricotta cheeses.
2. In a greased 13x9-in. baking dish, layer 2 cups turkey, 3 cups stuffing mixture and ricotta cheese mixture. Top with remaining turkey and stuffing mixture. Sprinkle with cheddar cheese.
3. Bake, covered, 40-45 minutes or until heated through. Bake, uncovered, 5 minutes longer. Let stand 10 minutes before serving.
1 piece: 418 cal., 24g fat (8g sat. fat), 91mg chol., 640mg sod., 26g carb. (10g sugars, 3g fiber), 27g pro.

APPLE CIDER-GLAZED HAM

When I wanted to try something new with our holiday ham, I created this cider glaze. It's slightly sweet but still has the spicy flavor my family craves.
—Rebecca LaWare, Canandaigua, NY

Prep: 15 min. • **Bake:** 2½ hours
Makes: 10 servings (1 cup sauce)

- 1 fully cooked bone-in ham (6 to 7 lbs.)
- 2 cups apple cider
- 1 cup honey
- ½ cup cider vinegar
- ¼ cup Dijon mustard
- 1 Tbsp. butter
- 2 tsp. chili powder
- ½ tsp. apple pie spice

1. Place ham on a rack in a shallow roasting pan. Score the surface of the ham, making diamond shapes ½ in. deep. Cover and bake at 325° for 2 hours.
2. Meanwhile, in a large saucepan, combine the cider, honey, vinegar and mustard; bring to a boil. Reduce heat; simmer, uncovered, for 15 minutes, stirring frequently. Stir in the butter, chili powder and apple pie spice. Set aside 1 cup for serving.
3. Cook the remaining sauce until thickened; spoon over ham. Bake, uncovered, until a thermometer reads 140°, 30-35 minutes longer. Warm the reserved sauce; serve with ham.
6 oz. cooked ham: 261 cal., 5g fat (2g sat. fat), 63mg chol., 877mg sod., 36g carb. (33g sugars, 0 fiber), 20g pro.

CREAMY TURKEY CASSEROLE

I sometimes make turkey just so I have the extras for this casserole!
—Mary Jo O'Brien, Hastings, MN

Prep: 15 min. • **Bake:** 40 min.
Makes: 12 servings

- 1 can (10¾ oz.) condensed cream of celery soup, undiluted
- 1 can (10¾ oz.) condensed cream of mushroom soup, undiluted
- 1 can (10¾ oz.) condensed cream of onion soup, undiluted
- 5 oz. process cheese (Velveeta), cubed
- ⅓ cup mayonnaise
- 3½ to 4 cups shredded cooked turkey
- 1 pkg. (16 oz.) frozen broccoli florets or cuts, thawed
- 1½ cups cooked white rice
- 1½ cups cooked wild rice
- 1 can (8 oz.) sliced water chestnuts, drained
- 1 jar (4 oz.) sliced mushrooms, drained
- 1½ to 2 cups salad croutons

1. Combine the soups, cheese and mayonnaise. Stir in the turkey, broccoli, rice, water chestnuts and mushrooms.
2. Transfer to a greased 13x9-in. baking dish. Bake casserole, uncovered, at 350° for 30 minutes; stir. Sprinkle with croutons. Bake until bubbly, 8-12 minutes longer.
¾ cup: 311 cal., 14g fat (4g sat. fat), 52mg chol., 846mg sod., 25g carb. (3g sugars, 3g fiber), 20g pro.

PITCHFORK PULLED PORK

Pile the spaghetti squash on top of these Italian-style pulled pork sandwiches so it looks like a haystack. It's so fun your kids won't know they're eating vegetables.
—Matthew Hass, Ellison Bay, WI

Prep: 15 min. • **Cook:** 6 hours
Makes: 12 servings

- 1 boneless pork shoulder butt roast (3 to 4 lbs.)
- 4½ tsp. Italian seasoning, divided
- 2½ tsp. salt, divided
- 1 cup water, divided
- 1 Tbsp. olive oil
- 1 medium onion, chopped
- 4 garlic cloves, minced
- 1 can (28 oz.) crushed tomatoes in puree
- 1 can (6 oz.) tomato paste
- 2 tsp. sugar
- ½ tsp. pepper
- 2 bay leaves
- 1 medium spaghetti squash (about 4 lbs.)
- 12 kaiser rolls, split

1. Sprinkle roast with 1½ tsp. Italian seasoning and 1½ tsp. salt. Place in a 4- or 5-qt. slow cooker; add ½ cup water. Cook, covered, on low 6-8 hours or until meat is tender.

2. Meanwhile, in a large saucepan, heat oil over medium heat. Add onion; cook and stir 4-5 minutes or until tender. Add garlic; cook 1 minute longer. Stir in tomatoes, tomato paste, sugar, pepper, bay leaves and remaining Italian seasoning, salt and water; bring to a boil. Reduce heat, simmer, uncovered, 15-20 minutes to allow flavors to blend. Discard bay leaves.

3. Cut squash lengthwise in half; discard seeds. Place squash on a microwave-safe plate, cut side down. Microwave, uncovered, on high 15-20 minutes or until tender. When squash is cool enough to handle, use a fork to separate strands.

4. Remove roast; discard cooking juices. When cool enough to handle, shred meat with 2 forks. Return meat to slow cooker. Stir in sauce; heat through.

5. Using tongs, place meat mixture on bun bottoms; top with squash. Replace tops.

1 sandwich: 450cal., 16g fat (5g sat. fat), 67mg chol., 1030mg sod., 50g carb. (6g sugars, 5g fiber), 28g pro.

BAKED BEEF TACOS

We give tacos a fresh approach by baking the shells upright in refried beans and tomatoes. The bottom gets soft, and the top stays crisp and crunchy.
—Patricia Stagich, Elizabeth, NJ

Prep: 15 min. • **Bake:** 20 min.
Makes: 12 servings

1½	lbs. ground beef
1	envelope taco seasoning
2	cans (10 oz. each) diced tomatoes and green chiles, divided
1	can (16 oz.) refried beans
2	cups shredded Mexican cheese blend, divided
¼	cup chopped fresh cilantro
1	tsp. hot pepper sauce, optional
12	taco shells
	Chopped green onions

1. Preheat oven to 425°. In a large skillet, cook beef over medium heat 6-8 minutes or until no longer pink, breaking into crumbles; drain. Stir in taco seasoning and 1 can of undrained tomatoes; heat through.
2. Meanwhile, in a bowl, mix beans, ½ cup cheese, fresh cilantro, remaining can of undrained tomatoes and, if desired, pepper sauce. Spread onto bottom of a greased 13x9-in. baking dish.
3. Stand taco shells upright over bean mixture. Fill each with 1 Tbsp. cheese and about ⅓ cup beef mixture. Bake, covered, 15 minutes.
4. Uncover; sprinkle with remaining cheese. Bake, uncovered, 5-7 minutes or until cheese is melted and shells are lightly browned. Sprinkle with green onions.
1 taco with ¼ cup bean mixture: 277 cal., 15g fat (7g sat. fat), 52mg chol., 836mg sod., 17g carb. (0 sugars, 3g fiber), 17g pro.

BLACK BEAN & CHICKEN ENCHILADA LASAGNA

Twice a month I make chicken enchiladas, lasagna-style. It's a regular with us because assembly is easy and my whole family gives it a thumbs-up.
—Cheryl Snavely, Hagerstown, MD

Prep: 30 min. • **Bake:** 25 min. + standing
Makes: 8 servings

- 2 cans (10 oz. each) enchilada sauce
- 12 corn tortillas (6 in.)
- 2 cups coarsely shredded rotisserie chicken
- 1 small onion, chopped
- 1 can (15 oz.) black beans, rinsed and drained
- 3 cans (4 oz. each) whole green chiles, drained and coarsely chopped
- 3 cups crumbled queso fresco or shredded Mexican cheese blend
- 2 medium ripe avocados
- 2 Tbsp. sour cream
- 2 Tbsp. lime juice
- ½ tsp. salt
  Chopped fresh tomatoes and cilantro

1. Preheat oven to 350°. Spread ½ cup enchilada sauce into a greasec 13x9-in. baking dish; top with 4 tortillas, 1 cup chicken, ¼ cup onion, ¼ cup beans, ⅓ cup green chiles and 1 cup cheese. Repeat layers. Drizzle with ½ cup enchilada sauce; top with the remaining tortillas, onion, beans, chiles, sauce and cheese.

2. Bake, uncovered, until lasagna is bubbly and cheese is melted, 25-30 minutes. Let stand 10 minutes before serving.

3. Meanwhile, pit and peel 1 avocado; place in a food processor. Add sour cream, lime juice and salt; process until smooth. Pit, peel and cut remaining the avocado into small cubes.

4. Top lasagna with tomatoes, cilantro and cubed avocado. Serve with avocado sauce.

1 piece with 1 Tbsp. sauce: 407 cal., 18g fat (7g sat. fat), 64mg chol., 857mg sod., 39g carb. (4g sugars, 8g fiber), 28g pro.

GRILLED BUTTERMILK CHICKEN

I created this recipe years ago after one of our farmers market customers, a chef, shared the idea of marinating chicken in buttermilk. The chicken is easy to prepare and always turns out moist and delicious! I bruise the thyme sprigs by twisting them before adding to the buttermilk mixture; this tends to release the oils in the leaves and flavor the chicken better.
—Sue Gronholz, Beaver Dam, WI

Prep: 10 min. + marinating • **Grill:** 10 min.
Makes: 12 servings

1½ cups buttermilk
4 fresh thyme sprigs
4 garlic cloves, halved
½ tsp. salt
12 boneless skinless chicken breast halves (about 4½ lbs.)

1. Place the buttermilk, thyme, garlic and salt in a large bowl or shallow dish. Add chicken and turn to coat. Refrigerate 8 hours or overnight, turning occasionally.
2. Drain chicken, discarding marinade. Grill, covered, over medium heat until a thermometer reads 165°, 5-7 minutes per side.
1 chicken breast half: 189 cal., 4g fat (1g sat. fat), 95mg chol., 168mg sod., 1g carb. (1g sugars, 0 fiber), 35g pro. **Diabetic exchanges:** 5 lean meat.

FIVE-CHEESE RIGATONI

Who can resist cheesy pasta hot from the oven? This ooey-gooey rigatoni boasts creamy homemade sauce that comes together in just a few minutes.
—Shirley Foltz, Dexter, KS

Prep: 25 min. • **Bake:** 25 min.
Makes: 9 servings

- 1 pkg. (16 oz.) rigatoni or large tube pasta
- 2 Tbsp. butter
- 3 Tbsp. all-purpose flour
- 1 tsp. salt
- ½ tsp. pepper
- 2½ cups whole milk
- ½ cup shredded Swiss cheese
- ½ cup shredded fontina cheese
- ½ cup shredded part-skim mozzarella cheese
- ½ cup grated Parmesan cheese, divided
- ½ cup grated Romano cheese, divided

1. Cook rigatoni according to package directions.
2. Preheat oven to 375°. In a large saucepan, melt butter. Stir in the flour, salt and pepper until smooth. Gradually stir in milk; bring to a boil. Cook and stir 1-2 minutes or until thickened. Stir in Swiss, fontina, mozzarella, ¼ cup Parmesan and ¼ cup Romano cheese until melted.
3. Drain rigatoni; stir in cheese sauce. Transfer to a greased 13x9-in. baking dish. Sprinkle with remaining Parmesan and Romano cheeses. Cover and bake for 20 minutes. Uncover; bake 5-10 minutes longer or until bubbly.
¾ cup: 362 cal., 14g fat (8g sat. fat), 40mg chol., 586mg sod., 42g carb. (5g sugars, 2g fiber), 18g pro.

SUNDAY PORK ROAST

Mom would prepare this delectable main dish for our family, friends and customers at the three restaurants she and Dad owned. The herb rub and vegetables give it a remarkable flavor.
—Sandi Pichon, Memphis, TN

Prep: 20 min.
Bake: 1 hour 10 min. + standing
Makes: 12 servings

2	medium onions, chopped
2	medium carrots, chopped
1	celery rib, chopped
4	Tbsp. all-purpose flour, divided
1	bay leaf, finely crushed
½	tsp. dried thyme
1¼	tsp. salt, divided
1¼	tsp. pepper, divided
1	boneless pork loin roast (3 to 4 lbs.)
⅓	cup packed brown sugar

1. Preheat oven to 350°. Place vegetables on bottom of a shallow roasting pan. Mix 2 Tbsp. flour, bay leaf, thyme, and 1 tsp. each salt and pepper; rub over roast. Place roast on top of vegetables, fat side up. Add 1 cup water to pan.

2. Roast 1 hour, basting once with pan juices if desired. Sprinkle brown sugar over roast. Roast 10-15 minutes longer or until a thermometer reads 140°. (Temperature of roast will continue to rise another 5-10° upon standing.)

3. Remove roast to a platter. Tent with foil; let stand 15 minutes before slicing.

4. Strain drippings from roasting pan into a measuring cup; skim fat. Add enough water to the drippings to measure 1½ cups.

5. In a small saucepan over medium heat, whisk remaining flour and ⅓ cup water until smooth. Gradually whisk in drippings mixture and remaining salt and pepper. Bring to a boil over medium-high heat, stirring constantly; cook and stir 2 minutes or until thickened. Serve roast with gravy.

Freeze option: Freeze cooled sliced pork and gravy in freezer containers. To use, partially thaw in refrigerator overnight. Heat through in a covered saucepan, gently stirring and adding a little broth or water if necessary.

3 oz. cooked pork with about 2 Tbsp. gravy: 174 cal., 5g fat (2g sat. fat), 57mg chol., 280mg sod., 8g carb. (6g sugars, 0 fiber), 22g pro. **Diabetic exchanges:** 3 lean meat, ½ starch.

> **TEST KITCHEN TIP**
> Dark brown sugar contains more molasses than light or golden brown sugar. The types are generally interchangeable in recipes. But if you prefer a bolder flavor, choose dark brown sugar.

ROADSIDE DINER CHEESEBURGER QUICHE

This unforgettable quiche tastes just like its burger counterpart. Easy and appealing, it's perfect for lunch guests and fun for the whole family.
—Barbara J. Miller, Oakdale, MN

- -

Prep: 20 min. • **Bake:** 50 min. + standing
Makes: 8 servings

1   sheet refrigerated pie crust
¾   lb. ground beef
2   plum tomatoes, seeded and chopped
1   medium onion, chopped
½   cup dill pickle relish
½   cup crumbled cooked bacon
5   large eggs
1   cup heavy whipping cream
½   cup 2% milk
2   tsp. prepared mustard
1   tsp. hot pepper sauce
½   tsp. salt
¼   tsp. pepper
1½   cups shredded cheddar cheese

½   cup shredded Parmesan cheese
     Optional garnishes: Mayonnaise, additional pickle relish, crumbled cooked bacon, and chopped onion and tomato

1. Unroll crust into a 9-in. deep-dish pie plate; flute edges and set aside. In a large skillet, cook beef over medium heat until no longer pink; drain. Stir in the tomatoes, onion, relish and bacon. Transfer to prepared crust.
2. In a large bowl, whisk the eggs, cream, milk, mustard, pepper sauce, salt and pepper. Pour over beef mixture. Sprinkle with cheeses.
3. Bake at 375° until a knife inserted in center comes out clean, 50-60 minutes. Cover edges with foil during the last 15 minutes to prevent overbrowning if necessary. Let stand for 10 minutes before cutting. Garnish with optional ingredients as desired.
1 piece: 502 cal., 35g fat (19g sat. fat), 236mg chol., 954mg sod., 24g carb. (8g sugars, 1g fiber), 23g pro.

VEGGIE NOODLE HAM CASSEROLE

This saucy main dish is really quite versatile. Without the ham, it can be a vegetarian entree or a hearty side dish.
—Judy Moody, Wheatley, ON

- -

Prep: 15 min. • **Bake:** 50 min.
Makes: 10 servings

1   pkg. (12 oz.) wide egg noodles
1   can (10¾ oz.) condensed cream of chicken soup, undiluted
1   can (10¾ oz.) condensed cream of broccoli soup, undiluted
1½   cups whole milk
2   cups frozen corn, thawed
1½   cups frozen California-blend vegetables, thawed
1½   cups cubed fully cooked ham
2   Tbsp. minced fresh parsley
½   tsp. pepper
¼   tsp. salt
1   cup shredded cheddar cheese, divided

1. Preheat oven to 350°. Cook the pasta according to package directions; drain. In a large bowl, combine soups and milk; stir in the noodles, corn, vegetables, ham, parsley, pepper, salt and ¾ cup of cheese.
2. Transfer to a greased 13x9-in. baking dish. Cover and bake 45 minutes. Uncover; sprinkle with remaining cheese. Bake for 5-10 minutes or until bubbly and cheese is melted.
Freeze option: Cool unbaked casserole; cover and freeze. To use, partially thaw in refrigerator overnight. Remove from refrigerator 30 minutes before baking. Preheat oven to 350°. Bake casserole as directed, increasing time as necessary to heat through and for a thermometer inserted in center to read 165°. Top with remaining cheese the last 5 minutes.
1 cup: 312 cal., 11g fat (5g sat. fat), 59mg chol., 828mg sod., 40g carb. (4g sugars, 3g fiber), 15g pro.

CHRISTMAS DAY CHICKEN

I've been making this comforting entree for Christmas dinner for more than 10 years. The chicken breasts marinate overnight, then you simply coat them with crumbs and bake. They come out crispy on the outside and tender and juicy on the inside.
—Marcia Larson, Batavia, IL

Prep: 15 min. + marinating • **Bake:** 30 min.
Makes: 16 servings

- 16 boneless skinless chicken breast halves (4 oz. each)
- 2 cups sour cream
- ¼ cup lemon juice
- 4 tsp. Worcestershire sauce
- 2 tsp. celery salt
- 2 tsp. pepper
- 2 tsp. paprika
- 1 tsp. seasoned salt
- 1 tsp. garlic salt
- 1½ to 2 cups crushed butter-flavored crackers
- ½ cup canola oil
- ½ cup butter, melted

1. Place the chicken in 2 large shallow bowls. In another bowl, combine sour cream, lemon juice, Worcestershire sauce and seasonings. Pour over chicken; turn to coat. Refrigerate overnight.

2. Preheat oven to 350°. Drain and discard marinade. Coat the chicken with cracker crumbs; place in 2 greased 13x9-in. baking dishes. Combine oil and butter; drizzle over the chicken.

3. Bake, uncovered, until a thermometer reads 165°, 30-35 minutes.

1 chicken breast half: 324 cal., 22g fat (8g sat. fat), 83mg chol., 464mg sod., 7g carb. (2g sugars, 0 fiber), 24g pro.

DOUBLE-CRUST PIZZA CASSEROLE

After my husband and I got married, this biscuit pizza solved the what's-for-dinner problem. As our family grew, I just made bigger and bigger batches.
—Pat Crane, Pine City, NY

Prep: 20 min. • **Bake:** 20 min.
Makes: 12 servings

- 2 lbs. lean ground beef (90% lean)
- 2 cans (15 oz. each) pizza sauce, divided
- 2 tsp. dried oregano
- 3 cups biscuit/baking mix
- 1¼ cups 2% milk
- 1 large egg, lightly beaten
- 2 cups shredded part-skim mozzarella cheese
- 1 cup sliced fresh mushrooms
- 1 medium green pepper, chopped
- 1 medium onion, chopped
- ¼ cup grated Parmesan cheese
- 1 plum tomato, chopped

1. Preheat oven to 400°. In a large skillet, cook beef over medium heat until no longer pink, 8-10 minutes, breaking into crumbles; drain. Stir in 1 can pizza sauce and oregano. Bring to a boil. Reduce heat; simmer, uncovered, until slightly thickened, 5-6 minutes, stirring occasionally. Remove from heat.

2. In a large bowl, stir biscuit mix, milk and egg just until moistened. Spread half the batter onto bottom of a greased 13x9-in. baking pan. Spread with remaining pizza sauce. Top with the mozzarella cheese, mushrooms, pepper, onion and beef mixture. Spoon remaining batter over top; sprinkle with Parmesan cheese.

3. Bake, uncovered, until golden brown, 20-25 minutes. Sprinkle with tomato. Let stand 5 minutes before serving.

1 piece: 369 cal., 16 g fat (7 g sat. fat), 78 mg chol., 710 mg sod., 30 g carb. (4 g sugars, 3 g fiber), 26 g pro.

EGGPLANT SAUSAGE CASSEROLE

If you want your kids to happily eat their eggplant, serve it in this lovely layered casserole. Our whole family enjoys it. Always a popular potluck item, it's a great company dish as well.
—Carol Mieske, Red Bluff, CA

- -

Prep: 45 min. • **Bake:** 45 min. + standing
Makes: 12 servings

- 1 pkg. (16 oz.) penne pasta
- 2 lbs. bulk Italian sausage
- 1 medium eggplant, peeled and cubed
- 1 large onion, chopped
- 2 Tbsp. olive oil
- 2 garlic cloves, minced
- 1 can (28 oz.) diced tomatoes, undrained
- 1 can (6 oz.) tomato paste
- 1 tsp. salt
- 1 tsp. dried basil
- 1 tsp. paprika
- 1 carton (15 oz.) ricotta cheese
- 4 cups shredded part-skim mozzarella cheese, divided

1. Cook pasta according to package directions. Meanwhile, in a large skillet, cook sausage over medium heat until no longer pink; drain. Set sausage aside.
2. In the same skillet, saute eggplant and onion in oil. Add garlic; cook 1 minute longer. Stir in the tomatoes, tomato paste, salt, basil and paprika; simmer, partially covered, for 15 minutes. Remove from the heat. Drain pasta; stir into eggplant mixture. Add sausage.
3. Spread half of the sausage mixture in a greased 13x9-in. baking dish. Spread with ricotta cheese. Top with half of the cheese and remaining sausage mixture.
4. Cover and bake at 350° for 40 minutes. Uncover; sprinkle with remaining cheese. Bake 5 minutes longer or until cheese is melted. Let casserole stand for 10 minutes before serving.
1 serving: 606 cal., 36g fat (15g sat. fat), 94mg chol., 1066mg sod., 41g carb. (11g sugars, 4g fiber), 31g pro.

MOM'S ROAST BEEF

Everyone loves slices of this fork-tender roast beef and its savory gravy. This well-seasoned roast is Mom's specialty. People always ask what her secret ingredients are. Now you have the delicious recipe for our family's favorite meat dish!
—Linda Gaido, New Brighton, PA

- -

Prep: 20 min. • **Cook:** 2½ hours + standing
Makes: 8 servings

- 1 Tbsp. canola oil
- 1 beef eye round roast (about 2½ lbs.)
- 1 garlic clove, minced
- 2 tsp. dried basil
- 1 tsp. salt
- 1 tsp. dried rosemary, crushed
- ½ tsp. pepper
- 1 medium onion, chopped
- 1 tsp. beef bouillon granules
- 1 cup brewed coffee
- ¾ cup water

GRAVY
- ¼ cup all-purpose flour
- ¼ cup cold water

1. In a Dutch oven, heat oil over medium heat; brown roast on all sides. Remove from pan. Mix garlic and seasonings; sprinkle over the roast.
2. Add onion to same pan; cook and stir over medium heat until tender; stir in bouillon, coffee and ¾ cup water. Add roast; bring to a boil. Reduce heat; simmer, covered, until meat is tender, about 2½ hours.
3. Remove roast from pan, reserving cooking juices. Tent with foil; let stand 10 minutes before slicing.
4. Mix flour and cold water until smooth; stir into cooking juices. Bring to a boil, stirring constantly. Cook and stir until thickened, 1-2 minutes. Serve with roast.
1 serving: 198 cal., 6g fat (2g sat. fat), 65mg chol., 453mg sod., 5g carb. (1g sugars, 1g fiber), 28g pro.

CASHEW-CHICKEN ROTINI SALAD

I've tried many chicken salad recipes over the years, but this is my favorite. It's fun, fruity and refreshing, and the cashews add wonderful crunch. Every time I serve it at a potluck or picnic, I get rave reviews and always come home with an empty bowl!
—Kara Cook, Elk Ridge, UT

Prep: 30 min. + chilling • **Makes:** 12 servings

- 1 pkg. (16 oz.) spiral or rotini pasta
- 4 cups cubed cooked chicken
- 1 can (20 oz.) pineapple tidbits, drained
- 1½ cups sliced celery
- ¾ cup thinly sliced green onions
- 1 cup seedless red grapes
- 1 cup seedless green grapes
- 1 pkg. (5 oz.) dried cranberries
- 1 cup ranch salad dressing
- ¾ cup mayonnaise
- 2 cups salted cashews

1. Cook pasta according to package directions. Meanwhile, in a large bowl, combine the chicken, pineapple, celery, onions, grapes and cranberries. Drain pasta and rinse in cold water; stir into chicken mixture.

2. In a small bowl, whisk the ranch dressing and mayonnaise. Pour over salad and toss to coat. Cover and refrigerate for at least 1 hour. Just before serving, stir in cashews.

1⅓ cups: 661 cal., 37g fat (6g sat. fat), 44mg chol., 451mg sod., 59g carb. (24g sugars, 4g fiber), 23g pro.

CALGARY STAMPEDE RIBS

"More, please!" is what I hear when I serve these zippy, finger-licking ribs to family or guests. The first time my husband and I tried them, we declared them the best ever. The recipe has its roots in the Calgary Stampede, an annual Western culture festival and exhibition in our province.
—Marian Misik, Sherwood Park, AB

Prep: 2¼ hours + marinating • **Grill:** 15 min.
Makes: 8 servings

- 4 lbs. pork baby back ribs, cut into serving-size pieces
- 3 garlic cloves, minced
- 1 Tbsp. sugar
- 2 tsp. salt
- 1 Tbsp. paprika
- 2 tsp. ground cumin
- 2 tsp. chili powder
- 2 tsp. pepper

BARBECUE SAUCE
- 2 Tbsp. butter
- 1 small onion, finely chopped
- 1 cup ketchup
- ¼ cup packed brown sugar
- 3 Tbsp. lemon juice
- 3 Tbsp. Worcestershire sauce
- 2 Tbsp. cider vinegar
- 1½ tsp. ground mustard
- 1 tsp. celery seed
- ⅛ tsp. cayenne pepper

1. Preheat oven to 325°. Rub ribs with garlic; place in a roasting pan. Bake, covered, until tender, about 2 hours.
2. Mix sugar, salt and seasonings; sprinkle over ribs. Remove from pan; cool slightly. Refrigerate, covered, 8 hours or overnight.
3. In a small saucepan, heat butter over medium heat; saute onion until tender. Stir in remaining ingredients; bring to a boil. Reduce heat; cook, uncovered, until thickened, about 10 minutes, stirring frequently.
4. Brush ribs with some of the sauce. Grill, covered, over medium heat until heated through, 12-15 minutes, turning and brushing occasionally with additional sauce. Serve with remaining sauce.
1 serving: 394 cal., 24g fat (9g sat. fat), 89mg chol., 1170mg sod., 21g carb. (18g sugars, 1g fiber), 23g pro.

PORK TENDERLOIN MEDALLIONS WITH STRAWBERRY SAUCE

Pork tenderloin paired with strawberries is a heavenly match, made even more special with a tangy feta garnish. Serve with roasted spring vegetables.
—Katherine Wollgast, Troy, MO

Prep: 15 min. • **Cook:** 20 min.
Makes: 8 servings

- 1½ cups reduced-sodium beef broth
- 2 cups chopped fresh strawberries, divided
- ½ cup white wine vinegar
- ¼ cup packed brown sugar
- ¼ cup reduced-sodium soy sauce
- 3 garlic cloves, minced
- 2 lbs. pork tenderloin, cut into ½-in. slices
- 1 tsp. garlic powder
- ½ tsp. salt
- ½ tsp. pepper
- 2 Tbsp. canola oil
- 2 Tbsp. cornstarch
- 2 Tbsp. cold water
- ½ cup crumbled feta cheese
- ½ cup chopped green onions

1. In a large saucepan, combine broth, 1 cup strawberries, vinegar, brown sugar, soy sauce and garlic; bring to a boil. Reduce heat; simmer, uncovered, 15 minutes or until slightly thickened. Strain mixture and set aside liquid, discarding solids.

2. Sprinkle pork with garlic powder, salt and pepper. In a large skillet, heat oil over medium heat. Brown pork in batches on both sides. Remove and keep warm.

3. Add broth mixture to the pan; bring to a boil. Combine cornstarch and water until smooth and gradually stir into skillet.

4. Return pork to the pan. Bring to a boil. Reduce heat; cook and stir 2 minutes or until sauce is thickened and pork is tender. Top each serving with cheese, onions and remaining strawberries.

1 serving: 244 cal., 9g fat (2g sat. fat), 68mg chol., 649mg sod., 15g carb. (9g sugars, 1g fiber), 25g pro. **Diabetic exchanges:** 3 lean meat, 1 starch, ½ fat.

CONTEST-WINNING GREEK PASTA BAKE

I've brought this dish to potlucks and it received rave reviews. There's never a morsel left. Best of all, it's a simple, healthy and hearty supper made with easy-to-find ingredients.
—Anne Taglienti, Kennett Square, PA

Prep: 20 min. • **Bake:** 25 min.
Makes: 8 servings

- 3⅓ cups uncooked whole grain spiral or penne pasta
- 4 cups cubed cooked chicken breast
- 1 can (29 oz.) tomato sauce
- 1 can (14½ oz.) no-salt-added diced tomatoes, drained
- 1 pkg. (10 oz.) frozen chopped spinach, thawed and squeezed dry
- 2 cans (2¼ oz. each) sliced ripe olives, drained
- ¼ cup thinly sliced red onion
- ¼ cup chopped green pepper
- 1 tsp. dried basil
- 1 tsp. dried oregano
- 1 cup shredded mozzarella cheese
- ½ cup crumbled feta cheese
  Chopped fresh oregano or basil, optional

1. Cook the pasta according to package directions; drain. In a large bowl, combine the pasta, chicken, tomato sauce, tomatoes, spinach, olives, onion, green pepper, basil and oregano.

2. Transfer to a 13x9-in. baking dish coated with cooking spray; top with cheeses. Bake, uncovered, at 400° for 25-30 minutes or until heated through and cheese is melted. If desired, sprinkle with oregano or basil.

Freeze option: Cool unbaked casserole; cover and freeze. To use, partially thaw in refrigerator overnight. Remove from refrigerator 30 minutes before baking. Preheat oven to 400°. Bake casserole as directed, increasing time as necessary to heat through and for a thermometer inserted in center to read 165°.

1½ cups: 398 cal., 10g fat (3g sat. fat), 67mg chol., 832mg sod., 47g carb. (5g sugars, 9g fiber), 34g pro. **Diabetic exchanges:** 3 lean meat, 3 very lean meat, 2½ starch, 1 vegetable, ½ fat.

★ ★ ★ ★ ★ **READER REVIEW**
"I added more cheese because all the guys in the house love cheese. I also used boneless skinless chicken thighs for more moisture. Very tasty, and it disappeared quickly."
TLCRAIGHEAD TASTEOFHOME.COM

BEEF & RICE ENCHILADAS

With a toddler in the house, I look for foods that are a snap to make. Loaded with beef, cheese and a flavorful rice mix, these enchiladas come together without any fuss. But they're so good that guests think I spent hours in the kitchen.
—Jennifer Smith, Colona, IL

Prep: 30 min. • **Bake:** 20 min.
Makes: 10 enchiladas

- 1 pkg. (6.8 oz.) Spanish rice and pasta mix
- 1 lb. ground beef
- 2 cans (10 oz. each) enchilada sauce, divided
- 10 flour tortillas (8 in.), warmed
- 1⅔ cups shredded cheddar cheese, divided

1. Prepare rice mix according to package directions. Meanwhile, in a large skillet, cook beef over medium heat until no longer pink; drain. Stir in Spanish rice and 1¼ cups enchilada sauce.
2. Spoon about ⅔ cup beef mixture down the center of each tortilla. Top each with 1 Tbsp. cheese; roll up.
3. Place in an ungreased 13x9-in. baking dish. Top with the remaining enchilada sauce and cheese. Bake, uncovered, at 350° until the cheese is melted, 20-25 minutes.
1 enchilada: 415 cal., 17g fat (8g sat. fat), 47mg chol., 1141mg sod., 46g carb. (3g sugars, 3g fiber), 20g pro.

BEER-BRAISED HAM FROM THE PRESSURE COOKER

To jazz up ham, I cook it in mustard and beer. Buns loaded with ham, pickles and mustard are perfect for a get-together.
—Ann R. Sheehy, Lawrence, MA

Prep: 10 min. • **Cook:** 25 min. + releasing
Makes: 16 servings

- 2 bottles (12 oz. each) beer or nonalcoholic beer
- ¾ cup German or Dijon mustard, divided
- ½ tsp. coarsely ground pepper
- 1 fully cooked bone-in ham (4 lbs.)
- 4 fresh rosemary sprigs
- 16 pretzel hamburger buns, split
  Dill pickle slices, optional

1. In a 6-qt. electric pressure cooker, whisk together beer, ½ cup mustard and pepper. Add ham and rosemary. Lock lid; make sure vent is closed. Select manual setting; adjust pressure to high and set time for 20 minutes. When finished cooking, allow pressure to naturally release for 10 minutes, then quick-release any remaining pressure.
2. Remove ham; cool slightly. Discard rosemary sprigs. Skim fat from liquid remaining in pressure cooker. Select saute setting and adjust for high heat. Bring liquid to a boil; cook for 5 minutes.
3. When ham is cool enough to handle, shred meat with 2 forks. Discard bone. Return ham to pressure cooker; heat through. To serve, place shredded ham on pretzel bun bottoms with remaining mustard and, if desired, dill pickle slices. Replace tops.
1 serving: 378 cal., 9g fat (1g sat. fat), 50mg chol., 1246mg sod., 50g carb. (4g sugars, 2g fiber), 25g pro.

Greek Breadsticks
page 116

Sides & Salads

Grazing goodness awaits in this chapter! From irresistible breads to crisp salads and colorful sides, you'll find just the thing to brighten up the buffet line.

SPINACH-ORZO SALAD WITH CHICKPEAS

The first version of this salad was an experiment in mixing together some random ingredients I had on hand. It was a success, and several people at the party asked for the recipe...which meant I had to re-create it! It's healthy, delicious and perfect for warm-weather days.
—Glen White, Kissimmee, FL

Takes: 25 min.
Makes: 12 servings

- 1 **can (14½ oz.) reduced-sodium chicken broth**
- 1½ **cups uncooked whole wheat orzo pasta**
- 4 **cups fresh baby spinach**
- 2 **cups grape tomatoes, halved**
- 2 **cans (15 oz. each) chickpeas or garbanzo beans, rinsed and drained**
- ¾ **cup chopped fresh parsley**
- 2 **green onions, chopped**

DRESSING
- ¼ **cup olive oil**
- 3 **Tbsp. lemon juice**
- ¾ **tsp. salt**
- ¼ **tsp. garlic powder**
- ¼ **tsp. hot pepper sauce**
- ¼ **tsp. pepper**

1. In a large saucepan, bring broth to a boil. Stir in orzo; return to a boil. Reduce heat; simmer, covered, until al dente, 8-10 minutes.
2. In a large bowl, toss spinach and warm orzo, allowing spinach to wilt slightly. Add tomatoes, chickpeas, parsley and green onions.
3. Whisk together dressing ingredients. Toss with salad.

¾ cup: 122 cal., 5g fat (1g sat. fat), 0 chol., 259mg sod., 16g carb. (1g sugars, 4g fiber), 4g pro. **Diabetic exchanges:** 1 starch, 1 fat.

PULL-APART GARLIC BREAD

People go wild over this golden, garlicky loaf whenever I serve it. There's intense flavor in every bite.
—Carol Shields, Summerville, PA

- -

Prep: 10 min. + rising • **Bake:** 30 min.
Makes: 16 servings

¼ cup butter, melted
1 Tbsp. dried parsley flakes
1 tsp. garlic powder
¼ tsp. garlic salt
1 loaf (1 lb.) frozen white bread dough, thawed

1. In a small bowl, combine the butter, parsley, garlic powder and garlic salt. Cut dough into 1-in. pieces; dip into butter mixture. Layer in a greased 9x5-in. loaf pan. Cover and let rise until doubled, about 1 hour.
2. Bake at 350° for 30 minutes or until golden brown.

1 serving: 104 cal., 4g fat (2g sat. fat), 8mg chol., 215mg sod., 15g carb. (1g sugars, 1g fiber), 3g pro.

★ ★ ★ ★ ★ **READER REVIEW**

"I made this bread for a family gathering and found it to be very easy to make and VERY tasty! I followed the recipe exactly and I don't believe I would change a thing except maybe to add a bit of grated Parmesan cheese to the butter mixture."

—BIKTASW, TASTEOFHOME.COM

OVERNIGHT FRUIT SALAD

I first tasted this rich fruit salad at my wedding reception almost 40 years ago. The ladies who did the cooking wouldn't share the recipe at the time, but I got it eventually. I've made it for many meals, and our daughters copied the recipe when they married.
—Eileen Duffeck, Lena, WI

- -

Prep: 30 min. + chilling • **Makes:** 16 servings

- 3 large eggs, beaten
- ¼ cup sugar
- ¼ cup white vinegar
- 2 Tbsp. butter
- 2 cups green grapes
- 2 cups miniature marshmallows
- 1 can (20 oz.) pineapple chunks, drained
- 1 can (15 oz.) mandarin oranges, drained
- 2 medium firm bananas, sliced
- 2 cups heavy whipping cream, whipped
- ½ cup chopped pecans

1. In a double boiler over medium heat, cook and stir eggs, sugar and vinegar until mixture is thickened and reaches 160°. Remove from the heat; stir in butter. Cool.
2. In a large serving bowl, combine grapes, marshmallows, pineapple, oranges and bananas; add cooled dressing and stir to coat. Refrigerate for 4 hours or overnight. Just before serving, fold in whipped cream and pecans.

½ cup: 244 cal., 16g fat (8g sat. fat), 84mg chol., 44mg sod., 24g carb. (21g sugars, 1g fiber), 3g pro.

MONTEREY SPAGHETTI

I'm a working mother with two young boys. Our family leads a very active life, so I make a lot of casseroles. It's so nice to have a hearty, tasty side dish the kids will eat. With two kinds of cheese and french-fried onions, it's always a hit at our house.
—Janet Hibler, Cameron, MO

- -

Prep: 15 min. • **Bake:** 35 min.
Makes: 8 servings

- 4 oz. spaghetti, broken into 2-in. pieces
- 1 large egg
- 1 cup sour cream
- ¼ cup grated Parmesan cheese
- ¼ tsp. garlic powder
- 2 cups shredded Monterey Jack cheese
- 1 pkg. (10 oz.) frozen chopped spinach, thawed and drained
- 1 can (2.8 oz.) french-fried onions, divided

1. Cook spaghetti according to package directions. Meanwhile, in a large bowl, beat egg. Add sour cream, Parmesan cheese and garlic powder.
2. Drain spaghetti; add to egg mixture with Monterey Jack cheese, spinach and half of the onions. Pour into a greased 2-qt. baking dish. Cover and bake at 350° for 30 minutes or until heated though. Top with remaining onions; return to the oven for 5 minutes or until onions are golden brown.

1 serving: 311 cal., 20g fat (11g sat. fat), 74mg chol., 333mg sod., 18g carb. (2g sugars, 1g fiber), 13g pro.

TEST KITCHEN TIP
A businessman from Monterey, California, named David Jacks made Monterey Jack cheese popular in the late 1800s by shipping it to San Francisco and other areas of the U.S.

TZATZIKI POTATO SALAD

My son has an egg allergy, so this potato salad is perfect for him. For extra color, add radishes, apple and garlic dill pickles.

—Cindy Romberg, Mississauga, ON

Prep: 25 min. + chilling • **Makes:** 12 servings

3 lbs. small red potatoes, halved
1 carton (12 oz.) refrigerated tzatziki sauce
2 celery ribs, thinly sliced
½ cup plain Greek yogurt
2 green onions, chopped
2 Tbsp. snipped fresh dill
2 Tbsp. minced fresh parsley
½ tsp. salt
¼ tsp. celery salt
¼ tsp. pepper
1 Tbsp. minced fresh mint, optional

1. Place potatoes in a Dutch oven; add water to cover. Bring to a boil. Reduce heat; cook, uncovered, until tender, 10-15 minutes. Drain; cool completely.
2. In a small bowl, mix the tzatziki sauce, celery, yogurt, green onions, dill, parsley, salt, celery salt, pepper and, if desired, mint. Spoon over the potatoes and toss to coat. Refrigerate, covered, until cold.

¾ cup: 128 cal., 3g fat (2g sat. fat), 7mg chol., 190mg sod., 21g carb. (3g sugars, 2g fiber), 4g pro. **Diabetic exchanges:** 1½ starch, ½ fat.

MANGO SALAD WITH MINT YOGURT DRESSING

An abundant planter full of mint inspired me to create this summery salad. The flavors pair so well, and the fruit really lets the freshness of the mint shine.
—Natalie Klein, Albuquerque, NM

- -

Prep: 25 min. + chilling • **Makes:** 8 servings

- 3 medium mangoes, peeled and cut into ¼-in. slices
- 3 medium Gala apples, cut into ¼-in. slices
- 2 Tbsp. lime juice, divided
- ½ cup plain yogurt
- 2 Tbsp. honey
- 1 tsp. minced fresh gingerroot
- ¼ tsp. salt
- ¼ cup fresh mint leaves, thinly sliced

1. In a large bowl combine the mangoes and apples. Drizzle with 1 Tbsp. lime juice; toss to coat.
2. In a small bowl, combine the yogurt, honey, ginger, salt and remaining lime juice. Stir into mango mixture. Sprinkle with mint and toss to coat. Refrigerate for at least 15 minutes before serving.

1 cup: 105 cal., 1g fat (0 sat. fat), 2mg chol., 84mg sod., 26g carb. (22g sugars, 3g fiber), 1g pro. **Diabetic exchanges:** 2 fruit.

SOUTHERN GREEN BEANS WITH APRICOTS

Green beans and apricots have become a family tradition. Enhanced with balsamic vinegar, this dish will make your taste buds pop.
—Ashley Davis, Easley, SC

- -

Prep: 15 min. • **Cook:** 20 min.
Makes: 8 servings

- 2 lbs. fresh green beans, trimmed
- 1 can (14½ oz.) chicken broth
- ½ lb. bacon strips, chopped
- 1 cup dried apricots, chopped
- ¼ cup balsamic vinegar
- ¾ tsp. salt
- ¾ tsp. garlic powder
- ¾ tsp. pepper

1. Place green beans and chicken broth in a large saucepan. Bring to a boil. Cook, covered, until beans are crisp-tender, 4-7 minutes; drain.
2. In a large skillet, cook chopped bacon over medium heat until crisp, stirring occasionally. Remove with a slotted spoon; drain on paper towels. Discard all but 1 Tbsp. drippings in pan.
3. Add apricots to drippings; cook and stir over medium heat until softened. Add vinegar, salt, garlic powder, pepper and beans; cook and stir until beans are coated, 2-3 minutes longer. Sprinkle with bacon.

¾ cup: 149 cal., 6g fat (2g sat. fat), 12mg chol., 464mg sod., 21g carb. (14g sugars, 5g fiber), 6g pro.

SPECTACULAR OVERNIGHT SLAW

To come up with this dish, I used a number of different recipes, plus some ideas of my own. It's great for a potluck because it's made the night before and the flavor keeps getting better. Whenever I serve it, I'm inundated with recipe requests.
—Ruth Lovett, Bay City, TX

Prep: 15 min. + chilling • **Makes:** 16 servings

- 1 medium head cabbage, shredded
- 1 medium red onion, thinly sliced
- ½ cup chopped green pepper
- ½ cup chopped sweet red pepper
- ½ cup sliced pimiento-stuffed olives
- ½ cup white wine vinegar
- ½ cup canola oil
- ½ cup sugar
- 2 tsp. Dijon mustard
- 1 tsp. salt
- 1 tsp. celery seed
- 1 tsp. mustard seed

Combine cabbage, onion, peppers and olives. In a large saucepan, mix remaining ingredients; bring to a boil. Cook and stir 1 minute. Pour over vegetables, and stir gently. Cover and refrigerate overnight. Mix well before serving.

¾ cup: 120 cal., 8g fat (1g sat. fat), 0 chol., 267mg sod., 12g carb. (9g sugars, 2g fiber), 1g pro.

BRING IT
A vinaigrette-based salad, like this one, is a good choice for hot-weather gatherings. You need to be extra careful with salads that have creamy or mayonnaise-based dressings. Keep salads cold on a bed of ice and out of the sun.

SPICY SWEET POTATO CHIPS & CILANTRO DIP

This cool, creamy dip is a perfect partner for the spicy sweet potato chips. These two are made for each other!
—Elizabeth Godecke, Chicago, IL

Prep: 20 min. • **Bake:** 25 min./batch
Makes: 12 servings (1½ cups dip)

- 2 to 3 large sweet potatoes (1¾ lbs.), peeled and cut into ⅛-in. slices
- 2 Tbsp. canola oil
- 1 tsp. chili powder
- ½ tsp. garlic powder
- ½ tsp. taco seasoning
- ¼ tsp. salt
- ¼ tsp. ground cumin
- ¼ tsp. pepper
- ⅛ tsp. cayenne pepper

DIP
- ¾ cup mayonnaise
- ½ cup sour cream
- 2 oz. cream cheese, softened
- 4½ tsp. minced fresh cilantro
- 1½ tsp. lemon juice
- ½ tsp. celery salt
- ⅛ tsp. pepper

1. Preheat oven to 400°. Place sweet potatoes in a large bowl. In a small bowl, mix oil and seasonings; drizzle over the potatoes and toss to coat.
2. Arrange half the sweet potatoes in a single layer in 2 ungreased 15x10x1-in. baking pans. Bake 25-30 minutes or until golden brown, turning once. Repeat with remaining sweet potatoes.
3. In a small bowl, beat dip ingredients until blended. Serve with chips.
½ cup chips with about 1 Tbsp. dip: 285 cal., 16g fat (4g sat. fat), 8mg chol., 217mg sod., 33g carb. (14g sugars, 4g fiber), 3g pro.

CRUNCHY COOL COLESLAW

This recipe is my version of the peanut slaw I love at Lucille's Smokehouse Bar-B-Que, a popular restaurant chain in California. I think it's a pretty close match to Lucille's!
—Elaine Hoffmann, Santa Ana, CA

- -

Takes: 30 min. • **Makes:** 16 servings

- 2 pkg. (16 oz. each) coleslaw mix
- 2 medium Honeycrisp apples, julienned
- 1 large carrot, shredded
- ¾ cup chopped red onion
- ½ cup chopped green pepper
- ½ cup cider vinegar
- ⅓ cup canola oil
- 1½ tsp. sugar
- ½ tsp. celery seed
- ½ tsp. salt
- ½ cup coarsely chopped dry-roasted peanuts or cashews

1. In a large bowl, combine the first 5 ingredients. In a small bowl, whisk the vinegar, oil, sugar, celery seed and salt.
2. Just before serving, pour dressing over salad; toss to coat. Sprinkle with peanuts.
1 cup: 100 cal., 7g fat (1g sat. fat), 0 chol., 128mg sod., 9g carb. (5g sugars, 2g fiber), 2g pro. **Diabetic exchanges:** 1½ fat, 1 vegetable.

MAKE AHEAD
FRESH CUCUMBER SALAD

Crisp, garden-fresh cukes are always in season when we hold our family reunion, and they really shine in this simple salad. The recipe can easily be expanded to make large quantities, too.
—Betsy Carlson, Rockforc, IL

- -

Prep: 10 min. + chilling • **Makes:** 10 servings

- 3 medium cucumbers, sliced
- 1 cup sugar
- ¾ cup water
- ½ cup white vinegar
- 3 Tbsp. minced fresh dill or parsley

Place cucumbers in a 1½- to 2-qt. glass container. In a jar with a tight-fitting lid, shake remaining ingredients until combined. Pour over cucumbers. Cover and refrigerate overnight. Serve with a slotted spoon.
½ cup: 87 cal., 0 fat (0 sat. fat), 0 chol., 0 sod., 22g carb. (21g sugars, 1g fiber), 1g pro.

WATERMELON & SPINACH SALAD

Summer's the perfect time to toss this watermelon salad. You'd never expect it, but spinach is awesome here. Eat it and feel cool on even the hottest days.
—Marjorie Au, Honolulu, HI

- -

Takes: 30 min. • **Makes:** 8 servings

- ¼ **cup rice vinegar or white wine vinegar**
- 1 **Tbsp. grated lime zest**
- 2 **Tbsp. lime juice**
- 2 **Tbsp. canola oil**
- 4 **tsp. minced fresh gingerroot**
- 2 **garlic cloves, minced**
- ½ **tsp. salt**
- ¼ **tsp. sugar**
- ¼ **tsp. pepper**

SALAD

- 4 **cups fresh baby spinach or arugula**
- 3 **cups cubed seedless watermelon**
- 2 **cups cubed cantaloupe**
- 2 **cups cubed English cucumber**
- ½ **cup chopped fresh cilantro**
- 2 **green onions, chopped**

In a small bowl, whisk the first 9 ingredients. In a large bowl, combine salad ingredients. Drizzle with dressing and toss to coat; serve immediately.

1 cup: 84 cal., 4g fat (0 sat. fat), 0 chol., 288mg sod., 13g carb. (10g sugars, 1g fiber), 1g pro. **Diabetic exchanges:** 1 vegetable, 1 fat, ½ fruit.

TEST KITCHEN TIP
Try adding a touch of honey to the dressing if your melon isn't super sweet. That will wake it right up!

LOUISIANA PECAN BACON BREAD

One Christmas, the babysitter brought gifts for my daughter and a basket of goodies, including pecan bread. Making it reminds me of that kind soul.
—Marina Castle Kelley
Canyon Country, CA

- -

Prep: 20 min. • **Bake:** 50 min. + cooling
Makes: 1 loaf (16 slices)

- 6 **bacon strips, chopped**
- 6 **oz. cream cheese, softened**
- ⅓ **cup sugar**
- 1 **large egg, room temperature**
- 2 **cups all-purpose flour**
- 2½ **tsp. baking powder**
- ½ **tsp. salt**
- ¾ **cup 2% milk**
- 1 **cup chopped pecans**
- ¼ **cup finely chopped onion**
- ¼ **cup chopped green pepper**

1. Preheat oven to 350°. In a large skillet, cook bacon over medium-low heat until crisp, stirring occasionally. Remove with a slotted spoon; drain on paper towels. Reserve drippings (about 2 Tbsp.); cool slightly.
2. In a large bowl, beat cream cheese, sugar and reserved drippings until smooth. Beat in egg. In another bowl, whisk flour, baking powder and salt; add to cream cheese mixture alternately with milk, beating well after each addition. Fold in pecans, onion, pepper and bacon. Transfer to a greased 9x5-in. loaf pan.
3. Bake until a toothpick inserted in center comes out clean, 50-60 minutes. Cool in pan 10 minutes before removing to a wire rack to cool.

Freeze option: Securely wrap cooled loaf and freeze. To use, thaw in the refrigerator.
1 slice: 198 cal., 12g fat (4g sat. fat), 29mg chol., 242mg sod., 18g carb. (6g sugars, 1g fiber), 5g pro.

CREAMY MAKE-AHEAD MASHED POTATOES

My recipe takes mashed potatoes to the next level with a savory topping of cheese, onions and bacon.
—JoAnn Koerkenmeier, Damiansville, IL

Prep: 35 min. + chilling • **Bake:** 40 min.
Makes: 10 servings

- 3 lbs. potatoes (about 9 medium), peeled and cubed
- 6 bacon strips, chopped
- 8 oz. cream cheese, softened
- ½ cup sour cream
- ½ cup butter, cubed
- ¼ cup 2% milk
- 1½ tsp. onion powder
- 1 tsp. salt
- 1 tsp. garlic powder
- ½ tsp. pepper
- 1 cup shredded cheddar cheese
- 3 green onions, chopped

1. Place potatoes in a Dutch oven; add water to cover. Bring to a boil. Reduce heat; cook, uncovered, 10-15 minutes or until tender.
2. Meanwhile, in a skillet, cook bacon over medium heat until crisp. Remove to paper towels with a slotted spoon; drain.
3. Drain potatoes; return to pan. Mash potatoes, gradually adding cream cheese, sour cream and butter. Stir in milk and seasonings. Transfer to a greased 13x9-in. baking dish; sprinkle with cheese, green onions and bacon. Refrigerate, covered, up to 1 day.
4. Preheat oven to 350°. Remove potatoes from refrigerator and let stand while oven heats. Bake, covered, about 30 minutes. Uncover; bake 10 minutes longer or until heated through.
¾ cup: 419 cal., 24g fat (15g sat. fat), 74mg chol., 544mg sod., 41g carb. (4g sugars, 4g fiber), 11g pro.

BALSAMIC GREEN BEAN SALAD

Serve fresh green beans in a whole new way! The tangy flavors and crunch of this tasty-looking side complement any special meal or potluck.
—Megan Spencer, Farmington Hills, MI

Prep: 30 min. + chilling
Makes: 16 servings (¾ cup each)

- 2 lbs. fresh green beans, trimmed and cut into 1½-in. pieces
- ¼ cup olive oil
- 3 Tbsp. lemon juice
- 3 Tbsp. balsamic vinegar
- ¼ tsp. salt
- ¼ tsp. garlic powder
- ¼ tsp. ground mustard
- ⅛ tsp. pepper
- 1 large red onion, chopped
- 4 cups cherry tomatoes, halved
- 1 cup (4 oz.) crumbled feta cheese

1. Place beans in a 6-qt. stockpot; add water to cover. Bring to a boil. Cook, covered, 8-10 minutes or until crisp-tender. Drain and immediately place in ice water. Drain and pat dry.
2. In a small bowl, whisk oil, lemon juice, vinegar, salt, garlic powder, mustard and pepper. Drizzle over beans. Add onion; toss to coat. Refrigerate, covered, at least 1 hour. Just before serving, stir in tomatoes and cheese.
¾ cup: 77 cal., 5g fat (1g sat. fat), 4mg chol., 112mg sod., 7g carb. (3g sugars, 3g fiber), 3g pro. **Diabetic exchanges:** 1 vegetable, 1 fat.

QUINOA TABBOULEH

When my mom and sister developed several food allergies, we had to modify many recipes. I substituted quinoa for couscous in this tabbouleh, and now we make it all the time.
—Jennifer Klann, Corbett, OR

Prep: 35 min. + chilling • **Makes:** 8 servings

- 2   cups water
- 1   cup quinoa, rinsed
- 1   can (15 oz.) black beans, rinsed and drained
- 1   small cucumber, peeled and chopped
- 1   small sweet red pepper, chopped
- ⅓   cup minced fresh parsley
- ¼   cup lemon juice
- 2   Tbsp. olive oil
- ½   tsp. salt
- ½   tsp. pepper

1. In a large saucepan, bring water to a boil. Add quinoa. Reduce heat; cover and simmer until liquid is absorbed, 12-15 minutes. Remove from the heat; fluff with a fork. Transfer to a bowl; cool completely.
2. Add the beans, cucumber, red pepper and parsley. In a small bowl, whisk the remaining ingredients; drizzle over salad and toss to coat. Refrigerate until chilled.
¾ cup: 159 cal., 5g fat (1g sat. fat), 0 chol., 255mg sod., 24g carb. (1g sugars, 4g fiber), 6g pro. **Diabetic exchanges:** 1½ starch, 1 fat.

MAKE AHEAD

MASHED CAULIFLOWER AU GRATIN

Unless someone tells you, you might not know you're eating cauliflower. Even my grandchildren love this buttery, cheesy, creamy dish that tastes like mashed potatoes.
—Sandie Parker, Elk Rapids, MI

Prep: 40 min. • **Cook:** 40 min.
Makes: 12 servings

- 2 large heads cauliflower, broken into florets
- 1½ cups shredded Parmesan cheese
- 1 cup shredded Colby-Monterey Jack cheese
- 6 Tbsp. butter, cubed
- ¾ tsp. garlic salt
- ½ tsp. Montreal steak seasoning
TOPPING
- 1 cup Italian-style panko bread crumbs
- ¼ cup butter, melted

1. Preheat oven to 350°. Place cauliflower in a stockpot; add water to cover. Bring to a boil. Reduce heat; simmer, uncovered, until very tender, 10-12 minutes. Drain; transfer to a large bowl. Mash cauliflower; stir in the cheeses, cubed butter and seasonings. Transfer to a greased 3-qt. or 13x9-in. baking dish.

2. In a small bowl, mix bread crumbs and melted butter until evenly coated; sprinkle over cauliflower mixture. Bake, uncovered, until heated through and topping is golden brown, 40-50 minutes.

Freeze option: Cool unbaked casserole; cover and freeze. To use, partially thaw in refrigerator overnight. Remove from refrigerator 30 minutes before baking. Preheat oven to 350°. Bake casserole as directed, increasing time as necessary to heat through and for a thermometer inserted in center to read 165°.

¾ cup: 238 cal., 17g fat (10g sat. fat), 41mg chol., 612mg sod., 14g carb. (3g sugars, 4g fiber), 9g pro.

Swiss Mashed Cauliflower: Cook and mash cauliflower as directed. Add 1 cup shredded Swiss cheese, 2 Tbsp. butter, 1 tsp. salt, ½ tsp. pepper, ¼ tsp. garlic powder and ¼-⅓ cup 2% milk. Place in baking dish, top, and bake as the recipe directs.

GREEK BREADSTICKS

Get ready for rave reviews when you serve these crispy Greek-inspired breadsticks. They're best served hot and fresh from the oven with your favorite tzatziki sauce. Great on an appetizer buffet, too.
—Jane Whittaker, Pensacola, FL

Prep: 20 min. • **Bake:** 15 min.
Makes: 32 breadsticks

¼ cup marinated quartered artichoke hearts, drained
2 Tbsp. pitted Greek olives
1 pkg. (17.3 oz.) frozen puff pastry, thawed
1 carton (6½ oz.) spreadable spinach and artichoke cream cheese
2 Tbsp. grated Parmesan cheese
1 large egg
1 Tbsp. water
2 tsp. sesame seeds
   Refrigerated tzatziki sauce, optional

1. Place artichokes and olives in a food processor; cover and pulse until finely chopped. Unfold 1 pastry sheet on a lightly floured surface; spread half of the cream cheese over half of pastry. Top with half of the artichoke mixture. Sprinkle with half of the Parmesan cheese. Fold plain half over filling; press gently to seal.
2. Repeat with remaining pastry, cream cheese, artichoke mixture and Parmesan cheese. Whisk egg and water; brush over tops. Sprinkle with sesame seeds. Cut each rectangle into sixteen ¾-in.-wide strips. Twist strips several times; place 2 in. apart on greased baking sheets.
3. Bake at 400° for 12-14 minutes or until golden brown. Serve warm, with tzatziki sauce if desired.
1 breadstick: 101 cal., 6g fat (2g sat. fat), 11mg chol., 104mg sod., 9g carb. (0 sugars, 1g fiber), 2g pro.

GRANDMOTHER'S ORANGE SALAD

This slightly sweet gelatin salad is a little bit tangy, too. It adds beautiful color to any meal and appeals to all ages.
—Ann Eastman, Santa Monica, CA

Prep: 20 min. + chilling • **Makes:** 10 servings

1 can (11 oz.) mandarin oranges
1 can (8 oz.) crushed pineapple
  Water
1 pkg. (6 oz.) orange gelatin
1 pint orange sherbet, softened
2 bananas, sliced

1. Drain oranges and pineapple, reserving juices. Set oranges and pineapple aside. Add water to juices to measure 2 cups. Place in a saucepan and bring to a boil; pour over gelatin in a large bowl. Stir until gelatin is dissolved. Stir in sherbet until smooth.
2. Chill until partially set (watch carefully). Fold in oranges, pineapple and bananas. Pour into an oiled 6-cup mold. Refrigerate until firm.

1 piece: 161 cal., 1g fat (0 sat. fat), 2mg chol., 55mg sod., 39g carb. (35g sugars, 1g fiber), 2g pro.

HONEY-LIME BERRY SALAD

I picked up this recipe a couple of years ago, and I really like the mint and fruit combo. Cilantro is one of my summer favorites, so sometimes I use it instead of mint.
—Kayla Spence, Wilber, NE

- -

Takes: 15 min. • **Makes:** 10 servings

   4   **cups fresh strawberries, halved**
   3   **cups fresh blueberries**
   3   **medium Granny Smith apples, cubed**
  ⅓   **cup lime juice**
  ¼   **to ⅓ cup honey**
   2   **Tbsp. minced fresh mint**

In a large bowl, combine strawberries, blueberries and apples. In a small bowl, whisk lime juice, honey and mint. Pour over fruit; toss to coat.

¾ cup: 93 cal., 0 fat (0 sat. fat), 0 chol., 2mg sod., 24g carb. (19g sugars, 3g fiber), 1g pro. **Diabetic exchanges:** 1 fruit, ½ starch.

CUBAN BLACK BEANS

This hearty side dish starts with sofrito, a combination of finely minced onions and green peppers. Tomato puree and sherry give the beans a distinctive flavor.
—Marina Castle Kelley
Canyon Country, CA

- -

Prep: 20 min. + soaking • **Cook:** 1¾ hours
Makes: 9 servings

   2   **cups dried black beans, rinsed**
   1   **bay leaf**
   3   **medium green peppers, chopped**
   2   **medium onions, chopped**
  ½   **cup olive oil**
   6   **garlic cloves, minced**
   1   **can (15 oz.) tomato puree**
  ½   **cup sherry or chicken broth**
   2   **Tbsp. sugar**
  ¾   **tsp. salt**

1. Rinse and sort beans; soak according to package directions. Drain and rinse beans, discarding liquid.
2. Place beans in a large saucepan; add 6 cups water and bay leaf. Bring to a boil. Reduce heat; cover and simmer until tender, 1½-2 hours.
3. Meanwhile, in a large skillet, saute the peppers and onions in oil until tender. Add minced garlic; cook 1 minute longer. Stir in the tomato puree, sherry, sugar and salt. Bring to a boil. Reduce heat; simmer, uncovered, until thickened, 8-10 minutes. Drain beans; discard bay leaf. Stir beans into tomato mixture.

¾ cup: 312 cal., 13g fat (2g sat. fat), 0 chol., 214mg sod., 38g carb. (8g sugars, 8g fiber), 11g pro.

ARTICHOKE TOMATO SALAD

For a little zip, crumble feta over the top of this salad. Or add shredded rotisserie chicken to make it a main dish.
—Deborah Williams, Peoria, AZ

- -

Takes: 20 min. • **Makes:** 8 servings

    5   large tomatoes (about
        2 lbs.), cut into wedges
    ¼   tsp. salt
    ¼   tsp. pepper
    1   jar (7½ oz.) marinated quartered
        artichoke hearts, drained
    1   can (2¼ oz.) sliced ripe olives,
        drained
    2   Tbsp. minced fresh parsley
    2   Tbsp. white wine vinegar
    2   garlic cloves, minced

Arrange tomato wedges on a large platter; sprinkle with salt and pepper. In a small bowl, toss remaining ingredients; spoon over tomatoes.
¾ cup: 74 cal., 5g fat (1g sat. fat), 0 chol., 241mg sod., 7g carb. (3g sugars, 2g fiber), 1g pro. **Diabetic exchanges:** 1 vegetable, 1 fat.

HOW TO KEEP PARSLEY FRESH
Trim stems and place in a tumbler of water. Be sure no leaves are in the water. Tie a produce bag around top to trap humidity; refrigerate. Each time you use parsley, change the water and turn the produce bag inside out so any moisture built up inside can escape.

RUSSIAN POTATO SALAD

This recipe is from my grandmother, who had written it down in Russian before she translated it for me when I was a teen. We made this every Easter, or for any event where there were family and friends.
—Gala McGaughey, Berryville, VA

- -

Prep: 40 min. + chilling **Makes:** 16 servings

    5   lbs. potatoes, peeled and cubed
        (about 8 cups)
    ⅓   cup sugar
    ⅓   cup cider vinegar
    ¼   cup canola oil
    1   can (14½ oz.) sliced carrots, drained
    1   medium onion, chopped
    2   jars (16 oz. each) pickled whole
        beets, drained and chopped
    1   cup chopped celery
    ½   cup chopped sweet pickles
    ½   cup chopped dill pickles
    1   cup mayonnaise
    1   tsp. salt
    ½   tsp. pepper

1. Place potatoes in a Dutch oven; cover with water. Bring to a boil. Reduce heat; cover and simmer until tender, 10-15 minutes. Drain and transfer to a large bowl.
2. Meanwhile, combine sugar and vinegar in a small saucepan. Cook and stir over medium heat until sugar is dissolved; pour over hot potatoes. Cool mixture to room temperature.
3. In a large skillet, heat oil over medium-high heat. Add carrots and onion; cook and stir until crisp-tender, 6-8 minutes. Add to potatoes. Stir in beets, celery and pickles. Combine mayonnaise, salt and pepper; gently stir into potato mixture. Refrigerate, covered, until chilled.
¾ cup: 269 cal., 14g fat (2g sat. fat), 1mg chol., 455mg sod., 35g carb. (15g sugars, 3g fiber), 2g pro.

ZUCCHINI IN DILL CREAM SAUCE

My husband and I were dairy farmers until we retired, so I always use fresh, real dairy products in my recipes. This creamy sauce combines all of our favorite foods!
—Josephine Vanden Heuvel, Hart, MI

Takes: 30 min. • **Makes:** 8 servings

- 7   cups sliced zucchini (¼-in. slices)
- ¼   cup finely chopped onion
- ½   cup water
- 1   tsp. salt
- 1   tsp. chicken bouillon granules or 1 chicken bouillon cube
- ½   tsp. dill weed
- 2   Tbsp. butter, melted
- 2   tsp. sugar
- 1   tsp. lemon juice
- 2   Tbsp. all-purpose flour
- ¼   cup sour cream

1. In Dutch oven, combine zucchini, onion, water, salt, bouillon and dill; bring to a boil. Add the butter, sugar and lemon juice; mix. Remove from heat; do not drain.
2. Combine flour and sour cream; stir half the mixture into hot zucchini. Return to heat; add remaining cream mixture and cook until thickened.
¾ cup: 73 cal., 4g fat, 11mg chol., 419mg sod., 8g carb., 2g pro. **Diabetic exchanges:** 1 vegetable, 1 fat.

STRAWBERRY SPINACH SALAD WITH CANDIED WALNUTS

This classic salad goes with just about anything you're serving. The juicy berries add a pop of color to the greens, and the sweet, crunchy nuts are good enough to eat all on their own!
—Susan Howell, Royal Oak, MI

Takes: 20 min. • **Makes:** 10 servings

- ½   cup sugar
- ¼   cup water
- ½   tsp. ground cinnamon
- ½   tsp. chili powder
- ¼   tsp. curry powder
- 2   cups walnut halves

SALAD
- 1   pkg. (9 oz.) fresh baby spinach
- 2   cups sliced fresh strawberries (about 1 lb.)
- 1   medium cucumber, halved and sliced

VINAIGRETTE
- ¼   cup olive oil
- 2   Tbsp. balsamic vinegar
- 2   Tbsp. seedless raspberry jam
- 1   tsp. lemon juice
- ¼   tsp. salt
- ⅛   tsp. pepper
- ⅓   cup grated Parmesan cheese

1. In a small heavy saucepan, combine the first 5 ingredients; stir gently to moisten all the sugar. Cook over medium-low heat, gently swirling pan occasionally, until sugar is dissolved. Cover; bring to a boil over medium heat. Cook 1 minute. Uncover pan; continue to boil and gently swirl pan until syrup turns a deep amber color, about 2-3 minutes. Immediately remove from heat and carefully stir in walnuts until evenly coated. Spread onto foil to cool completely. Break into pieces.
2. In a large bowl, combine spinach, strawberries and cucumber. In a small bowl, whisk the first 6 vinaigrette ingredients. Drizzle over salad; toss to coat. Sprinkle with Parmesan cheese and walnuts. Serve immediately.
1 cup: 262 cal., 19g fat (2g sat. fat), 2mg chol., 132mg sod., 21g carb. (16g sugars, 3g fiber), 5g pro.

SOUTHWESTERN RICE

I created this colorful side dish after eating something similar at a restaurant. It complements any Tex-Mex meal wonderfully. Sometimes I add cubed grilled chicken breast to the rice to make it a meal in itself.
—Michelle Dennis, Clarks Hill, IN

Takes: 30 min. • **Makes:** 8 servings

- 1 Tbsp. olive oil
- 1 medium green pepper, diced
- 1 medium onion, chopped
- 2 garlic cloves, minced
- 1 cup uncooked long grain rice
- ½ tsp. ground cumin
- ⅛ tsp. ground turmeric
- 1 can (14½ oz.) reduced-sodium chicken broth
- 2 cups frozen corn (about 10 oz.), thawed
- 1 can (15 oz.) black beans, rinsed and drained
- 1 can (10 oz.) diced tomatoes and green chiles, undrained

1. In a large nonstick skillet, heat oil over medium-high heat; saute pepper and onion 3 minutes. Add garlic; cook and stir 1 minute.
2. Stir in rice, spices and broth; bring to a boil. Reduce heat; simmer, covered, until rice is tender, about 15 minutes. Stir in remaining ingredients; cook, covered, until heated through.
¾ cup: 198 cal., 3g fat (1g sat. fat), 1mg chol., 339mg sod., 37g carb. (0 sugars, 5g fiber), 7g pro.

CELERY ROOT & PEAR SLAW

Crunchy celery root is an underappreciated yet completely delicious veggie. It lends sweetness tc this tangy slaw, which I like to serve on holidays with pork roast or baked ham.
—Roxanne Chan, Albany, CA

Prep: 40 min. • **Makes:** 16 servings

- 1 medium celery root, peeled and julienned
- 3 cups shredded red cabbage
- 3 medium pears, thinly sliced
- ⅓ cup golden raisins
- ¼ cup chopped red onion
- ¼ cup minced fresh parsley
- ¼ cup sliced almonds
- ¾ cup sour cream
- ⅓ cup mayonnaise
- 4 tsp. poppy seeds
- 4 tsp. prepared horseradish
- 2 garlic cloves, minced
- 1½ tsp. honey
- ¾ tsp. pepper
- ¾ tsp. grated lemon zest
- 4 tsp. lemon juice
- ½ cup crumbled blue cheese

Combine the first 7 ingredients. In another bowl, combine the next 9 ingredients; pour over slaw, tossing to coat. Sprinkle with blue cheese.
¾ cup: 128 cal., 8g fat (3g sat. fat), 6mg chol., 114mg sod., 13g carb. (7g sugars, 3g fiber), 3g pro. **Diabetic exchanges:** 1½ fat, 1 starch.

FRIED CHICKEN & PULLED PORK CORNBREAD POPPERS

These fun little corn muffins are an instant conversation starter wherever they're served. We love them on game day, but they'd be a hit at brunch, too.
—Crystal Schlueter, Northglenn, CO

- -

Takes: 25 min. • **Makes:** 2 dozen

- 2 oz. frozen popcorn chicken
- 1 pkg. (8½ oz.) cornbread/muffin mix
- 4 seeded jalapeno peppers or pickled jalapeno peppers, cut into 6 slices each
- ¼ cup refrigerated fully cooked barbecued pulled pork
- ½ cup maple syrup or honey
- 1 tsp. Sriracha chili sauce, optional

1. Preheat oven to 400°. Bake popcorn chicken according to package directions. When cool enough to handle, cut chicken into 12 pieces.
2. Meanwhile, prepare cornbread mix according to package directions. Place a jalapeno slice in each of 24 foil-lined mini muffin cups. Fill each cup with 1 Tbsp. batter. Gently press a piece of popcorn chicken into the centers of half the cups. Spoon 1 tsp. pulled pork into the centers of remaining cups.
3. Bake muffins until golden brown, about 12 minutes. Serve with maple syrup; if desired, whisk chili sauce into syrup.
1 mini muffin: 74 cal., 2g fat (1g sat. fat), 10mg chol., 120mg sod., 13g carb. (7g sugars, 1g fiber), 2g pro.

GRECIAN POTATO CUPS

If you like stuffed potato skins, you'll love these little cups filled with feta cheese, spinach, onion, garlic and more. They're easy for guests to take and enjoy from a buffet.

—Nicole Filizetti, Stevens Point, WI

Prep: 25 min. • **Bake:** 70 min.
Makes: 8 servings

8	medium red potatoes (about 2¼ lbs.)
4	Tbsp. olive oil, divided
1	tsp. salt
¾	tsp. pepper
1	medium onion, finely chopped
1	tsp. dried oregano
2	garlic cloves, minced
1	pkg. (10 oz.) frozen chopped spinach, thawed and squeezed dry
1	Tbsp. lemon juice
1½	cups (6 oz.) crumbled feta cheese

1. Preheat oven to 425°. Scrub potatoes; pierce several times with a fork. Place in a foil-lined 15x10x1-in. baking pan; bake until tender, 40-45 minutes.

2. Increase oven setting to 450°. When cool enough to handle, cut each potato crosswise in half. Scoop out pulp, leaving ¼-in.-thick shells. (Save removed potato for another use.) If necessary, carefully trim bottom of cups so potatoes will sit upright. Rub 3 Tbsp. olive oil over the inside and outside of potatoes.

3. Place potato cups on two 15x10x1-in. baking pans, cut side down; sprinkle with salt and pepper. Bake until skin is crisp, 8-10 minutes. Turn potatoes over; bake until golden brown, 10-12 minutes longer. Remove from oven. Reduce oven setting to 350°.

4. In a large skillet, heat remaining olive oil over medium-high heat. Add onion and oregano; cook and stir until onion is tender, 2-3 minutes. Add garlic; cook 1 minute longer. Stir in spinach and lemon juice; heat through. Remove from heat; stir in cheese. Spoon into potato cups. Bake until heated through, 8-10 minutes.

2 potato cups: 212 cal., 11g fat (3g sat. fat), 11mg chol., 531mg sod., 22g carb. (2g sugars, 4g fiber), 7g pro. **Diabetic exchanges:** 2 fat, 1½ starch.

CRAN-ORANGE COUSCOUS SALAD

I often create salads for summer using a variety of satisfying, good-for-you grains. This version with tender couscous is amped up by the bright flavors of oranges, cranberries, basil and a touch of fennel.
—Kristen Heigl, Staten Island, NY

Prep: 25 min. • **Cook:** 15 min.
Makes: 12 servings

- 3 cups uncooked pearl (Israeli) couscous
- 2 cans (14 oz. each) garbanzo beans or chickpeas, rinsed and drained
- 2 large navel oranges, peeled and chopped
- 2 cups fresh baby spinach
- 1 cup crumbled goat cheese
- 1 small red onion, chopped
- ¾ cup dried cranberries
- ½ cup fennel bulb, thinly sliced, fronds reserved
- ½ cup chopped pecans, toasted
- 8 fresh basil leaves, chopped, plus more for garnish

VINAIGRETTE
- ½ cup olive oil
- ¼ cup orange juice
- ¼ cup balsamic vinegar
- 1 Tbsp. grated orange zest
- 2 tsp. honey
- 1 tsp. salt
- ½ tsp. pepper

Prepare couscous according to package directions. Fluff with a fork; cool. In a bowl, combine couscous and the next 9 ingredients. In a small bowl, whisk together vinaigrette ingredients until blended. Pour over salad; toss to coat. Garnish with additional chopped basil and reserved fennel fronds.
¾ cup: 403 cal., 16g fat (3g sat. fat), 12mg chol., 335mg sod., 57g carb. (15g sugars, 5g fiber), 10g pro.

CORN PUDDING

The pleasing flavor of this golden corn pudding side dish makes it real comfort food. And because the recipe starts with a mix, it's easy to prepare.
—P. Lauren Fay-Neri, Syracuse, NY

Prep: 20 min. • **Bake:** 45 min.
Makes: 8 servings

- ½ cup butter, softened
- ½ cup sugar
- 2 large eggs, room temperature
- 1 cup sour cream
- 1 pkg. (8½ oz.) cornbread/muffin mix
- ½ cup 2% milk
- 1 can (15¼ oz.) whole kernel corn, drained
- 1 can (14¾ oz.) cream-style corn

1. Preheat oven to 325°. In a large bowl, cream butter and sugar until light and fluffy, 5-7 minutes. Add eggs, 1 at a time, beating well after each addition. Beat in sour cream. Gradually add muffin mix alternately with milk. Fold in the corn.
2. Pour into a greased 3-qt. baking dish or 13x9-in. baking pan. Bake, uncovered, until set and lightly browned, 45-50 minutes.
¾ cup: 435 cal., 22g fat (12g sat. fat), 112mg chol., 700mg sod., 52g carb. (24g sugars, 2g fiber), 7g pro.

SWEET ONION PIE

Loaded with sweet onions, this creamy pie makes a scrumptious addition to the buffet. By using less butter to cook the onions and substituting some lighter ingredients, I cut calories and fat from the tasty dish.

—Barbara Reese, Catawissa, PA

Prep: 35 min. • **Bake:** 30 min.
Makes: 8 servings

- 2   sweet onions, halved and sliced
- 1   Tbsp. butter
- 1   frozen deep-dish pie crust
- 1   cup egg substitute
- 1   cup fat-free evaporated milk
- 1   tsp. salt
- ¼   tsp. pepper

1. In a large nonstick skillet, cook onions in butter over medium-low heat until very tender, 30 minutes. Meanwhile, line unpricked crust with a double thickness of heavy-duty foil.
2. Bake at 450° for 6 minutes. Remove foil; cool on a wire rack. Reduce heat to 425°.
3. Spoon onions into crust. In a small bowl, whisk the egg substitute, milk, salt and pepper; pour over onions. Bake until a knife inserted in the center comes out clean, 30-35 minutes. Let stand for 5-10 minutes before cutting.
1 piece: 169 cal., 7g fat (2g sat. fat), 5mg chol., 487mg sod., 21g carb. (8g sugars, 1g fiber), 7g pro. **Diabetic exchanges:** 1 starch, 1 lean meat, 1 fat.

ROASTED SWEET POTATO & PROSCIUTTO SALAD

I still think there's no better combo than sweet potatoes with pork, or prosciutto in this case. I'm a retired physician and am glad that sweet potatoes are being given their due as nutritional powerhouses.

—Helen Conwell, Portland, OR

Prep: 20 min. • **Bake:** 40 min. + cooling
Makes: 8 servings

- 3   medium sweet potatoes (about 2½ lbs.), peeled and cut into 1-in. pieces
- 4   Tbsp. olive oil, divided
- ½   tsp. salt, divided
- ⅛   tsp. pepper
- 3   oz. thinly sliced prosciutto, julienned
- ½   cup sliced radishes
- ⅓   cup chopped pecans, toasted
- ¼   cup finely chopped sweet red pepper
- 2   green onions, sliced, divided
- 1   Tbsp. lemon juice
- 1   tsp. honey

1. Preheat oven to 400°. Place sweet potatoes in a greased 15x10x1-in. baking pan. Drizzle with 2 Tbsp. oil and sprinkle with ¼ tsp. salt and pepper; toss to coat. Roast 30 minutes, stirring occasionally.
2. Sprinkle prosciutto over sweet potatoes; roast 10-15 minutes longer or until potatoes are tender and prosciutto is crisp. Transfer to a large bowl; cool slightly.
3. Add radishes, pecans, red pepper and half of the green onions. In a small bowl, whisk lemon juice, honey, and remaining oil and salt until blended. Drizzle over salad; toss to combine. Sprinkle with remaining green onion.
¾ cup: 167 cal., 12g fat (2g sat. fat), 9mg chol., 360mg sod., 13g carb. (6g sugars, 2g fiber), 4g pro. **Diabetic exchanges:** 2 fat, 1 starch.

Sausage
Bacon Bites
page 159

Big Batch Dishes

Got a large group to feed? Turn here for big-batch cooking at its best, from breakfast dishes to sweets and everything in between.

STUFFED MUSHROOMS

These stuffed mushrooms are can't-stop-eating-them good. I sometimes substitute venison or crabmeat for the pork sausage in the stuffing.
—Sheryl Siemonsma, Sioux Falls, SD

Prep: 15 min. • **Bake:** 20 min.
Makes: 4 dozen

- 48 **large fresh mushrooms**
- 2 **large eggs, lightly beaten**
- 1 **lb. bulk pork sausage, cooked and crumbled**
- 1 **cup shredded Swiss cheese**
- ¼ **cup mayonnaise**
- 3 **Tbsp. butter, melted**
- 2 **Tbsp. finely chopped onion**
- 2 **tsp. spicy brown or horseradish mustard**
- 1 **tsp. garlic salt**
- 1 **tsp. Cajun seasoning**
- 1 **tsp. Worcestershire sauce**

1. Remove mushroom stems (discard or save for another use); set caps aside. In a large bowl, combine remaining ingredients. Stuff into mushroom caps.
2. Place in 2 greased 13x9-in. baking dishes. Bake, uncovered, at 350° until heated through, 16-20 minutes.
1 stuffed mushroom: 53 cal., 4g fat (2g sat. fat), 17mg chol., 129mg sod., 1g carb. (0 sugars, 0 fiber), 2g pro.

BRING IT
This crowd-sized offering keeps on giving! Serve one pan and keep the second in the fridge to refresh the buffet as the party goes on. For convenience, bring the mushrooms in two stacking pans with lids. (If using disposable foil pans, you may need to decrease bake time slightly.)

CREAM CHEESE MASHED POTATOES

When I serve this easy mash, the bowl is always scraped clean. Before a big feast, I make it early and keep it warm in a slow cooker so I can focus on last-minute details.
—Jill Thomas, Washington, IN

Prep: 20 min. • **Cook:** 15 min.
Makes: 20 servings

- 8 **lbs. russet potatoes**
- 1 **pkg. (8 oz.) cream cheese, softened**
- ½ **cup butter, melted**
- 2 **tsp. salt**
- ¾ **tsp. pepper**
  Additional melted butter, optional
- ¼ **cup finely chopped green onions**

1. Peel and cube potatoes. Place in a large stockpot; add water to cover. Bring to a boil. Reduce heat; cook, uncovered, until tender, 12-15 minutes. Drain.
2. With a mixer, beat the cream cheese, ½ cup melted butter, salt and pepper until smooth. Add potatoes; beat until light and fluffy. If desired, top with additional melted butter. Sprinkle with green onions.
¾ cup: 185 cal., 9g fat (5g sat. fat), 25mg chol., 318mg sod., 25g carb. (2g sugars, 2g fiber), 3g pro.

CHEESEBURGER MINI MUFFINS

I invented these cute little muffins so I could enjoy the flavor of cheeseburgers without resorting to fast food. I often freeze a batch and reheat however many I need. They're also great as appetizers.
—Teresa Kraus, Cortez, CO

Prep: 20 min. • **Bake:** 15 min./batch
Makes: 5 dozen

½	lb. ground beef
1	small onion, finely chopped
2½	cups all-purpose flour
1	Tbsp. sugar
2	tsp. baking powder
1	tsp. salt
¾	cup ketchup
¾	cup 2% milk
½	cup butter, melted
2	large eggs
1	tsp. prepared mustard
2	cups shredded cheddar cheese

1. In a large skillet, cook beef and onion over medium heat until meat is no longer pink; drain.

2. In a small bowl, combine the flour, sugar, baking powder and salt. In another bowl, combine the ketchup, milk, butter, eggs and mustard; stir into the dry ingredients just until moistened. Fold in the beef mixture and cheese.

3. Fill greased miniature muffin cups three-fourths full. Bake at 425° until a toothpick comes out clean, 15-18 minutes. Cool for 5 minutes before removing from pans to wire racks. Serve warm. Refrigerate any leftovers.

Note: Muffins may be baked in regular-size muffin cups for 20-25 minutes; recipe makes 2 dozen.

1 mini muffin: 62 cal., 3g fat (2g sat. fat), 16mg chol., 137mg sod., 5g carb. (1g sugars, 0 fiber), 2g pro.

CARROT SHEET CAKE

We sold pieces of this to-die-for carrot cake at an art show and before long, sold out of the 10 cakes we had made!
—Dottie Cosgrove, South El Monte, CA

- -

Prep: 20 min. • **Bake:** 35 min. + cooling
Makes: 30 servings

4   large eggs, room temperature
1   cup canola oil
2   cups sugar
2   cups all-purpose flour
2   tsp. baking soda
¼   tsp. baking powder
2   tsp. ground cinnamon
½   tsp. salt
3   cups shredded carrots
⅔   cup chopped walnuts
FROSTING
1   pkg. (8 oz.) cream cheese, softened
½   cup butter, softened
1   tsp. vanilla extract
4   cups confectioners' sugar
⅔   cup chopped walnuts

1. In a bowl, beat eggs, oil and sugar until smooth. Combine flour, baking soda, baking powder, cinnamon and salt; add to egg mixture and beat well. Stir in carrots and walnuts. Pour into a greased 15x10x1-in. baking pan. Bake at 350° until a toothpick inserted in the center comes out clean, about 35 minutes. Cool on a wire rack.
2. For frosting, beat cream cheese, butter and vanilla in a bowl until smooth; beat in sugar. Spread over cake. Sprinkle with nuts. Decorate as desired.

1 piece: 311 cal., 17g fat (5g sat. fat), 45mg chol., 193mg sod., 38g carb. (29g sugars, 1g fiber), 4g pro.

TEST KITCHEN TIP
Use an offset spatula to get a smooth, professional-looking finish to your frosting.

PECAN PIE BARS

These bars are decadently rich—just like pecan pie! They're sure to disappear from the dessert table at your next gathering, so you might want to save a piece for later.
—Carolyn Custer, Clifton Park, NY

Prep: 10 min. • **Bake:** 35 min. + chilling
Makes: 4 dozen

- 2 cups all-purpose flour
- ½ cup confectioners' sugar
- 1 cup butter, softened

- 1 can (14 oz.) sweetened condensed milk
- 1 large egg, room temperature
- 1 tsp. vanilla extract
  Pinch salt
- 1 pkg. (8 oz.) milk chocolate English toffee bits
- 1 cup chopped pecans

1. In a large bowl, combine flour and sugar. Cut in butter until mixture resembles coarse meal. Press firmly onto the bottom of a greased 13x9-in. baking dish. Bake at 350° for 15 minutes.

2. Meanwhile, in large bowl, beat the milk, egg, vanilla and salt until smooth. Stir in toffee bits and pecans; spread evenly over baked crust.

3. Bake until lightly browned, 20-25 minutes longer. Cool. Cover and chill; cut into bars. Store in refrigerator.

1 bar: 127 cal., 8g fat (4g sat. fat), 18mg chol., 100mg sod., 13g carb. (9g sugars, 0 fiber), 2g pro.

TEST KITCHEN TIP
Pecans have a higher fat content than other nuts, so they're more prone to going rancid. They'll stay fresh for twice as long in the freezer as they would at room temperature.

RED VELVET PANCAKES

The recipe makes mix for five batches of pancakes, so you can make one or more batches at a time, depending on how large your crowd is. Our Christmastime tradition is to enjoy a lazy pancake breakfast and read J.R.R. Tolkien's Letters from Father Christmas, *fables he wrote for his children.*
—Sue Brown, West Bend, WI

Prep: 30 min. • **Cook:** 15 min./batch
Makes: 16 pancakes per batch

- 10 cups all-purpose flour
- 1¼ cups sugar
- ⅔ cup baking cocoa
- 6 tsp. baking soda
- 4 tsp. baking powder
- 5 tsp. salt

ADDITIONAL INGREDIENTS (EACH BATCH)
- 2 cups buttermilk
- 2 large eggs
- 2 Tbsp. red food coloring
  Butter and maple syrup

1. In a large bowl, combine the first 6 ingredients. Place 2 cups mix in each of 5 resealable containers. Store in a cool, dry place for up to 6 months. Makes: 5 batches (10 cups mix).
2. To prepare pancakes, pour mix into a large bowl. In a small bowl, whisk the buttermilk, eggs and food coloring. Stir into dry ingredients just until moistened.
3. Pour batter by ¼ cupfuls onto a greased hot griddle; turn when bubbles form on top. Cook until the second side is golden brown. Serve with butter and syrup.
2 pancakes: 619 cal., 33g fat (17g sat. fat), 183mg chol., 700mg sod., 64g carb. (22g sugars, 1g fiber), 16g pro.

SAUSAGE CRESCENT ROLLS

I love the pigs in a blanket appetizer and thought I could turn it into an amazing breakfast dish. Boy, was I right. These rolls are now on the menu for every family gathering.
—Jimmie Harvey, Bedias, TX

Prep: 25 min. + rising • **Bake:** 15 min.
Makes: 3 dozen

- 36 frozen fully cooked breakfast sausage links
- 1 pkg. (¼ oz.) active dry yeast
- 1 cup warm water (110° to 115°)
- ½ cup sugar
- ½ cup butter, melted
- 3 large eggs, room temperature
- 1 tsp. salt
- 5½ to 6 cups all-purpose flour

TOPPING
- 1 large egg white
- 1 Tbsp. water
- 3 Tbsp. sesame seeds, toasted

1. In a large skillet, cook sausage links over medium heat just until browned, turning frequently. Cool slightly; refrigerate.
2. Dissolve yeast in warm water. Add sugar, butter, eggs, salt and 2 cups flour. Beat on medium speed until smooth. Stir in enough of the remaining flour to form a soft dough. Refrigerate, covered, overnight.
3. Turn dough onto a lightly floured surface; divide into 6 portions. Roll each portion into a 10-in. circle; cut each circle into 6 wedges. Place a sausage at wide end of each wedge; roll up from wide ends. Place point sides down, 2 in. apart, on greased baking sheets. Cover with a kitchen towel; let rise in a warm place until doubled, about 1 hour.
4. Preheat oven to 350°. Beat egg white and water; brush over rolls. Sprinkle with sesame seeds. Bake until lightly browned, 12-14 minutes. Serve warm.
1 roll: 165 cal., 9g fat (4g sat. fat), 30mg chol., 218mg sod., 18g carb. (3g sugars, 1g fiber), 5g pro.

2 Tbsp. grated Parmesan cheese
2 Tbsp. Italian seasoning
1 Tbsp. sugar
2 tsp. garlic salt
1 tsp. dried parsley flakes
1 tsp. pepper
Hot cooked spaghetti and additional Parmesan cheese

1. In a Dutch oven, cook beef, sausage and onion over medium heat until meat is no longer pink; drain. Stir in tomatoes, water, tomato paste, mushrooms, pepperoni, cheese, Italian seasoning, sugar, garlic salt, parsley and pepper. Bring to a boil. Reduce heat; cover and simmer for 30 minutes.
2. Serve desired amount with spaghetti and sprinkle with additional cheese. Cool remaining sauce. Freeze sauce in freezer containers for up to 3 months.
To use frozen sauce: Thaw in refrigerator overnight. Place in a saucepan; heat through. Serve over spaghetti and sprinkle with Parmesan cheese.
½ cup: 121 cal., 8g fat (3g sat. fat), 23mg chol., 467mg sod., 6g carb. (2g sugars, 1g fiber), 8g pro.

SALAMI ROLL-UPS
These bite-sized appetizers are a cinch to make with just four ingredients—even your kids can help you with them!
—Jean Baffuto, Apache Junction, AZ

- -

Takes: 25 min. • **Makes:** 3½ dozen

1 carton (8 oz.) whipped cream cheese
¼ lb. hard salami, finely chopped
2 Tbsp. dill pickle relish
4 flour tortillas (10 in.), room temperature

1. In a small bowl, combine cream cheese, salami and pickle relish.
2. Spread over tortillas. Roll up tightly; wrap in plastic. Refrigerate 15 minutes. Unwrap and cut each tortilla into 1-in. slices.
1 piece: 49 cal., 3g fat (2g sat. fat), 9mg chol., 120mg sod., 4g carb. (0 sugars, 1g fiber), 2g pro.

THREE-MEAT SPAGHETTI SAUCE
I simmer this hearty sauce in large batches, then freeze it and use it for spaghetti, lasagna, mostaccioli and pizza. I experimented with the original recipe until I came up with the perfect sauce.
—Ellen Stringer, Bourbonnais, IL

- -

Prep: 10 min. • **Cook:** 55 min.
Makes: 11½ cups

1 lb. ground beef
1 lb. bulk Italian sausage
1 cup chopped onion
1 can (28 oz.) crushed tomatoes
3 cups water
2 cans (6 oz. each) tomato paste
2 jars (4½ oz. each) sliced mushrooms, drained
1 cup chopped pepperoni

★ ★ ★ ★ ★ **READER REVIEW**
"We love this hearty sauce! Over the years, I have changed things a bit: I use lean ground beef, hot Italian turkey sausage and turkey pepperoni. I also simmer it without the lid on and never have a problem with runny sauce. We appreciate the freezer convenience!"

HBASELY TASTEOFHOME.COM

HAMBURGER BAKED BEANS

I serve this satisfying ground beef and bean bake when I need to feed a crowd. I keep an extra pan of it in my freezer for occasions when there's no time to cook.
—Louann Sherbach, Wantagh, NY

Prep: 15 min. • **Bake:** 45 min.
Makes: 2 casseroles (12 servings each)

- 3 lbs. ground beef
- 4 cans (15¾ oz. each) pork and beans
- 2 cups ketchup
- 1 cup water
- 2 envelopes onion soup mix
- ¼ cup packed brown sugar
- ¼ cup ground mustard
- ¼ cup molasses
- 1 Tbsp. white vinegar
- 1 tsp. garlic powder
- ½ tsp. ground cloves

1. In a Dutch oven, cook ground beef over medium heat until no longer pink; drain. Stir in the remaining ingredients; heat through. Transfer to 2 greased 2-qt. baking dishes. Cover and freeze 1 dish for up to 3 months.
2. Cover and bake the second dish at 400° for 30 minutes. Uncover; bake until bubbly, 10-15 minutes longer.
To use frozen casserole: Thaw in the refrigerator. Cover and bake at 400° for 40 minutes. Uncover; bake until bubbly, 15-20 minutes longer.
1 serving: 157 cal., 6g fat (2g sat. fat), 28mg chol., 544mg sod., 15g carb. (8g sugars, 1g fiber), 12g pro.

GINGER-CREAM BARS

I rediscovered this nearly forgotten old-time recipe recently and found it's everyone's favorite. Even 4-year-olds have asked for these frosted bars as nursery treats.
—Carol Nagelkirk, Holland, MI

Prep: 20 min. • **Bake:** 20 min.
Makes: 5 dozen

- 1 cup butter, softened
- 1 cup sugar
- 2 cups all-purpose flour
- 1 tsp. salt
- 2 tsp. baking soda
- 1 Tbsp. ground cinnamon
- 1 Tbsp. ground cloves
- 1 Tbsp. ground ginger
- 2 large eggs, room temperature
- ½ cup molasses
- 1 cup hot brewed coffee

FROSTING
- ½ cup butter, softened
- 3 oz. cream cheese, softened
- 2 cups confectioners' sugar
- 2 tsp. vanilla extract
  Chopped nuts, optional

1. Preheat oven to 350°. Cream butter and sugar. Sift together flour, salt, baking soda and spices; add to creamed mixture. Add eggs, 1 at a time, beating well after each addition, and molasses. Blend in coffee. Spread in a 15x10x1-in. baking pan.
2. Bake 20-25 minutes. Cool. For frosting, cream butter and cream cheese; add confectioners' sugar and vanilla. Spread over bars. If desired, top with nuts.
1 bar: 101 cal., 5g fat (3g sat. fat), 20mg chol., 126mg sod., 13g carb. (9g sugars, 0 fiber), 1g pro.

WINTER SQUASH, SAUSAGE & FETA BAKE

I can't resist butternut squash because of its bright color and fall flavor. I make this casserole for potlucks. It's always a guaranteed hit.
—Craig Simpson, Savannah, GA

Prep: 30 min. • **Bake:** 45 min.
Makes: 20 servings

- 1 lb. bulk Italian sausage
- 2 large onions, chopped
- ½ tsp. crushed red pepper flakes, divided
- ¼ cup olive oil
- 2 tsp. minced fresh rosemary
- 1½ tsp. salt
- 1 tsp. Worcestershire sauce
- 1 tsp. pepper
- 1 medium butternut squash (about 4 lbs.), peeled and cut into 1-in. cubes
- 1 medium acorn squash, peeled and cut into 1-in. cubes
- 2 cups crumbled feta cheese
- 2 small sweet red peppers, chopped

1. Preheat oven to 375°. In a large skillet, cook the sausage, onions and ¼ tsp. pepper flakes over medium heat 8-10 minutes or until sausage is no longer pink and onions are tender, breaking up the sausage into crumbles; drain.

2. In a large bowl, combine oil, rosemary, salt, Worcestershire sauce, pepper and remaining pepper flakes. Add butternut and acorn squash, cheese, red peppers and sausage mixture; toss to coat.

3. Transfer to an ungreased shallow roasting pan. Cover and bake 35 minutes. Uncover; bake 10-15 minutes longer or until squash is tender.

¾ cup: 160 cal., 10g fat (4g sat. fat), 22mg chol., 481mg sod., 10g carb. (3g sugars, 3g fiber), 7g pro.

SPICE-RUBBED HAM

Now this is a ham—it's sweet and smoky, with just the right hint of cloves and ginger.
—Sharon Tipton, Casselberry, FL

Prep: 15 min. • **Bake:** 3¼ hours + standing
Makes: 24 servings

- 1 fully cooked semi-boneless ham (8 to 10 lbs.)
- ½ cup spicy brown mustard
- ¼ cup packed brown sugar
- ¼ tsp. ground ginger
- ¼ tsp. ground cinnamon
  Whole cloves

1. Place ham on a rack in a shallow roasting pan. Score the surface of the ham, making diamond shapes ½ in. deep. Combine the mustard, brown sugar, ground ginger and cinnamon; rub over surface of ham. Insert a clove in each diamond.

2. Bake, uncovered, at 325° for 1½ hours. Cover and bake 1¾-2 hours longer or until a thermometer reads 140°. Discard cloves. Let stand for 10 minutes before slicing.

3 oz. cooked ham: 139 cal., 4g fat (1g sat. fat), 66mg chol., 858mg sod., 3g carb. (3g sugars, 0 fiber), 22g pro. **Diabetic exchanges:** 3 lean meat.

GLAZED SPICED RUM POUND CAKES

My recipe makes two loaf-size treats, perfect for sharing. The spiced rum flavor in both the cake and the glaze really comes through.
—Christine Russell, Littleton, NH

Prep: 30 min. • **Bake:** 45 min. + cooling
Makes: 2 loaves (16 slices each)

- 1 cup butter, softened
- 2 cups packed brown sugar
- 5 large eggs, room temperature
- ⅓ cup spiced rum
- 2 tsp. vanilla extract
- 3½ cups all-purpose flour
- 2 tsp. baking powder
- ½ tsp. baking soda
- ½ tsp. salt
- ½ cup 2% milk

GLAZE
- ½ cup sugar
- ¼ cup butter, cubed
- 2 tsp. water
- 2 tsp. spiced rum
- ½ cup chopped pecans, toasted

1. Preheat oven to 350°. Grease and flour two 9x5-in. loaf pans. In a large bowl, cream butter and brown sugar until light and fluffy, 5-7 minutes. Add eggs, 1 at a time, beating well after each addition. Beat in rum and vanilla. In another bowl, whisk flour, baking powder, baking soda and salt; add to creamed mixture alternately with milk, beating well after each addition.
2. Spoon batter into prepared pans. Bake 45-50 minutes or until a toothpick inserted in center comes out clean. Cool in pans for 10 minutes before removing to wire racks to cool.
3. Meanwhile, in a small saucepan, combine sugar, butter, water and rum. Bring to a boil. Remove from heat; drizzle over warm cakes. Sprinkle with chopped pecans. Cool completely on wire racks.
1 slice: 209 cal., 9g fat (5g sat. fat), 48mg chol., 161mg sod., 28g carb. (17g sugars, 1g fiber), 3g pro.

MAKE AHEAD
HAM & CHEESE PUFF

For brunch, lunch or anytime, people really seem to go for the big chunks of ham combined with the flavors of mustard and cheese. Assembled the night before, it's a great make-ahead potluck dish.
—Nina Clark, Wareham, MA

Prep: 15 min. + chilling • **Bake:** 55 min.
Makes: 2 casseroles (12 servings each)

- 2 loaves (1 lb. each) Italian bread, cut into 1-in. cubes
- 6 cups cubed fully cooked ham
- 1½ lbs. Monterey Jack or Muenster cheese, cubed
- 1 medium onion, chopped
- ¼ cup butter
- 16 large eggs
- 7 cups whole milk
- ½ cup prepared mustard

1. Toss bread, ham and cheese; divide between 2 greased 13x9-in. baking dishes. In a skillet, saute onion in butter until tender; transfer to a bowl. Add eggs, milk and mustard; mix well. Pour over bread mixture. Cover and refrigerate overnight.
2. Remove from the refrigerator 30 minutes before baking. Bake, uncovered, at 350° for 55-65 minutes or until a knife inserted in the center comes out clean. Serve immediately.
1 piece: 369 cal., 19g fat (9g sat. fat), 187mg chol., 949mg sod., 24g carb. (5g sugars, 1g fiber), 25g pro.

KAHLUA DREAM BARS

I always double this recipe so everyone gets a piece. For a glaze with deeper flavor, use 1 ounce of unsweetened chocolate and 2 ounces of semisweet.
—Lorraine Caland, Shuniah, ON

Prep: 30 min. + chilling • **Makes:** 6 dozen

- 1 cup butter, cubed
- ½ cup baking cocoa
- 1 large egg yolk, room temperature
- 2 cups graham cracker crumbs
- ½ cup confectioners' sugar
- 1 tsp. vanilla extract

FILLING
- ½ cup butter, melted
- ⅓ cup Kahlua (coffee liqueur)
- 3 cups confectioners' sugar

GLAZE
- ¼ cup butter, cubed
- 3 oz. semisweet chocolate, chopped

1. In large heavy saucepan, melt butter over medium-low heat; stir in cocoa until blended. Whisk a small amount of hot mixture into egg yolk; return all to the pan, whisking constantly. Cook, stirring constantly, until mixture thickens and a thermometer reads 160°, 2-3 minutes. Remove from heat. Stir in cracker crumbs, confectioners' sugar and vanilla. Press into a greased 13x9-in. pan.

2. For filling, in a large bowl, combine butter and Kahlua. Stir in confectioners' sugar. Spread over crust. Refrigerate until set.

3. For glaze, in a microwave, melt the butter and chocolate; stir until smooth. Spread over filling. Refrigerate until set. Cut into bars.

1 bar: 88 cal., 5g fat (3g sat. fat), 14mg chol., 49mg sod., 9g carb. (7g sugars, 0 fiber), 0 pro.

DILLED MUSHROOM TURNOVERS

My bite-sized mushroom pastries are hard to resist. For parties, I prep and freeze them, then pop them in the oven when guests are on the way.
—Isabella Michel-Clark, Sparks, NV

Prep: 1 hour + chilling • **Bake:** 15 min./batch
Makes: about 5 dozen

- 1 cup butter, softened
- 2 pkg. (8 oz. each) cream cheese, softened
- 3 cups all-purpose flour

FILLING

- 3 Tbsp. butter
- ½ lb. fresh mushrooms, finely chopped
- 1 large onion, finely chopped
- ¼ cup sour cream
- 2 Tbsp. all-purpose flour
- 1 tsp. salt
- 1 tsp. snipped fresh dill
- 1 large egg, beaten

1. In a large bowl, cream butter and cream cheese until smooth. Gradually beat flour into creamed mixture. Divide dough in half. Shape each half into a disk; wrap in plastic. Refrigerate for 1 hour or until firm enough to handle.

2. Meanwhile, in a large skillet, heat butter over medium heat. Add mushrooms and onion; cook and stir until vegetables are tender, 6-8 minutes. Remove from heat; stir in sour cream, flour, salt and dill. Cool to room temperature.

3. Preheat oven to 400°. On a lightly floured surface, roll dough to ⅛-in. thickness. Cut circles with a floured 2½-in. round cookie cutter. Place about 1 tsp. filling on one side of each. Brush edges with egg; fold dough over filling. Press edges with a fork to seal.

4. Place on ungreased baking sheets; brush egg over tops. Bake until edges are golden brown, 12-14 minutes.

Freeze option: Cover and freeze unbaked turnovers on waxed paper-lined baking sheets until firm. Transfer to freezer containers; cover and return to freezer. To use, bake turnovers as directed, increasing time by 2-3 minutes.

1 turnover: 87 cal., 7g fat (4g sat. fat), 22mg chol., 98mg sod., 6g carb. (0 sugars, 0 fiber), 1g pro.

MAKE AHEAD

BROCCOLI SALAD SUPREME

People can't get enough of the sweet grapes and crunchy broccoli in this colorful salad. I appreciate its make-ahead convenience.

—Terri Twyman, Bonanza, OR

- -

Takes: 10 min. • **Makes:** about 20 servings

- 10 cups broccoli florets (about 3½ lbs.)
- 6 cups seedless red grapes (about 3 lbs.)
- 1 cup sliced celery
- 6 green onions, sliced
- 2 cups mayonnaise
- ⅔ cup sugar
- 2 Tbsp. cider vinegar
- 1 lb. sliced bacon, cooked and crumbled
- 1⅓ cups slivered almonds, toasted

1. In a large salad bowl, combine broccoli, grapes, celery and green onions. In a small bowl, combine the mayonnaise, sugar and vinegar. Pour over broccoli mixture and toss to coat.

2. Cover and refrigerate for at least 4 hours or overnight. Just before serving, gently stir in bacon and almonds.

1 cup: 344 cal., 26g fat (4g sat. fat), 14mg chol., 268mg sod., 25g carb. (20g sugars, 4g fiber), 7g pro.

APPLE RAISIN BREAD

I've been making this bread for many years. It smells so good in the oven and tastes even better. I make bread almost every Saturday, and it doesn't stay around long when our sons are home from college in the summer.

—Perlene Hoekema, Lynden, WA

- -

Prep: 25 min. + rising • **Bake:** 30 min.
Makes: 3 loaves (16 slices each)

- 2 pkg. (¼ oz. each) active dry yeast
- 1½ cups warm water (110° to 115°), divided
- 1 tsp. sugar
- 3 large eggs, room temperature, beaten
- 1 cup applesauce
- ½ cup honey
- ½ cup canola oil
- 2 tsp. salt
- 8 to 9 cups all-purpose flour
- 1½ cups diced peeled apples
- 1½ cups raisins
- 2 Tbsp. lemon juice
- 2 Tbsp. cornmeal

GLAZE
- 1 large egg, beaten
  Sugar

1. In a small bowl, combine yeast, ½ cup water and sugar; set aside. In a large bowl, combine eggs, applesauce, honey, oil, salt and remaining water; mix well. Stir in yeast mixture. Gradually add enough flour to form a soft dough. Knead on a floured surface until smooth and elastic, about 10 minutes. Place dough in a greased bowl, turning once to grease top. Cover and let rise in a warm place until doubled, about 1 hour.

2. Punch dough down and turn over in bowl. Cover and let rise 30 minutes. In a small bowl, combine the apples, raisins and lemon juice. Divide dough into 3 parts; knead a third of the apple mixture into each part. Shape each into a round flat ball. Place each in a greased 8-in. round baking pan that has been sprinkled with cornmeal. Cover and let rise until doubled, about 1 hour.

3. Brush each loaf with egg and sprinkle with sugar. Bake at 350° for 30-35 minutes or until bread sounds hollow when tapped.

1 slice: 135 cal., 3g fat (0 sat. fat), 18mg chol., 105mg sod., 25g carb. (8g sugars, 1g fiber), 3g pro.

SPICY CHUNKY SALSA

Vinegar adds a refreshing tang to this sweet tomato salsa. It's wonderful as is, but for more heat, leave in some hot pepper seeds.

—Donna Larae Goutermont, Sequim, WA

Prep: 1½ hours • **Process:** 15 min.
Makes: 8 pints

- 6 lbs. tomatoes
- 3 large green peppers, chopped
- 3 large onions, chopped
- 2 cups white vinegar
- 1 large sweet red pepper, chopped
- 1 can (12 oz.) tomato paste
- 4 jalapeno peppers, seeded and chopped
- 2 serrano peppers, seeded and chopped
- ½ cup sugar
- ½ cup minced fresh cilantro
- ½ cup bottled lemon juice
- 3 garlic cloves, minced
- 4 tsp. ground cumin
- 1 Tbsp. salt
- 2 tsp. dried oregano
- 1 tsp. hot pepper sauce

1. In a Dutch oven, bring 2 qt. water to a boil. Using a slotted spoon, place tomatoes, a few at a time, in boiling water for 30-60 seconds. Remove each tomato and immediately plunge into ice water. Drain and pat dry. Peel and finely chop tomatoes to measure 9 cups; place in a stockpot.
2. Stir in remaining ingredients. Add water to cover; bring to a boil. Reduce heat; simmer, uncovered, until slightly thickened, about 30 minutes.
3. Ladle hot mixture into hot 1-pint jars, leaving ½-in. headspace. Remove air bubbles and adjust headspace, if necessary, by adding hot mixture. Wipe jar rims. Center lids on jars; screw on bands until fingertip tight.
4. Place jars into canner with simmering water, ensuring that they are completely covered with water. Bring to a boil; process for 15 minutes. Remove jars and cool.

Note: When cutting hot peppers, disposable gloves are recommended. Avoid touching your face. The processing time listed is for altitudes of 1,000 feet or less. For altitudes up to 3,000 feet, add 5 minutes; 6,000 feet, add 10 minutes; 8,000 feet, add 15 minutes; 10,000 feet, add 20 minutes.
¼ cup: 25 cal., 0 fat (0 sat. fat), 0 chol., 117mg sod., 6g carb. (4g sugars, 1g fiber), 1g pro. **Diabetic exchanges:** ½ starch.

MINI SPINACH FRITTATAS

These mini frittatas are a cinch to make and just delicious. The recipe doubles easily for a crowd; they even freeze well for added convenience.

—Nancy Statkevicus, Tucson, AZ

Takes: 30 min. • **Makes:** 2 dozen

- 1 cup whole-milk ricotta cheese
- ¾ cup grated Parmesan cheese
- ⅔ cup chopped fresh mushrooms
- 1 pkg. (10 oz.) frozen chopped spinach, thawed and squeezed dry
- 1 large egg
- ½ tsp. dried oregano
- ¼ tsp. salt
- ¼ tsp. pepper
- 24 slices pepperoni

1. Preheat oven to 375°. In a small bowl, combine the first 8 ingredients. Place a pepperoni slice in each of 24 greased mini-muffin cups; fill three-fourths full with cheese mixture.
2. Bake for 20-25 minutes or until completely set. Carefully run a knife around sides of muffin cups to loosen frittatas. Serve warm.
1 mini frittata: 128 cal., 9g fat (5g sat. fat), 50mg chol., 396mg sod., 4g carb. (2g sugars, 1g fiber), 10g pro.

EVELYN'S SOUR CREAM TWISTS

Keep some of these terrific flaky twists in your freezer to serve in a pinch at breakfast, lunch or dinner.
—Linda Welch, North Platte, NE

Prep: 40 min. + chilling • **Bake:** 15 min.
Makes: 4 dozen

- 1 pkg. (¼ oz.) active dry yeast
- ¼ cup warm water (110° to 115°)
- 3 cups all-purpose flour
- 1½ tsp. salt
- ½ cup cold butter
- ½ cup shortening
- 2 large eggs, room temperature
- ½ cup sour cream
- 3 tsp. vanilla extract, divided
- 1½ cups sugar

1. In a small bowl, dissolve yeast in water. In a bowl, combine flour and salt. Cut in butter and shortening until the mixture resembles coarse crumbs. Stir in eggs, sour cream, 1 tsp. vanilla and the yeast mixture; mix thoroughly. Cover and refrigerate overnight.
2. Combine sugar and remaining vanilla; lightly sprinkle ½ cup over a pastry cloth or countertop surface. On the sugared surface, roll half the dough into a 12x8-in. rectangle; refrigerate remaining dough. Sprinkle rolled dough with about 1 Tbsp. of the sugar mixture. Fold the rectangle into thirds.
3. Give dough a quarter turn and repeat rolling, sugaring and folding 2 more times. Roll into a 12x8-in. rectangle. Cut into 4x1-in. strips; twist each strip 2 or 3 times. Place on chilled ungreased baking sheets. Repeat with the remaining sugar mixture and dough.
4. Bake at 375° until lightly browned, 12-14 minutes. Immediately remove from pan to wire racks to cool.
1 twist: 97 cal., 5g fat (2g sat. fat), 16mg chol., 97mg sod., 12g carb. (6g sugars, 0 fiber), 1g pro.

LOADED BAKED POTATO SALAD

I revamped my mother's potato salad recipe to taste more like baked potatoes with all the fixin's, which I love. It's now the most requested dish at family gatherings. Even my mother asked for the recipe!
—Jackie Deckard, Solsberry, IN

Prep: 20 min. • **Bake:** 40 min. + cooling
Makes: 20 servings

- 5 lbs. small unpeeled red potatoes, cubed
- 1 tsp. salt
- ½ tsp. pepper
- 8 hard-boiled large eggs, chopped
- 1 lb. sliced bacon, cooked and crumbled
- 2 cups shredded cheddar cheese
- 1 sweet onion, chopped
- 3 dill pickles, chopped
- 1½ cups sour cream
- 1 cup mayonnaise
- 2 to 3 tsp. prepared mustard

1. Preheat oven to 425°. Sprinkle potatoes with salt and pepper; bake, uncovered, in a greased 15x10x1-in. baking pan until tender, 40-45 minutes. Cool in pan on a wire rack.
2. Combine the potatoes with the next 5 ingredients. In another bowl, combine sour cream, mayonnaise and mustard; pour over potato mixture, tossing to coat. Refrigerate until serving.
¾ cup: 315 cal., 21g fat (7g sat. fat), 99mg chol., 587mg sod., 21g carb. (3g sugars, 2g fiber), 11g pro.

LEMON COCONUT BITES

The tangy lemon flavor of this no-fuss bar dessert is especially delicious on a warm day. It reminds me of selling lemonade on the sidewalk as a little girl.
—Donna Biddle, Elmira, NY

Prep: 25 min. • **Bake:** 20 min. + cooling
Makes: 4 dozen

1½ cups all-purpose flour
½ cup confectioners' sugar
¾ cup cold butter, cubed
4 large eggs, room temperature
1½ cups sugar
½ cup lemon juice
1 tsp. baking powder
¾ cup sweetened shredded coconut

1. In a small bowl, combine flour and confectioners' sugar; cut in butter until crumbly. Press into a lightly greased 13x9-in. baking pan. Bake at 350° for 15 minutes.

2. Meanwhile, in another small bowl, beat the eggs, sugar, lemon juice and baking powder until combined. Pour over crust; sprinkle with coconut.

3. Bake at 350° until golden brown, 20-25 minutes. Cool on a wire rack. Cut into bars.

1 bar: 82 cal., 4g fat (2g sat. fat), 25mg chol., 46mg sod., 11g carb. (8g sugars, 0 fiber), ˉg pro.

MAKE AHEAD

APPETIZER TORTILLA PINWHEELS

A friend gave me this recipe, and whenever I serve these pretty and delicious appetizers, people ask me for the recipe, too! Besides being attractive and tasty, the pinwheels can be made ahead of time and sliced just before serving, leaving you time for other last-minute party preparations.

—Pat Waymire, Yellow Springs, OH

Prep: 20 min. + chilling
Makes: about 4 dozen

- 1 pkg. (8 oz.) cream cheese, softened
- 1 cup shredded cheddar cheese
- 1 cup sour cream
- 1 can (4¼ oz.) chopped ripe olives
- 1 can (4 oz.) chopped green chiles, well drained
- ½ cup chopped green onions
  Garlic powder to taste
  Seasoned salt to taste
- 5 flour tortillas (10 in.)
  Salsa, optional

1. Beat cream cheese, cheddar cheese and sour cream until blended. Stir in olives, green chiles, green onions and seasonings.
2. Spread over tortillas; roll up tightly. Wrap each roll in plastic, twisting ends to seal; refrigerate several hours or overnight.
3. Unwrap. Cut into ½- to ¾-in. slices, using a serrated knife. If desired, serve with salsa.
1 pinwheel: 63 cal., 4g fat (2g sat. fat), 8mg chol., 119mg sod., 5g carb. (1g sugars, 0 fiber), 2g pro.

CORNBREAD CONFETTI SALAD

This colorful and tasty salad is always well received at picnics and potlucks. Cornbread salads have long been popular in the South but may be new to people in other regions. No matter where you live, I think you'll like this one!
—Jennifer Horst, Goose Creek, SC

Prep: 15 min. • **Bake:** 15 min. + cooling
Makes: 22 servings

- 1 pkg. (8½ oz.) cornbread/muffin mix
- 2 cans (15½ oz. each) whole kernel corn, drained
- 2 cans (15 oz. each) pinto beans, rinsed and drained
- 1 can (15 oz.) black beans, rinsed and drained
- 3 small tomatoes, chopped
- 1 medium green pepper, chopped
- 1 medium sweet red pepper, chopped
- ½ cup chopped green onions
- 10 bacon strips, cooked and crumbled
- 2 cups shredded cheddar cheese

DRESSING
- 1 cup sour cream
- 1 cup mayonnaise
- 1 envelope ranch salad dressing mix

1. Prepare cornbread according to package directions. Cool completely; crumble.
2. In a large bowl, combine the corn, beans, tomatoes, peppers, onions, bacon, cheese and crumbled cornbread.
3. In a small bowl, whisk the dressing ingredients. Just before serving, pour dressing over salad and toss to coat.
¾ cup: 285 cal., 16g fat (5g sat. fat), 38mg chol., 582mg sod., 24g carb. (6g sugars, 3g fiber), 9g pro.

GOOEY CHOCOLATE CARAMEL BARS

These rich, gooey bars are my most requested treats. They're popular at school functions, family barbecues and picnics. We like them alone or topped off with a scoop of ice cream.
—Betty Hagerty, Philadelphia, PA

Prep: 25 min. • **Bake:** 20 min. + cooling
Makes: about 4½ dozen

- 2¼ cups all-purpose flour, divided
- 2 cups quick-cooking oats
- 1½ cups packed brown sugar
- 1 tsp. baking soda
- ½ tsp. salt
- 1½ cups cold butter, cubed
- 2 cups semisweet chocolate chips
- 1 cup chopped pecans
- 1 jar (12 oz.) caramel ice cream topping

1. In a large bowl, combine 2 cups flour, oats, brown sugar, baking soda and salt. Cut in butter until crumbly. Set half of mixture aside for topping.
2. Press the remaining crumb mixture into a greased 13x9-in. baking pan. Bake at 350° for 15 minutes. Sprinkle with the chocolate chips and pecans.
3. Whisk caramel topping and remaining flour until smooth; drizzle over top. Sprinkle with the reserved crumb mixture. Bake for 18-20 minutes or until golden brown. Cool on a wire rack for 2 hours before cutting.
1 bar: 156 cal., 9g fat (5g sat. fat), 14mg chol., 110mg sod., 20g carb. (13g sugars, 1g fiber), 2g pro.

LAYERED MINT CANDIES

These incredible melt-in-your-mouth candies have the perfect amount of mint nestled between layers of mild chocolate. Even when I make a double batch for everyone to enjoy, the supply never lasts long at Christmas!
—Rhonda Vauble, Sac City, IA

Prep: 15 min. + chilling
Makes: about 2 lbs. (about 9½ dozen)

1 Tbsp. butter
1½ lbs. white candy coating, coarsely chopped, divided
1 cup semisweet chocolate chips
1 tsp. peppermint extract
4 drops green food coloring, optional
3 Tbsp. heavy whipping cream

1. Line a 13x9-in. pan with foil. Grease foil with butter.
2. Microwave 1 lb. candy coating and chocolate chips until smooth, stirring every 30 seconds. Spread half into prepared pan, reserving half. Microwave remaining white candy coating until melted; stir in extract and, if desired, food coloring. Stir in cream until smooth (mixture will be stiff). Spread over first layer; refrigerate until firm, about 10 minutes. Warm the reserved chocolate mixture if necessary; spread over mint layer. Refrigerate until firm, about 1 hour.
3. Using foil, lift candy out of pan, then remove foil. Cut candy into 1-in. squares. Refrigerate in an airtight container.

1 piece: 41 cal., 2g fat (2g sat. fat), 1mg chol., 1mg sod., 5g carb. (5g sugars, 0 fiber), 0 pro.

TEXAS-STYLE BRISKET

This is the quintessential brisket here in the Lone Star State. Even my husband's six-generation Texas family is impressed! Grilling with wood chips takes a little extra effort, but I promise it's worth it. Each bite tastes like heaven on a plate.
—Renee Morgan, Taylor, TX

Prep: 35 min. + chilling
Cook: 6 hours + standing
Makes: 20 servings

- 1 whole fresh beef brisket (12 to 14 lbs.)
- ½ cup pepper
- ¼ cup kosher salt
  Large disposable foil pan
  About 6 cups wood chips, preferably oak

1. Trim fat on brisket to ½-in. thickness. Rub brisket with pepper and salt; place in a large disposable foil pan, fat side up. Refrigerate, covered, for several hours or overnight. Meanwhile, soak wood chips in water.

2. To prepare grill for slow indirect cooking, adjust grill vents so top vent is half open and bottom vent is open only one-quarter of the way. Make 2 arrangements of 45 unlit coals on opposite sides of the grill, leaving center of the grill open. Light 20 additional coals until ash-covered; distribute over unlit coals. Sprinkle 2 cups soaked wood chips over lit coals.

3. Replace grill rack. Close grill and allow temperature in grill to reach 275°, about 15 minutes.

4. Place foil pan with brisket in center of grill rack; cover grill and cook 3 hours (do not open grill). Check temperature of grill periodically to maintain a temperature of 275° throughout cooking. Heat level may be adjusted by opening vents to raise temperature and closing vents partway to decrease temperature.

5. Add another 10 unlit coals and 1 cup wood chips to each side of the grill. Cook brisket, covered, 3-4 hours longer or until fork-tender (a thermometer inserted in brisket should read about 190°); add coals and wood chips as needed to maintain a grill temperature of 275°.

6. Remove brisket from grill. Cover tightly with foil; let stand 30-60 minutes. Cut brisket across the grain into slices.

Note: If your charcoal grill does not have a built-in thermometer, the grill temperature may be checked by inserting the stem of a food thermometer through the top vent.

5 oz. cooked beef: 351 cal., 12g fat (4g sat. fat), 116mg chol., 1243mg sod., 2g carb. (0 sugars, 1g fiber), 56g pro.

2. Turn onto a floured surface; knead until smooth and elastic, about 10 minutes. Cover and let rest 15 minutes.

3. Divide dough into thirds. Roll each portion into a 20-in. rope. Cut each into 20 pieces; shape each into a ball. Grease three 9-in. round baking pans; arrange 20 balls in each pan. Cover and refrigerate overnight.

4. Let rise in a warm place until doubled, about 1¼ hours. Bake at 350° until golden brown, 18-22 minutes. Meanwhile, in a small bowl, cream butter. Add honey; beat until light and fluffy. Remove rolls from pans to wire racks. Combine glaze ingredients; brush over warm rolls. Serve with honey butter.

1 roll with about 1 tsp. honey butter: 114 cal., 7g fat (4g sat. fat), 24mg chol., 107mg sod., 12g carb. (4g sugars, 1g fiber), 2g pro.

DEVILED EGGS EXTRAORDINAIRE

Featuring a mild mustard flavor, these deviled eggs are perfect for summertime picnics. They would be good for formal occasions, too.
—Carol Ross, Anchorage, AK

Prep: 40 min. • **Makes:** 4 dozen

- 24 hard-boiled large eggs
- 4   oz. cream cheese, softened
- ½   cup mayonnaise
- 2   Tbsp. prepared mustard
- 1   tsp. cider vinegar
- ¼   tsp. salt
- ¼   tsp. onion powder

Cut eggs in half lengthwise. Remove yolks; set whites aside. In a small bowl, mash yolks. Add the cream cheese, mayonnaise, mustard, vinegar, salt and onion powder; mix well. Stuff or pipe into egg whites. Refrigerate until serving.

1 stuffed egg half: 64 cal., 5g fat (2g sat. fat), 109mg chol., 70mg sod., 0 carb. (0 sugars, 0 fiber), 3g pro.

HONEY WHOLE WHEAT PAN ROLLS

With their pleasant wheat flavor and a honey of a glaze, these rolls impress my guests. Every time I take them to potluck dinners, I come home with an empty pan.
—Nancye Thompson, Paducah, KY

Prep: 35 min. + chilling • **Bake:** 20 min.
Makes: 5 dozen (1¼ cups honey butter)

- 4   to 5 cups bread flour
- ¼   cup sugar
- 2   pkg. (¼ oz. each) active dry yeast
- 1   tsp. salt
- 1   cup 2% milk
- 1   cup butter, cubed
- ½   cup water
- 2   large eggs, room temperature
- 2   cups whole wheat flour

HONEY BUTTER
- 1   cup butter, softened
- 7   Tbsp. honey

HONEY GLAZE
- 2   Tbsp. honey
- 1   Tbsp. butter, melted

1. In a large bowl, combine 2 cups bread flour, sugar, yeast and salt. In a small saucepan, heat the milk, butter and water to 120°-130°. Add to dry ingredients; beat just until moistened. Beat in eggs. Stir in whole wheat flour and enough remaining bread flour to form a soft dough.

MAKE AHEAD

MEXICAN CHICKEN MEATBALLS

These low-fat meatballs taste fabulous on their own, but if you want to take things up a notch, serve them with a dip of hot Velveeta cheese and salsa. You could also substitute ground turkey for the chicken.
—Katrina Lopes, Lyman, SC

Prep: 20 min. • **Bake:** 15 min.
Makes: about 5 dozen

½ cup egg substitute
1 can (4 oz.) chopped green chiles
1 cup crushed cornflakes
1 cup shredded reduced-fat Mexican cheese blend
½ tsp. seasoned salt
¼ tsp. cayenne pepper
1 lb. ground chicken
   Salsa, optional

In a large bowl, combine first 6 ingredients. Crumble ground chicken over mixture and mix well. Shape into 1-in. balls. Place on baking sheets coated with cooking spray. Bake at 375°, turning occasionally, until a thermometer reads 165° and juices run clear, 12-15 minutes. Serve with salsa if desired.
Freeze option: Freeze cooled meatballs in freezer containers. To use, partially thaw in refrigerator overnight. Microwave, covered, on high in a microwave-safe dish until heated through, gently stirring and adding a little broth or water if necessary.
1 serving: 21 cal., 1g fat (0 sat. fat), 6mg chol., 49mg sod., 1g carb. (0 sugars, 0 fiber), 2g pro.

MAKE AHEAD

SAUSAGE BACON BITES

These tasty morsels are perfect for brunch with almost any egg dish or as finger foods that party guests can just pop into their mouths.
—Pat Waymire, Yellow Springs, OH

Prep: 20 min. + chilling • **Bake:** 35 min.
Makes: about 3½ dozen

¾ lb. sliced bacon
2 pkg. (8 oz. each) frozen fully cooked breakfast sausage links, thawed
½ cup plus 2 Tbsp. packed brown sugar, divided

1. Preheat oven to 350°. Cut bacon strips widthwise in half; cut sausage links in half. Wrap a piece of bacon around each piece of sausage. Place ½ cup brown sugar in a shallow bowl; roll sausages in sugar. Secure each with a toothpick. Place in a foil-lined 15x10x1-in. baking pan. Cover; refrigerate 4 hours or overnight.
2. Sprinkle with 1 Tbsp. brown sugar. Bake until bacon is crisp, 35-40 minutes, turning once. Sprinkle with remaining brown sugar.
1 piece: 51 cal., 4g fat (1g sat. fat), 6mg chol., 100mg sod., 4g carb. (4g sugars, 0 fiber), 2g pro.

PIZZA ROLL-UPS

This has been a regular after-school snack in my house since I first got the recipe through our local 4-H club. These bite-sized pizza treats, made with refrigerated crescent rolls, are especially good served with spaghetti sauce for dipping.
—Donna Klettke, Wheatland, MO

Prep: 20 min. • **Bake:** 15 min.
Makes: 2 dozen

- ½ lb. ground beef
- 1 can (8 oz.) tomato sauce
- ½ cup shredded part-skim mozzarella cheese
- ½ tsp. dried oregano
- 2 tubes (8 oz. each) refrigerated crescent rolls

1. In a large skillet, cook beef over medium heat until no longer pink; drain. Remove from the heat. Add the tomato sauce, mozzarella cheese and oregano.

2. Separate the crescent dough into 8 rectangles, pinching seams together. Place about 3 Tbsp. of meat mixture along 1 long side of each rectangle. Roll up, jelly-roll style, starting with a long side. Cut each roll into 3 pieces.

3. Place, seam side down, 2 in. apart on greased baking sheets. Bake at 375° for 15 minutes or until golden brown.

1 appetizer: 94 cal., 5g fat (1g sat. fat), 7mg chol., 206mg sod., 9g carb. (2g sugars, 0 fiber), 4g pro.

LATTICE-TOPPED PEAR SLAB PIE

A lattice top makes a charming frame for this dessert of pears and candied fruit—perfect for the fall and winter. Dollop the slices with whipped cream if you like.
—Johnna Johnson, Scottsdale, AZ

Prep: 30 min. + chilling
Bake: 40 min. + cooling • **Makes:** 2 dozen

- 1 cup butter, softened
- 1 pkg. (8 oz.) cream cheese, softened
- 2 Tbsp. sugar
- ½ tsp. salt
- 2¼ cups all-purpose flour

FILLING
- ¾ cup sugar
- 3 Tbsp. all-purpose flour
- 2 tsp. grated lemon zest
- 8 cups thinly sliced peeled fresh pears (about 7 medium)
- 1 cup chopped mixed candied fruit
- 1 Tbsp. 2% milk
- 3 Tbsp. coarse sugar

1. In a small bowl, beat butter, cream cheese, sugar and salt until blended. Gradually beat in flour. Divide dough in 2 portions so that 1 portion is slightly larger than the other. Shape each into a rectangle; wrap and refrigerate 1 hour or overnight.

2. Preheat oven to 350°. For filling, in a large bowl, combine sugar, flour and lemon zest. Add pears and candied fruit; toss to coat.

3. On a lightly floured surface, roll out larger portion of dough into an 18x13-in. rectangle. Transfer to a greased 15x10x1-in. baking pan. Press onto the bottom and up the sides of pan; add filling.

4. Roll out the remaining dough to a ⅛-in.-thick rectangle; cut into ½-in.-wide strips. Arrange over filling in a lattice pattern. Trim and seal strips to edge of bottom pastry. Brush pastry with milk; sprinkle with coarse sugar.

5. Bake 40-45 minutes or until crust is golden brown and filling is bubbly. Cool on a wire rack.

1 piece: 239 cal., 11g fat (7g sat. fat), 30mg chol., 151mg sod., 35g carb. (21g sugars, 2g fiber), 2g pro.

SEASONED TACO MEAT

I got this recipe from the restaurant where I work. Everyone in town loves the blend of different seasonings, and now the secret is out!
—Denise Mumm, Dixon, IA

- -

Prep: 10 min. • **Cook:** 35 min.
Makes: 6½ cups

- 3 lbs. ground beef
- 2 large onions, chopped
- 2 cups water
- 5 Tbsp. chili powder
- 2 tsp. salt
- 1 tsp. ground cumin
- ¾ tsp. garlic powder
- ¼ to ½ tsp. crushed red pepper flakes

In a large cast-iron skillet or Dutch oven, cook beef and onion over medium heat until meat is no longer pink; drain. Add water and seasonings. Bring to a boil. Reduce heat; simmer, uncovered, until the water is evaporated, about 15 minutes.

¼ cup: 113 cal., 7g fat (3g sat. fat), 35mg chol., 277mg sod., 2g carb. (1g sugars, 1g fiber), 10g pro.

BRING IT
You can serve the taco meat in a variety of ways. Use it as a filling for tacos or enchiladas, as a topping for nachos or for a build-your-own pizza or baked potato bar.

PEANUT BUTTER SHEET CAKE

I received the recipe for this incredible sheet cake from a minister's wife, and my family loves it.
—Brenda Jackson, Garden City, KS

- -

Prep: 15 min. • **Bake:** 20 min. + cooling
Makes: 24 servings

2	cups all-purpose flour
2	cups sugar
1	tsp. baking soda
½	tsp. salt
1	cup water
¾	cup butter, cubed
½	cup chunky peanut butter
¼	cup canola oil
2	large eggs, room temperature
½	cup buttermilk
1	tsp. vanilla extract

GLAZE

⅔	cup sugar
⅓	cup evaporated milk
1	Tbsp. butter
⅓	cup chunky peanut butter
⅓	cup miniature marshmallows
½	tsp. vanilla extract

1. Preheat oven to 350°. Grease a 15x10x1-in. baking pan.

2. In a large bowl, whisk flour, sugar, baking soda and salt. In a small saucepan, combine water and butter; bring just to a boil. Stir in peanut butter and oil until blended. Stir into flour mixture. In a small bowl, whisk eggs, buttermilk and vanilla until blended; add to flour mixture, whisking constantly.

3. Transfer to prepared pan. Bake until a toothpick inserted in center comes out clean, 20-25 minutes.

4. Meanwhile, for glaze, combine sugar, milk and butter in a saucepan. Bring to a boil, stirring constantly; cook and stir 2 minutes. Remove from heat; stir in peanut butter, marshmallows and vanilla until blended. Spoon over warm cake, spreading evenly. Cool on a wire rack.

1 piece: 266 cal., 14g fat (5g sat. fat), 36mg chol., 222mg sod., 33g carb. (23g sugars, 1g fiber), 4g pro.

SEAFOOD GUMBO

Gumbo is one of the dishes that makes Louisiana cuisine so famous. We live across the border in Texas and can't get enough of this traditional Cajun dish featuring okra, shrimp, spicy seasonings and the holy trinity—onions, green peppers and celery.
—Ruth Aubey, San Antonio, TX

Prep: 20 min. • **Cook:** 30 min.
Makes: 24 servings (6 qt.)

- 1 cup all-purpose flour
- 1 cup canola oil
- 4 cups chopped onion
- 2 cups chopped celery
- 2 cups chopped green pepper
- 1 cup sliced green onion and tops
- 4 cups chicken broth
- 8 cups water
- 4 cups sliced okra
- 2 Tbsp. paprika
- 1 Tbsp. salt
- 2 tsp. oregano
- 1 tsp. ground black pepper
- 6 cups small shrimp, rinsed and drained, or seafood of your choice
- 1 cup minced fresh parsley
- 2 Tbsp. Cajun seasoning

1. In a heavy Dutch oven, combine flour and oil until smooth. Cook over medium-high heat for 5 minutes, stirring constantly. Reduce heat to medium. Cook and stir about 10 minutes more, or until mixture is reddish brown.
2. Add the onion, celery, green pepper and green onions; cook and stir for 5 minutes. Add the chicken broth, water, okra, paprika, salt, oregano and pepper. Bring to boil; reduce heat and simmer, covered, for 10 minutes.
3. Add shrimp and fresh parsley. Simmer, uncovered, about 5 minutes more or until seafood is done. Remove from heat; stir in Cajun seasoning.
1 cup: 166 cal., 10g fat (1g sat. fat), 96mg chol., 900mg sod., 10g carb. (2g sugars, 2g fiber), 10g pro.

GARLIC-HERB MINI QUICHES

Looking for a wonderful little bite to dress up the brunch buffet? These delectable tartlets are irresistible!
—Josephine Piro, Easton, PA

Takes: 25 min. • **Makes:** 45 mini quiches

- 1 pkg. (6½ oz.) reduced-fat garlic-herb spreadable cheese
- ¼ cup fat-free milk
- 2 large eggs
- 3 pkg. (1.9 oz. each) frozen miniature phyllo tart shells
- 2 Tbsp. minced fresh parsley
  Minced chives, optional

1. In a small bowl, beat the spreadable cheese, milk and eggs. Place tart shells on an ungreased baking sheet; fill each with 2 tsp. mixture. Sprinkle with parsley.
2. Bake at 350° for 10-12 minutes or until filling is set and shells are lightly browned. Sprinkle with chives if desired. Serve warm.
1 mini quiche: 31 cal., 2g fat (0 sat. fat), 12mg chol., 32mg sod., 2g carb. (0 sugars, 0 fiber), 1g pro.

Crab Rangoon Tartlets: Substitute whipped cream cheese and 2 Tbsp. sour cream for the spreadable cheese and milk. Omit eggs. Stir in ½ cup fresh crab. Bake as directed; serve with sweet-and-sour sauce.

Smoky Apricot Tarts: Heat 2¼ cups apricot preserves, 1½ tsp. pumpkin pie spice and 3 Tbsp. brown sugar until sugar is dissolved. Spoon into tart shells. Sprinkle with 1½ cups shredded smoked mozzarella cheese and 3 Tbsp. brown sugar. Bake 5-7 minutes or until cheese is melted.

Slow-Cooker
Cheese Dip
page 182

Slow Cooker

Everybody loves the make-and-take convenience of the slow cooker. Good get-togethers become great ones thanks to hot dips, sandwiches and breakfasts you wake up to. Here are 33 reasons to celebrate!

CHAMPIONSHIP BEAN DIP

My friends and neighbors expect me to bring this irresistible dip to every gathering. When I arrive, they ask, "You brought your bean dip, didn't you?" If there are any leftovers, we use them to make bean and cheese burritos the next day.

—Wendi Wavrin Law, Omaha, NE

Prep: 10 min. • **Cook:** 2 hours
Makes: 4½ cups

- 1 can (16 oz.) vegetarian refried beans
- 1 cup picante sauce
- 1 cup shredded Monterey Jack cheese
- 1 cup shredded cheddar cheese
- ¾ cup sour cream
- 3 oz. cream cheese, softened
- 1 Tbsp. chili powder
- ¼ tsp. ground cumin
  Tortilla chips and salsa

In a large bowl, combine the first 8 ingredients; transfer to a 1½-qt. slow cooker. Cover and cook on high for 2 hours or until heated through, stirring once or twice. Serve with tortilla chips and salsa.

2 Tbsp.: 57 cal., 4g fat (2g sat. fat), 12mg chol., 151mg sod., 3g carb. (1g sugars, 1g fiber), 2g pro.

STUFFING FROM THE SLOW COOKER

If you're hosting a big Thanksgiving dinner, add this simple stuffing to your menu to ease entertaining. The recipe comes in handy when you run out of oven space at large gatherings. I use it often.

—Donald Seiler, Macon, MS

Prep: 30 min. • **Cook:** 3 hours
Makes: 10 servings

- 1 cup chopped onion
- 1 cup chopped celery
- ¼ cup butter
- 6 cups cubed day-old white bread
- 6 cups cubed day-old whole wheat bread
- 1 tsp. salt
- 1 tsp. poultry seasoning
- 1 tsp. rubbed sage
- ½ tsp. pepper
- 1 can (14½ oz.) reduced-sodium chicken broth or vegetable broth
- 2 large eggs, beaten

1. In a small nonstick skillet over medium heat, cook the onion and celery in butter until tender.

2. In a large bowl, combine the bread cubes, salt, poultry seasoning, sage and pepper. Stir in onion mixture. Combine broth and eggs; add to bread mixture and toss to coat.

3. Transfer to a 3-qt. slow cooker coated with cooking spray. Cover and cook on low for 3-4 hours or until a thermometer reads 160°.

¾ cup: 178 cal., 7g fat (4g sat. fat), 49mg chol., 635mg sod., 23g carb. (3g sugars, 3g fiber), 6g pro. **Diabetic exchanges:** 1½ starch, 1 fat.

SLOW-COOKER CAPONATA

This Italian eggplant dip preps quickly and actually gets better as it stands. Serve it warm or at room temperature. Try adding a little leftover caponata to scrambled eggs for a savory breakfast.
—Nancy Beckman, Helena, MT

Prep: 20 min. • **Cook:** 5 hours
Makes: 6 cups

- 2 medium eggplants, cut into ½-in. pieces
- 1 medium onion, chopped
- 1 can (14½ oz.) diced tomatoes, undrained
- 12 garlic cloves, sliced
- ½ cup dry red wine
- 3 Tbsp. extra virgin olive oil
- 2 Tbsp. red wine vinegar
- 4 tsp. capers, undrained
- 5 bay leaves
- 1½ tsp. salt
- ¼ tsp. coarsely ground pepper
  French bread baguette slices, toasted
  Optional: Fresh basil leaves, toasted pine nuts and additional olive oil

Place first 11 ingredients in a 6-qt. slow cooker (do not stir). Cook, covered, on high for 3 hours. Stir gently; replace cover. Cook on high about 2 hours longer or until the vegetables are tender. Cool slightly; discard bay leaves. Serve with toasted baguette slices, adding toppings as desired.
¼ cup: 34 cal., 2g fat (0 sat. fat), 0 chol., 189mg sod., 4g carb. (2g sugars, 2g fiber), 1g pro.

TEST KITCHEN TIP
For easy entertaining, serve warm directly from the slow cooker or at room temperature.

MINISTER'S DELIGHT

A friend gave me this recipe several years ago. She said a local minister's wife fixed it every Sunday, so she named it accordingly.
—Mary Ann Potter, Blue Springs, MO

Prep: 5 min. • **Cook:** 2 hours
Makes: 12 servings

- 1 can (21 oz.) cherry or apple pie filling
- 1 pkg. yellow cake mix (regular size)
- ½ cup butter, melted
- ⅓ cup chopped walnuts, optional

Place pie filling in a 1½-qt. slow cooker. Combine cake mix and butter (mixture will be crumbly); sprinkle over filling. Sprinkle with walnuts if desired. Cover and cook on low for 2-3 hours. Serve in bowls.
1 serving: 304 cal., 12g fat (6g sat. fat), 20mg chol., 357mg sod., 48g carb. (31g sugars, 1g fiber), 2g pro.

MAKE AHEAD

BBQ BEEF BRISKET

A friend tried this recipe and liked it, so I thought I would try it, too. When my husband told me how much he liked it, I knew I'd be making it often.
—Vivian Warner, Elkhart, KS

- -

Prep: 25 min. + marinating • **Cook:** 6½ hours
Makes: 12 servings

- 3 Tbsp. Worcestershire sauce
- 1 Tbsp. chili powder
- 2 bay leaves
- 2 garlic cloves, minced
- 1 tsp. celery salt
- 1 tsp. pepper
- 1 tsp. liquid smoke, optional
- 1 fresh beef brisket (6 lbs.)
- ½ cup beef broth

BARBECUE SAUCE
- 1 medium onion, chopped
- 2 Tbsp. canola oil
- 2 garlic cloves, minced
- 1 cup ketchup
- ½ cup molasses
- ¼ cup cider vinegar
- 2 tsp. chili powder
- ½ tsp. ground mustard

1. In a large shallow bowl, combine the Worcestershire sauce, chili powder, bay leaves, garlic, celery salt, pepper and, if desired, liquid smoke. Cut the brisket in half; add to the bowl and turn to coat. Cover and refrigerate overnight.
2. Transfer brisket to a 5- or 6-qt. slow cooker; add broth. Cover and cook on low for 6-8 hours or until tender.
3. For sauce, in a small saucepan, saute onion in oil until tender. Add garlic; cook 1 minute longer. Stir in the remaining ingredients; heat through.
4. Remove brisket from the slow cooker; discard bay leaves. Place 1 cup cooking juices in a measuring cup; skim fat. Add to the barbecue sauce. Discard remaining cooking juices.

5. Return brisket to the slow cooker; top with sauce mixture. Cover and cook on high for 30 minutes to allow flavors to blend. Thinly slice beef across the grain; serve with sauce.
Freeze option: Place individual portions of sliced brisket in freezer containers; top with cooking sauce. Cool and freeze. To use, partially thaw in refrigerator overnight. Heat through in a covered saucepan, gently stirring and adding a little water if necessary.
6 oz. cooked beef with ¼ cup sauce: 381 cal., 12g fat (4g sat. fat), 96mg chol., 548mg sod., 18g carb. (14g sugars, 1g fiber), 47g pro.

HOT FRUIT SALAD

If you're looking for something easy to round out a brunch, try this spiced fruit salad. With its pretty color, it's perfect around the holidays or for any special occasion.
—Barb Vande Voort, New Sharon, IA

- -

Prep: 10 min. • **Cook:** 3 hours
Makes: 16 servings

- 1 jar (25 oz.) unsweetened applesauce
- 1 can (21 oz.) cherry pie filling
- 1 can (20 oz.) unsweetened pineapple chunks, undrained
- 1 can (15 oz.) sliced peaches in juice, undrained
- 1 can (15 oz.) reduced-sugar apricot halves, undrained
- 1 can (15 oz.) mandarin oranges, undrained
- ¼ cup packed brown sugar
- 1 tsp. ground cinnamon

Combine first 6 ingredients in a 5-qt. slow cooker. Mix brown sugar and cinnamon; sprinkle over fruit mixture. Cook, covered, on low 3-4 hours or until heated through.
¾ cup: 141 cal., 0 fat (0 sat. fat), 0 chol., 13mg sod., 35g carb. (23g sugars, 2g fiber), 1g pro.

SLOW-COOKER BREAKFAST CASSEROLE

Here's a breakfast casserole that is very easy on the cook. I can do all the prep work the night before and it's ready in the morning. It's the perfect recipe when I have weekend guests.
—Ellie Stutheit, Las Vegas, NV

Prep: 25 min. • **Cook:** 7 hours
Makes: 12 servings

1	pkg. (30 oz.) frozen shredded hash brown potatoes
1	lb. bulk pork sausage, cooked and drained
1	medium onion, chopped
1	can (4 oz.) chopped green chiles
1½	cups shredded cheddar cheese
12	large eggs
1	cup 2% milk
½	tsp. salt
½	tsp. pepper

1. In a greased 5- or 6-qt. slow cooker, layer half of the potatoes, sausage, onion, chiles and cheese. Repeat layers.
2. In a large bowl, whisk the eggs, milk, salt and pepper; pour over top. Cover and cook on low for 7-9 hours or until eggs are set.
1 cup: 272 cal., 16g fat (7g sat. fat), 242mg chol., 466mg sod., 16g carb. (3g sugars, 1g fiber), 15g pro.

HONEY PULLED PORK SUBS

Honey and ground ginger are the flavor boosters behind my delicious no-stress sandwiches. A bottle of barbecue sauce quickly ties it all together.
—Denise Davis, Porter, ME

- -

Prep: 15 min. • **Cook:** 5 hours
Makes: 16 servings

1　small onion, finely chopped
1　boneless pork shoulder butt roast (2½ lbs.)
1　bottle (18 oz.) barbecue sauce
½　cup water
¼　cup honey
6　garlic cloves, minced
1　tsp. seasoned salt
1　tsp. ground ginger
8　submarine buns, split

Place onion and roast in a 5-qt. slow cooker. In a small bowl, combine the barbecue sauce, water, honey, garlic, seasoned salt and ginger; pour over meat. Cover and cook on high 5-6 hours or until meat is tender. Remove meat; cool slightly. Shred meat with 2 forks and return to the slow cooker; heat through. Serve on submarine buns. Cut sandwiches in half.

Freeze option: Place individual portions of cooled meat mixture in freezer containers. To use, partially thaw in the refrigerator overnight. Microwave, covered, on high in a microwave-safe dish until heated through, gently stirring and adding a little water if necessary. Serve on buns.

½ sandwich: 417 cal., 13g fat (4g sat. fat), 81mg chol., 867mg sod., 44g carb. (12g sugars, 2g fiber), 29g pro.

Italian Pulled Pork: Omit all ingredients except roast and buns. Combine 1 Tbsp. crushed fennel seed, 1 Tbsp. steak seasoning and ½ tsp. cayenne. Rub mixture over roast. In a skillet, brown roast on all sides in 1 Tbsp. olive oil. Place roast in slow cooker. Add 2 thinly sliced medium green or sweet red peppers, 2 thinly sliced medium onions and 1 can (14½ oz.) diced tomatoes with liquid. Proceed as recipe directs.

CHIPOTLE PULLED CHICKEN

I love chicken that has a chipotle kick to it. This is a go-to meal when I'm looking for something extra tasty.
—Tamra Parker, Manlius, NY

- -

Prep: 15 min. • **Cook:** 3 hours
Makes: 12 servings

<blockquote>

2 cups ketchup
1 small onion, finely chopped
¼ cup Worcestershire sauce
3 Tbsp. reduced-sodium soy sauce
2 Tbsp. brown sugar
2 Tbsp. cider vinegar
3 garlic cloves, minced
1 Tbsp. molasses
2 tsp. dried oregano
2 tsp. minced chipotle pepper in adobo sauce plus 1 tsp. sauce
1 tsp. ground cumin
1 tsp. smoked paprika
¼ tsp. salt
¼ tsp. crushed red pepper flakes
2½ lbs. boneless skinless chicken breasts
12 sesame seed hamburger buns, split and toasted

</blockquote>

In a 3-qt. slow cooker, combine the first 14 ingredients; add chicken. Cook, covered, on low 3-4 hours or until chicken is tender (a thermometer should read at least 165°). Remove chicken from slow cooker. Shred with 2 forks; return to slow cooker. Using tongs, place the chicken mixture on bun bottoms. Replace tops.
Freeze option: Freeze cooled meat mixture and sauce in freezer containers. To use, partially thaw in refrigerator overnight. Heat through in a saucepan, stirring occasionally.
1 sandwich: 298 cal., 5g fat (2g sat. fat), 52mg chol., 1031mg sod., 39g carb. (18g sugars, 1g fiber), 24g pro.

COUNTRY BACON-BEEF MAC & CHEESE

This extra meaty mac and cheese is super easy to make in the slow cooker. Kids love it, and I like to sneak in some veggies.
—Nancy Heishman, Las Vegas, NV

- -

Prep: 35 min. • **Cook:** 1½ hours
Makes: 8 servings

<blockquote>

5 bacon strips, chopped
1½ lbs. ground beef
1 medium onion, chopped
3 garlic cloves, minced
1 medium sweet red pepper, chopped
1 large carrot, coarsely grated
1 Tbsp. dried parsley flakes
¼ tsp. salt
1 tsp. pepper
3 cups uncooked protein-enriched or whole wheat elbow macaroni
1 can (14½ oz.) reduced-sodium beef broth
1 cup sour cream
2 cups shredded sharp cheddar cheese
2 cups shredded part-skim mozzarella cheese

</blockquote>

1. In a large skillet, cook bacon, stirring occasionally, over medium heat until crisp, 5-6 minutes. Remove with a slotted spoon; drain on paper towels. Discard all but 1 Tbsp. of drippings. Brown ground beef in drippings; remove from pan. Add onion to skillet; cook and stir until translucent, 2-3 minutes. Add the garlic and cook 1 minute longer.
2. Combine red pepper, carrot, seasonings and pasta in a 4-qt. slow cooker. Layer with ground beef, bacon and onion mixture (do not stir). Pour in broth.
3. Cook, covered, on low for about 1 hour, until meat and vegetables are tender. Thirty minutes before serving, stir in sour cream and cheeses.
1½ cups: 591 cal., 36g fat (17g sat. fat), 113mg chol., 719mg sod., 29g carb. (5g sugars, 3g fiber), 38g pro.

HOT WING DIP

Since I usually have all the ingredients on hand, this is a great go-to snack for entertaining friends and family.
—Coleen Corner, Grove City, PA

Prep: 10 min. • **Cook:** 1 hour
Makes: 4½ cups

- 2 cups shredded cooked chicken
- 1 pkg. (8 oz.) cream cheese, cubed
- 2 cups shredded cheddar cheese
- 1 cup ranch salad dressing
- ½ cup Louisiana-style hot sauce
  Tortilla chips and celery sticks
  Minced fresh parsley, optional

In a 3-qt. slow cooker, mix the first 5 ingredients. Cook, covered, on low for 1-2 hours or until cheese is melted. Serve with chips and celery. If desired, sprinkle with parsley.

¼ cup: 186 cal., 16g fat (7g sat. fat), 43mg chol., 235mg sod., 2g carb. (1g sugars, 0 fiber), 8g pro.

Baked Hot Wing Dip: Preheat oven to 350°. Spread dip mixture into an ungreased 9-in. square baking dish. Bake, uncovered, 20-25 minutes or until heated through.

★ ★ ★ ★ ★ **READER REVIEW**

"Great recipe! I used two 10-oz. cans of chicken and 2 packages of cream cheese. This is totally awesome. Great with chicken-flavored crackers."

LACEYEST TASTEOFHOME.COM

SHREDDED STEAK SANDWICHES

I received this recipe when I was a newlywed, and it's been a favorite since then. The saucy steak barbecue makes a quick meal served on sliced buns or over rice, potatoes or buttered noodles.
—Lee Steinmetz, Lansing, MI

Prep: 15 min. • **Cook:** 6 hours
Makes: 14 servings

- 3 lbs. beef top round steak, cut into large pieces
- 2 large onions, chopped
- ¾ cup thinly sliced celery
- 1½ cups ketchup
- ½ to ¾ cup water
- ⅓ cup lemon juice
- ⅓ cup Worcestershire sauce
- 3 Tbsp. brown sugar
- 3 Tbsp. cider vinegar
- 2 to 3 tsp. salt
- 2 tsp. prepared mustard
- 1½ tsp. paprika
- 1 tsp. chili powder
- ½ tsp. pepper
- ⅛ to ¼ tsp. hot pepper sauce
- 14 sandwich rolls, split

1. Place meat in a 5-qt. slow cooker. Add onions and celery. In a bowl, combine the ketchup, water, lemon juice, Worcestershire sauce, brown sugar, vinegar, salt, mustard, paprika, chili powder, pepper and hot pepper sauce. Pour over meat.
2. Cover and cook on high for 6-8 hours. Remove meat; cool slightly. Shred meat with 2 forks. Return to the slow cooker and heat through. Serve on rolls.

1 sandwich: 347 cal., 7g fat (2g sat. fat), 39mg chol., 1100mg sod., 44g carb. (13g sugars, 2g fiber), 27g pro.

MULLED DR PEPPER

When neighbors or friends visit us on a chilly evening, I'll serve this warm beverage with ham sandwiches and deviled eggs.
—Bernice Morris, Marshfield, MO

Prep: 10 min. • **Cook:** 2 hours
Makes: 10 servings

8   cups Dr Pepper
¼   cup packed brown sugar
¼   cup lemon juice
½   tsp. ground allspice
½   tsp. whole cloves
¼   tsp. salt
¼   tsp. ground nutmeg
3   cinnamon sticks (3 in.)

1. In a 3-qt. slow cooker, combine all ingredients.
2. Cover and cook on low about 2 hours or until heated through. Discard cloves and cinnamon sticks.

¾ cup: 105 cal., 0 fat (0 sat. fat), 0 chol., 69mg sod., 27g carb. (26g sugars, 0 fiber), 0 pro.

HOW TO MAKE A SPICE BAG

A spice bag makes it easy to discard seasonings after they've flavored the recipe. To make, place spices on a double thickness of cheesecloth. Bring up edges and tie securely with ktichen string. A cloth tea sachet (available in tea shops) also makes a great spice bag.

MAKE AHEAD
BUTTER CHICKEN MEATBALLS

My husband and I love meatballs, and we love butter chicken. Before a party, we had the brilliant idea to combine these two loves, and they got rave reviews! Want them as a main dish? Just serve with basmati rice.
—Shannon Dobos, Calgary, AB

Prep: 30 min. • **Cook:** 3 hours
Makes: about 3 dozen

1½   lbs. ground chicken or turkey
1   large egg, lightly beaten
½   cup soft bread crumbs
1   tsp. garam masala
½   tsp. tandoori masala seasoning
½   tsp. salt
¼   tsp. cayenne pepper
3   Tbsp. minced fresh cilantro, divided
1   jar (14.1 oz.) butter chicken sauce

1. Combine the first 7 ingredients plus 2 Tbsp. cilantro; mix lightly but thoroughly. With wet hands, shape into 1-in. balls. Place meatballs in a 3-qt. slow cooker coated with cooking spray. Pour butter sauce over top.
2. Cook, covered, on low until meatballs are cooked through, 3-4 hours. Top with remaining cilantro.

Note: Look for butter chicken sauce in the Indian foods section.

Freeze option: Omitting remaining cilantro, freeze cooled meatball mixture in freezer containers. To use, partially thaw in the refrigerator overnight. Microwave, covered, on high in a microwave-safe dish until heated through, stirring gently and adding a little water if necessary.

1 meatball: 40 cal., 2g fat (1g sat. fat), 18mg chol., 87mg sod., 1g carb. (1g sugars, 0 fiber), 3g pro.

CHICKEN SLIDERS WITH SESAME SLAW

Everyone loves barbecue chicken sliders. My version has an Asian twist with tangy, spicy flavors. At our potlucks, they quickly vanish.
—Priscilla Yee, Concord, CA

- -

Prep: 25 min. • **Cook:** 6 hours
Makes: 20 servings

1	medium onion, coarsely chopped
3	lbs. boneless skinless chicken thighs
½	cup ketchup
¼	cup reduced-sodium teriyaki sauce
2	Tbsp. dry sherry or reduced-sodium chicken broth
2	Tbsp. minced fresh gingerroot
½	tsp. salt

SESAME SLAW

¼	cup mayonnaise
1	Tbsp. rice wine vinegar
1	Tbsp. sesame oil
1	tsp. Sriracha chili sauce
3	cups coleslaw mix
⅓	cup dried cherries or cranberries
2	Tbsp. minced fresh cilantro
20	slider buns or dinner rolls, split

1. Place onion and chicken in a 4-qt. slow cooker. In a small bowl, mix ketchup, teriyaki sauce, sherry, ginger and salt. Pour over chicken. Cook, covered, on low for 6-7 hours or until a thermometer reads 170°.
2. Remove chicken; cool slightly. Skim fat from cooking juices. Shred chicken with 2 forks. Return chicken to slow cooker.
3. Meanwhile, in a small bowl, whisk mayonnaise, vinegar, sesame oil and chili sauce until blended. Stir in coleslaw mix, cherries and cilantro. Using a slotted spoon, place ¼ cup chicken mixture on each bun bottom; top with about 2 Tbsp. slaw. Replace tops.
1 slider: 255 cal., 10g fat (2g sat. fat), 63mg chol., 493mg sod., 24g carb. (6g sugars, 2g fiber), 16g pro.

SLOW-COOKER BBQ BAKED BEANS

I was under doctor's orders to reduce the amount sodium I was eating, but I just couldn't part with some of my favorite foods. After experimenting, I came up with this potluck favorite. Now everyone's happy!
—Sherrel Hendrix, Arkadelphia, AR

- -

Prep: 10 min. + soaking • **Cook:** 8½ hours
Makes: 12 servings

- 1 pkg. (16 oz.) dried great northern beans
- 2 smoked ham hocks (about ½ lb. each)
- 2 cups water
- 1 medium onion, chopped
- 2 tsp. garlic powder, divided
- 2 tsp. onion powder, divided
- 1 cup barbecue sauce
- ¾ cup packed brown sugar
- ½ tsp. ground nutmeg
- ¼ tsp. ground cloves
- 2 tsp. hot pepper sauce, optional

1. Rinse and sort beans; soak according to package directions. Drain and rinse beans, discarding liquid.

2. In a 4-qt. slow cooker, combine beans, ham hocks, water, onion, 1 tsp. garlic powder and 1 tsp. onion powder. Cook, covered, on low 8-10 hours or until beans are tender.

3. Remove ham hocks; cool slightly. Cut meat into small cubes, discarding bones; return meat to slow cooker. Stir in the barbecue sauce, brown sugar, nutmeg, cloves, remaining garlic powder, remaining onion powder and, if desired, pepper sauce. Cook, covered, on high about 30 minutes or until heated through.

½ cup: 238 cal., 1g fat (0 sat. fat), 4mg chol., 347mg sod., 48g carb. (22g sugars, 8g fiber), 10g pro.

TEST KITCHEN TIP
Using hot sauce to flavor foods can be a smart alternative to salt, but make sure you check the nutrition labels. We recommend Tabasco. It has only 26 milligrams of sodium per 5-7 drops.

SIMMERED SMOKED LINKS

No one can resist the sweet and spicy glaze on these bite-sized sausages. They're effortless to prepare, and make the perfect party nibbler. Serve them with frilled toothpicks to make them extra fancy.
—Maxine Cenker, Weirton, WV

Prep: 5 min. • **Cook:** 4 hours
Makes: about 6½ dozen

- 2 pkg. (16 oz. each) miniature smoked sausage links
- 1 cup packed brown sugar
- ½ cup ketchup
- ¼ cup prepared horseradish

Place sausages in a 3-qt. slow cooker. Combine the brown sugar, ketchup and horseradish; pour over sausages. Cover and cook on low for 4 hours.

1 sausage: 46 cal., 3g fat (1g sat. fat), 7mg chol., 136mg sod., 3g carb. (3g sugars, 0 fiber), 1g pro.

SLOW-COOKER CHEESE DIP

I brought this slightly spicy cheese dip to a gathering with friends and it was a huge hit. The spicy pork sausage provides just the right zip!
—Marion Bartone, Conneaut, OH

Prep: 15 min. • **Cook:** 4 hours • **Makes:** 2 qt.

- 1 lb. ground beef
- ½ lb. bulk spicy pork sausage
- 2 lbs. cubed Velveeta
- 2 cans (10 oz. each) diced tomatoes and green chiles
  Tortilla chip scoops, red pepper and cucumber sticks

1. In a large skillet, cook beef and sausage over medium heat until no longer pink; drain. Transfer to a 3- or 4-qt. slow cooker. Stir in cheese and tomatoes.

2. Cover and cook on low for 4-5 hours or until cheese is melted, stirring occasionally. Serve with tortilla chips.

¼ cup: 139 cal., 10g fat (5g sat. fat), 40mg chol., 486mg sod., 3g carb. (2g sugars, 0 fiber), 8g pro.

BRING IT
Be the hero of the potluck...and not just because you brought the tastiest dip! How? Simply keep an extra extension cord or power strip in your car. You never know when friends might need more outlets to plug in their offerings.

TEXAS BEEF BARBECUE

These shredded beef sandwiches are a family favorite. The beef simmers for hours in a slightly sweet sauce with plenty of spices.

—Jennifer Bauer, Lansing, MI

Prep: 15 min. • **Cook:** 8 hours
Makes: 16 servings

1	beef sirloin tip roast (4 lbs.)
1	can (5½ oz.) spicy hot V8 juice
½	cup water
¼	cup white vinegar
¼	cup ketchup
2	Tbsp. Worcestershire sauce
½	cup packed brown sugar
1	tsp. salt
1	tsp. ground mustard
1	tsp. paprika
¼	tsp. chili powder
⅛	tsp. pepper
16	kaiser rolls, split

1. Cut roast in half; place in a 5-qt. slow cooker. Combine the V8 juice, water, vinegar, ketchup, Worcestershire sauce, brown sugar and seasonings; pour over roast. Cover and cook on low 8-10 hours or until meat is tender.

2. Remove meat and shred with 2 forks; return to slow cooker and heat through. Spoon ½ cup meat mixture onto each roll.

1 sandwich: 339 cal., 8g fat (2g sat. fat), 60mg chol., 606mg sod., 39g carb. (10g sugars, 1g fiber), 27g pro. **Diabetic exchanges:** 3 lean meat, 2½ starch.

SLOW-COOKER SAUSAGE & WAFFLE BAKE

Here's an easy dish guaranteed to create excitement at the breakfast table! Nothing is missing from this sweet and savory combination. It's so wrong, it's right!
—Courtney Lentz, Boston, MA

- -

Prep: 20 min. • **Cook:** 5 hours + standing
Makes: 12 servings

- 2 lbs. bulk spicy breakfast pork sausage
- 1 Tbsp. rubbed sage
- ½ tsp. fennel seed
- 1 pkg. (12.3 oz.) frozen waffles, cut into bite-sized pieces
- 8 large eggs
- 1¼ cups half-and-half cream
- ¼ cup maple syrup
- ¼ tsp. salt
- ¼ tsp. pepper
- 2 cups shredded cheddar cheese
   Additional maple syrup

1. Fold two 18-in.-long pieces of foil into two 18x4-in. strips. Line the sides around the perimeter of a 5-qt. slow cooker with foil strips; spray with cooking spray.
2. In a large skillet, cook and crumble sausage over medium heat; drain. Add sage and fennel.
3. Place waffles in slow cooker; top with sausage. In a bowl, mix eggs, cream, syrup and seasonings. Pour over sausage and waffles. Top with cheese. Cook, covered, on low 5-6 hours or until set. Remove insert and let stand, uncovered, 15 minutes. Serve with additional maple syrup.
1 serving: 442 cal., 31g fat (12g sat. fat), 200mg chol., 878mg sod., 20g carb. (7g sugars, 1g fiber), 19g pro.

MAKE AHEAD
CHINESE MEATBALLS

These were a huge hit at a cookout I attended recently. You can use 2 tablespoons of chopped crystallized ginger in place of the fresh ginger if you like.
—Pat Barnes, Panama City, FL

- -

Prep: 35 min. • **Cook:** 3 hours
Makes: about 6 dozen

- 2 large eggs, lightly beaten
- 2 Tbsp. soy sauce
- 1 tsp. salt
- 6 green onions, sliced
- 2 lbs. lean ground pork
- 2 cans (8 oz. each) sliced water chestnuts, drained and chopped
- 1 cup dry bread crumbs

SAUCE
- ¼ cup cornstarch
- 1 cup pineapple juice
- ⅓ cup sugar
- 4 tsp. minced fresh gingerroot
- 1 can (10½ oz.) condensed beef consomme, undiluted
- ½ cup white vinegar

1. Preheat oven to 400°. In a large bowl, combine first 4 ingredients. Add pork, water chestnuts and bread crumbs; mix lightly but thoroughly. Shape mixture into 1-in. balls. Place in a greased 15x10x1-in. pan. Bake 15 minutes.
2. In a 5- or 6-qt. slow cooker, mix the cornstarch and juice until smooth. Stir in remaining ingredients. Add meatballs; stir gently to coat. Cook, covered, on low for 3-4 hours or until meatballs are cooked through and sauce is thickened.
Freeze option: Freeze cooled meatball mixture in freezer containers. To use, partially thaw in refrigerator overnight. Heat through in a covered saucepan, stirring gently and adding a little broth if necessary.
1 meatball: 41 cal., 2g fat (1g sat. fat), 12mg chol., 109mg sod., 4g carb. (2g sugars, 0 fiber), 3g pro.

3. Remove from refrigerator 30 minutes before cooking. Cook, covered, on low for 3-4 hours or until a knife inserted in the center comes out clean.

4. For syrup, in a small saucepan, mix sugar and cornstarch; stir in water until smooth. Stir in ¼ cup blueberries. Bring to a boil; cook and stir until berries pop, about 3 minutes. Remove from heat; stir in butter, lemon juice and remaining berries. Serve warm with French toast.

1 cup with about 2 Tbsp. sauce: 390 cal., 17g fat (9g sat. fat), 182mg chol., 371mg sod., 49g carb. (28g sugars, 2g fiber), 12g pro.

SLOW-COOKED SLOPPY JOES

Slow-cook your way to a crowd-pleasing sandwich! Ground beef is transformed into a classic sandwich filling with just a few pantry staples.

—Joeanne Steras, Garrett, PA

Prep: 15 min. • **Cook:** 4 hours
Makes: 12 servings

- 2 lbs. ground beef
- 1 cup chopped green pepper
- ⅔ cup chopped onion
- 2 cups ketchup
- 2 envelopes sloppy joe mix
- 2 Tbsp. brown sugar
- 1 tsp. prepared mustard
- 12 hamburger buns, split

1. In a large skillet, cook the beef, pepper and onion over medium heat until meat is no longer pink; drain. Stir in the ketchup, sloppy joe mix, brown sugar and mustard.

2. Transfer to a 3-qt. slow cooker. Cover and cook on low for 4-5 hours or until flavors are blended. Spoon ½ cup onto each bun.

1 sandwich: 337 cal., 9g fat (4g sat. fat), 37mg chol., 1251mg sod., 47g carb. (23g sugars, 1g fiber), 18g pro.

MAKE AHEAD
SLOW-COOKED BLUEBERRY FRENCH TOAST

Your slow cooker can be your best friend on a busy morning. Just get this recipe going, run some errands and come back to the aroma of hot French toast ready to eat.

—Elizabeth Lorenz, Peru, IN

Prep: 30 min. + chilling • **Cook:** 3 hours
Makes: 12 servings (2 cups syrup)

- 8 large eggs
- ½ cup plain yogurt
- ⅓ cup sour cream
- 1 tsp. vanilla extract
- ½ tsp. ground cinnamon
- 1 cup 2% milk
- ⅓ cup maple syrup
- 1 loaf (1 lb.) French bread, cubed
- 1½ cups fresh or frozen blueberries
- 12 oz. cream cheese, cubed

BLUEBERRY SYRUP
- 1 cup sugar
- 2 Tbsp. cornstarch
- 1 cup cold water
- ¾ cup fresh or frozen blueberries, divided
- 1 Tbsp. butter
- 1 Tbsp. lemon juice

1. In a large bowl, whisk eggs, yogurt, sour cream, vanilla and cinnamon. Gradually whisk in milk and maple syrup until blended.

2. Place half of the bread in a greased 5- or 6-qt. slow cooker; layer with half of the blueberries, cream cheese and egg mixture. Repeat layers. Refrigerate, covered, overnight.

PULLED PORK NACHOS

While home from college, my daughter made these tempting pork nachos, her first recipe ever. My son and I couldn't get enough.
—Carol Kurpjuweit, Humansville, MO

- -

Prep: 30 min. • **Cook:** 8 hours
Makes: 16 servings

- 1 tsp. garlic powder
- 1 tsp. mesquite seasoning
- ¼ tsp. pepper
- ⅛ tsp. celery salt
- 3 lbs. boneless pork shoulder butt roast
- 1 medium green pepper, chopped
- 1 medium sweet red pepper, chopped
- 1 medium onion, chopped
- 1 can (16 oz.) baked beans
- 1 cup barbecue sauce
- 1 cup shredded cheddar cheese
   Corn or tortilla chips
   Optional toppings: Chopped tomatoes, shredded lettuce and chopped green onions

1. In a small bowl, mix the seasoning ingredients. Place pork roast in a 5- or 6-qt. slow cooker; rub with seasonings. Add peppers and onion. Cook, covered, on low 8-10 hours.

2. Remove roast; cool slightly. Strain cooking juices, reserving vegetables and ½ cup juices; discard remaining juices. Skim fat from reserved juices. Shred pork with 2 forks.

3. Return the pork, reserved juices and vegetables to slow cooker. Stir in beans, barbecue sauce and cheese; heat through. Serve over chips with toppings as desired.

Freeze option: Freeze cooled pork mixture in freezer containers. To use, partially thaw in refrigerator overnight. Heat through in a saucepan, stirring occasionally and adding a little broth or water if necessary.

½ cup pork mixture: 233 cal., 11g fat (5g sat. fat), 60mg chol., 416mg sod., 14g carb. (6g sugars, 2g fiber), 18g pro.

HOT CRAB DIP

I have a large family, work full time and also coach soccer and football, so I appreciate recipes that are easy to assemble. The rich, creamy dip is a fun appetizer to whip up for any gathering.
—Teri Rasey, Cadillac, MI

- -

Prep: 10 min. • **Cook:** 3 hours
Makes: about 5 cups

- ½ cup whole milk
- ⅓ cup salsa
- 3 pkg. (8 oz. each) cream cheese, cubed
- 2 pkg. (8 oz. each) imitation crabmeat, flaked
- 1 cup thinly sliced green onions
- 1 can (4 oz.) chopped green chiles
   Assorted crackers or fresh vegetables

In a small bowl, combine milk and salsa. Transfer to a greased 3-qt. slow cooker. Stir in cream cheese, crab, onions and chiles. Cover and cook on low for 3-4 hours, stirring every 30 minutes. Serve with crackers.

¼ cup: 148 cal., 12g fat (7g sat. fat), 38mg chol., 274mg sod., 6g carb. (2g sugars, 0 fiber), 5g pro.

LIME-CHIPOTLE CARNITAS TOSTADAS

Here's a terrific recipe for your next party! Set out various toppings and garnishes so guests can customize their own tostadas with the lime-kissed shredded pork.
—Jan Valdez, Chicago, IL

Prep: 20 min. • **Cook:** 8 hours
Makes: 16 servings

½ cup chicken broth
4 tsp. ground chipotle pepper
4 tsp. ground cumin
1 tsp. salt
1 boneless pork shoulder roast (4 to 5 lbs.), halved
1 large onion, peeled and halved
8 garlic cloves, peeled
1 to 2 limes, halved
16 tostada shells
   Optional toppings: Warmed refried beans, salsa, sour cream, shredded lettuce, chopped avocado, crumbled queso fresco and minced fresh cilantro
   Lime wedges

1. Add broth to a 5-qt. slow cooker. Mix seasonings; rub over all sides of pork. Place in slow cooker. Add onion and garlic cloves. Cook, covered, on low 8-10 hours or until meat is tender, .
2. Remove pork; cool slightly. Strain cooking juices, reserving garlic cloves; discard onion. Skim fat from cooking juices. Mash garlic with a fork. Shred pork with 2 forks.
3. Return cooking juices, garlic and pork to slow cooker. Squeeze lime juice over pork; heat through, stirring to combine. Layer tostada shells with pork mixture and toppings as desired. Serve with lime wedges.

1 tostada: 269 cal., 15g fat (5g sat. fat), 76mg chol., 279mg sod., 9g carb. (1g sugars, 1g fiber), 23g pro. **Diabetic exchanges:** 3 medium-fat meat, ½ starch.

BUTTERSCOTCH FRUIT DIP

If you like the sweetness of butterscotch chips, you'll enjoy this hot rum-flavored fruit dip. I serve it with apple and pear wedges. It holds up for up to two hours in the slow cooker.
—Jeaune Hadl Van Meter, Lexington, KY

Prep: 5 min. • **Cook:** 45 min.
Makes: about 3 cups

2 pkg. (10 to 11 oz. each) butterscotch chips
⅔ cup evaporated milk
⅔ cup chopped pecans
1 Tbsp. rum extract
   Apple and pear wedges

In a 1½-qt. slow cooker, combine the butterscotch chips and milk. Cover and cook on low for 45-50 minutes or until chips are softened; stir until smooth. Stir in pecans and extract. Serve warm with fruit.

¼ cup: 197 cal., 13g fat (7g sat. fat), 6mg chol., 32mg sod., 17g carb. (16g sugars, 1g fiber), 2g pro.

SLOW-COOKER REUBEN SPREAD

My daughter shared this recipe with me for a hearty spread that tastes just like a Reuben sandwich. Serve it from a slow cooker set to warm.
—Rosalie Fuchs, Paynesville, MN

Prep: 5 min. • **Cook:** 2 hours
Makes: 3½ cups

- 1   can (14 oz.) sauerkraut, rinsed and well drained
- 1   pkg. (8 oz.) cream cheese, cubed
- 2   cups shredded Swiss cheese
- 1   pkg. (3 oz.) deli corned beef, chopped
- 3   Tbsp. prepared Thousand Island salad dressing
  Snack rye bread or crackers

In a 1½-qt. slow cooker, combine the first 5 ingredients. Cover and cook on low for 2-3 hours or until cheeses are melted; stir to blend. Serve warm with bread or crackers.
2 Tbsp.: 69 cal., 6g fat (3g sat. fat), 18mg chol., 203mg sod., 1g carb. (1g sugars, 0 fiber), 3g pro.

CARIBBEAN BREAD PUDDING

A completely unexpected dessert from the slow cooker, this is moist and sweet with plump, juicy raisins and the wonderful tropical accents of pineapple and coconut.
—Elizabeth Doss, California City, CA

Prep: 30 min. • **Cook:** 4 hours
Makes: 16 servings

- 1 cup raisins
- 1 can (8 oz.) crushed pineapple, undrained
- 2 large firm bananas, halved
- 1 can (12 oz.) evaporated milk
- 1 can (10 oz.) frozen nonalcoholic pina colada mix
- 1 can (6 oz.) unsweetened pineapple juice
- 3 large eggs, room temperature
- ½ cup cream of coconut
- ¼ cup light rum, optional
- 1 loaf (1 lb.) French bread, cut into 1-in. cubes
  Whipped cream and maraschino cherries, optional

1. In a small bowl, combine raisins and pineapple; set aside. In a blender, combine the halved bananas, milk, pina colada mix, pineapple juice, eggs, cream of coconut and, if desired, rum. Cover and process until smooth.

2. Place two-thirds of the bread in a greased 6-qt. slow cooker. Top with 1 cup raisin mixture. Layer with remaining bread and raisin mixture. Pour banana mixture into slow cooker. Cover and cook on low for 4-5 hours or until a knife inserted in the center comes out clean. Serve warm, with whipped cream and cherries if desired.

¾ cup: 254 cal., 5g fat (3g sat. fat), 42mg chol., 214mg sod., 45g carb. (27g sugars, 2g fiber), 6g pro.

SWEET & SPICY CHICKEN WINGS

The meat literally falls off the bones of these chicken wings! Spice lovers will get a kick out of the big sprinkling of red pepper flakes.
—Sue Bayless, Prior Lake, MN

Prep: 25 min. • **Cook:** 5 hours
Makes: about 2½ dozen

- 3 lbs. chicken wings
- 1½ cups ketchup
- 1 cup packed brown sugar
- 1 small onion, finely chopped
- ¼ cup finely chopped sweet red pepper
- 2 Tbsp. chili powder
- 2 Tbsp. Worcestershire sauce
- 1½ tsp. crushed red pepper flakes
- 1 tsp. ground mustard
- 1 tsp. dried basil
- 1 tsp. dried thyme
- 1 tsp. pepper
  Ranch dressing and celery stalks, optional

1. Cut wings into 3 sections; discard the wing tip sections. Place chicken in a 4-qt. slow cooker.

2. In a small bowl, combine the remaining ingredients. Pour over chicken; stir until coated. Cover and cook on low 5-6 hours or until chicken is no longer pink. If desired, serve with ranch dressing and celery stalks.

1 piece: 95 cal., 3g fat (1g sat. fat), 14mg chol., 195mg sod., 11g carb. (11g sugars, 0 fiber), 5g pro.

SLOW-COOKER SPINACH & ARTICHOKE DIP

With this creamy dip, I can get my daughters to eat spinach and artichokes. We serve it with chips, toasted pita bread or fresh veggies.
—Jennifer Stowell, Deep River, IA

Prep: 10 min. • **Cook:** 2 hours
Makes: 8 cups

- 2 cans (14 oz. each) water-packed artichoke hearts, drained and chopped
- 2 pkg. (10 oz. each) frozen chopped spinach, thawed and squeezed dry
- 1 jar (15 oz.) Alfredo sauce
- 1 pkg. (8 oz.) cream cheese, cubed
- 2 cups shredded Italian cheese blend
- 1 cup shredded part-skim mozzarella cheese
- 1 cup shredded Parmesan cheese
- 1 cup 2% milk
- 2 garlic cloves, minced
  Assorted crackers and/or cucumber slices

In a greased 4-qt. slow cooker, combine the first 9 ingredients. Cook, covered, on low 2-3 hours or until heated through. Serve with crackers and/or cucumber slices.

¼ cup: 105 cal., 7g fat (4g sat. fat), 21mg chol., 276mg sod., 5g carb. (1g sugars, 1g fiber), 6g pro.

1. In a 5-qt. slow cooker, combine the first 13 ingredients. Add chicken, jalapeno and bay leaf. Cook, covered, on low 4 hours or until chicken is tender. Remove jalapeno and bay leaf.

2. In a small bowl, mix cornstarch and cream until smooth; gradually stir into sauce. Cook, covered, on high 15-20 minutes or until sauce is thickened. Serve with rice. If desired, sprinkle with cilantro.

1¼ cups chicken mixture: 381 cal., 19g fat (9g sat. fat), 118mg chol., 864mg sod., 13g carb. (5g sugars, 2g fiber), 33g pro.

SLOW-COOKER KEY LIME FONDUE

Love fondue but want something other than milk chocolate? Dip into my luscious white chocolate Key lime fondue with graham crackers, fresh fruit and cubed pound cake.

—Elisabeth Larsen, Pleasant Grove, UT

- -

Prep: 5 min. • **Cook:** 50 min. • **Makes:** 3 cups

  1   can (14 oz.) sweetened condensed milk
 12   oz. white baking chocolate, finely chopped
  ½   cup Key lime or regular lime juice
  1   Tbsp. grated lime zest
      Graham crackers, macaroon cookies, fresh strawberries and sliced ripe bananas

1. In a 1½-qt. slow cooker, combine milk, white chocolate and lime juice.

2. Cook, covered, on low 50-60 minutes or until chocolate is melted. Stir in lime zest. Serve with graham crackers, cookies and fruit.

¼ cup: 251 cal., 11g fat (8g sat. fat), 11mg chol., 62mg sod., 37g carb. (36g sugars, 0 fiber), 5g pro.

CHICKEN TIKKA MASALA

This Indian-style dish has flavors that keep me coming back for more. It's a simple dish spiced with garam masala, cumin and gingerroot that's truly amazing.

—Jaclyn Bell, Logan, UT

- -

Prep: 25 min. • **Cook:** 4¼ hours
Makes: 8 servings

  1   can (29 oz.) tomato puree
 1½   cups plain yogurt
  ½   large onion, finely chopped
  2   Tbsp. olive oil
 4½   tsp. minced fresh gingerroot
  4   garlic cloves, minced
  1   Tbsp. garam masala
 2½   tsp. salt
 1½   tsp. ground cumin
  1   tsp. paprika
  ¾   tsp. pepper
  ½   tsp. cayenne pepper
  ¼   tsp. ground cinnamon
 2½   lbs. boneless skinless chicken breasts, cut into 1½-in. cubes
  1   jalapeno pepper, halved and seeded
  1   bay leaf
  1   Tbsp. cornstarch
  1   cup heavy whipping cream
      Hot cooked basmati rice
      Chopped fresh cilantro, optional

Strawberry
Poke Cake
page 225

The Sweetest Treats

And now, the stars of the show: pretty cakes, luscious pies, munchable cookies and all the other sweets that make the dessert table the liveliest place to be.

GRANDMA KRAUSE'S COCONUT COOKIES

When my two daughters were young, their great-grandma made them cookies with oats and coconut. Thankfully, she shared the recipe.
—Debra J. Dorn, Dunnellon, FL

- -

Prep: 40 min. + freezing
Bake: 10 min./batch • **Makes:** about 4 dozen

- 1   **cup shortening**
- 1   **cup sugar**
- 1   **cup packed brown sugar**
- 2   **large eggs, room temperature**
- 1   **tsp. vanilla extract**
- 2   **cups all-purpose flour**
- 1   **tsp. baking powder**
- 1   **tsp. baking soda**
- ¼   **tsp. salt**
- 1   **cup old-fashioned oats**
- 1   **cup sweetened shredded coconut**

1. In a large bowl, beat shortening and sugars until blended. Beat in eggs and vanilla. In another bowl, whisk flour, baking powder, baking soda and salt; gradually beat into sugar mixture. Stir in oats and coconut.
2. Divide dough into 4 portions. On a lightly floured surface, shape each into a 6-in.-long log. Wrap in plastic; freeze for 2 hours or until firm.
3. Preheat oven to 350°. Unwrap and cut dough crosswise into ½-in. slices, reshaping as needed. Place 2 in. apart on ungreased baking sheets. Bake 10-12 minutes or until golden brown. Cool on pans 5 minutes. Remove to wire racks to cool.
Freeze option: Place wrapped logs in freezer container; return to freezer. To use, unwrap frozen logs and cut into slices. If necessary, let dough stand a few minutes at room temperature before cutting. Prepare and bake as directed.
1 cookie: 109 cal., 5g fat (2g sat. fat), 8mg chol., 56mg sod., 15g carb. (10g sugars, 0 fiber), 1g pro.

HEAVENLY BLUEBERRY TART

Mmm—this tart is bursting with the fresh flavor of blueberries! Not only do I bake the berries with the crust, but after taking the tart out of the oven, I top it with just-picked fruit.
—Lyin Schramm, Berwick, ME

- -

Prep: 20 min. • **Bake:** 40 min. + cooling
Makes: 6 servings

- 1   **cup all-purpose flour**
- 2   **Tbsp. sugar**
- ⅛   **tsp. salt**
- ½   **cup cold butter**
- 1   **Tbsp. vinegar**
- **FILLING**
- 4   **cups fresh blueberries, divided**
- ⅔   **cup sugar**
- 2   **Tbsp. all-purpose flour**
- ½   **tsp. ground cinnamon**
- ⅛   **tsp. ground nutmeg**

1. In a small bowl, combine flour, sugar and salt; cut in butter until crumbly. Add vinegar, tossing with a fork to moisten. Press onto bottom and up the sides of a lightly greased 9-in. tart pan with removable bottom.
2. For filling, lightly smash 2 cups blueberries in a bowl. Combine the sugar, flour, cinnamon and nutmeg; stir into smashed blueberries. Spread mixture evenly into crust; sprinkle with 1 cup of the remaining whole blueberries. Place tart pan on a baking sheet.
3. Bake at 400° for 40-45 minutes or until crust is browned and filling is bubbly. Remove from the oven; arrange remaining berries over top. Cool on a wire rack. Store in the refrigerator.
1 slice: 380 cal., 16g fat (10g sat. fat), 41mg chol., 173mg sod., 59g carb. (36g sugars, 3g fiber), 3g pro.

OREO CUPCAKES WITH COOKIES & CREAM FROSTING

Kids and adults alike will find these Oreo cupcakes irresistible. If you want to pipe the frosting, be sure to thoroughly crush the cookies.

—*Taste of Home* Test Kitchen

Prep: 20 min. • **Bake:** 20 min. + cooling
Makes: 2 dozen

⅔ cup butter, softened
1¾ cups sugar
2 large eggs, room temperature
1½ tsp. vanilla extract
2½ cups all-purpose flour
2½ tsp. baking powder
½ tsp. salt
1¼ cups 2% milk
2 cups coarsely crushed Oreo cookies

FROSTING

1 cup butter, softened
3 cups confectioners' sugar
2 Tbsp. 2% milk
1 tsp. vanilla extract
1½ cups finely crushed Oreo cookie crumbs
24 mini Oreo cookies

1. Preheat oven to 350°. Line 24 muffin cups with paper liners.

2. In a large bowl, cream butter and sugar until light and fluffy, 5-7 minutes. Add eggs, 1 at a time, beating well after each addition. Beat in vanilla. In another bowl, whisk flour, baking powder and salt; add to creamed mixture alternately with milk, beating well after each addition. Fold in crushed cookies.

3. Fill prepared cups three-fourths full. Bake 20-22 minutes or until a toothpick inserted in center comes out clean. Cool in pans 10 minutes before removing to wire racks to cool completely.

4. In a large bowl, combine the butter, confectioners' sugar, milk and vanilla; beat until smooth. Fold in cookie crumbs. Pipe or spread frosting over cupcakes. If desired, sprinkle with additional cookie crumbs and garnish with mini Oreo cookies.

1 cupcake: 411 cal., 19g fat (10g sat. fat), 51mg chol., 346mg sod., 58g carb. (40g sugars, 2g fiber), 4g pro.

SOFT TRIED & TRUE PEANUT BUTTER COOKIES

When I want to offer friends and family soft and chewy peanut butter cookies, this is the recipe I always turn to. You can use either creamy or crunchy peanut butter with the same delicious results. These are the best, and my family can't get enough.
—Emma Lee Granger, La Pine, OR

Prep: 15 min. • **Bake:** 15 min./batch
Makes: about 5 dozen

- 1 cup butter-flavored shortening
- 1 cup creamy peanut butter
- ¾ cup sugar
- ¾ cup packed brown sugar
- 2 large eggs, room temperature
- 1 tsp. vanilla extract
- ½ tsp. water
- 2¼ cups all-purpose flour
- 1 tsp. baking soda
- 1 tsp. salt

1. In a large bowl, cream the shortening, peanut butter and sugars until light and fluffy, about 4 minutes. Add eggs, 1 at a time, beating well after each addition. Beat in vanilla and water. Combine the flour, baking soda and salt; gradually add to the creamed mixture and mix well.
2. Drop by Tbsp. 2 in. apart onto ungreased baking sheets. Flatten with a fork. Bake at 350° until golden brown, 12-15 minutes. Remove to wire racks to cool.
1 cookie: 105 cal., 6g fat (1g sat. fat), 7mg chol., 91mg sod., 11g carb. (6g sugars, 0 fiber), 2g pro.

> **TEST KITCHEN TIP**
> Because shortening melts at a higher temperature than butter, it's useful for baking cookies that you want to have a nice uniform shape.

SKY-HIGH STRAWBERRY PIE

This dessert is my specialty. It's fairly simple to make but so dramatic to serve. The ultimate taste of spring, the luscious pie has a big, fresh berry taste. I've had many requests to bring it to gatherings.
—Janet Mooberry, Peoria, IL

Prep: 20 min. • **Cook:** 5 min. + chilling
Makes: 10 servings

- 3 qt. fresh strawberries, divided
- 1½ cups sugar
- 6 Tbsp. cornstarch
- ⅔ cup water
  Red food coloring, optional
- 1 deep-dish pie crust (10 in.), baked
- 1 cup heavy whipping cream
- 4½ tsp. instant vanilla pudding mix

1. In a large bowl, mash enough berries to equal 3 cups. In a large saucepan, combine sugar and cornstarch. Stir in mashed berries and water. Bring to a boil over medium heat, stirring constantly. Cook and stir for 2 minutes or until thickened.
2. Remove from the heat; add food coloring if desired. Pour into a large bowl. Chill for 20 minutes, stirring occasionally, until mixture is just slightly warm. Fold in the remaining berries. Pile into the pie crust. Chill for 2-3 hours.
3. In a small bowl, whip cream until soft peaks form. Sprinkle dry pudding mix over cream and whip until stiff. Pipe around edge of pie or dollop on individual slices.
1 piece: 350 cal., 13g fat (6g sat. fat), 27mg chol., 82mg sod., 59g carb. (40g sugars, 4g fiber), 3g pro.

QUICK & EASY BAKLAVA SQUARES

I love baklava but rarely indulged because it takes so much time to make. Then a friend gave me this simple recipe. I've made these squares for family, friends and co-workers—they can't get enough. I'm always asked to bring them to special gatherings and parties, and I even give them as gifts during the holidays.
—Paula Marchesi, Lenhartsville, PA

Prep: 20 min. • **Bake:** 30 min. + cooling
Makes: 2 dozen

- 1 lb. (4 cups) chopped walnuts
- 1½ tsp. ground cinnamon
- 1 pkg. (16 oz., 14x9-in. sheets) frozen phyllo dough, thawed
- 1 cup butter, melted
- 1 cup honey

1. Preheat oven to 350°. Coat a 13x9-in. baking dish with cooking spray. Combine walnuts and cinnamon.

2. Unroll phyllo dough. Layer 2 sheets of phyllo in prepared pan; brush with butter. Repeat with 6 more sheets of phyllo, brushing every other one with butter. (Keep remaining phyllo covered with a damp towel to prevent it from drying out.)

3. Sprinkle ½ cup nut mixture in pan; drizzle with 2 Tbsp. honey. Add 2 more phyllo sheets, brushing with butter; sprinkle another ½ cup nut mixture and 2 Tbsp. honey over phyllo. Repeat layers 6 times. Top with remaining phyllo sheets, brushing every other one with butter.

4. Using a sharp knife, score surface to make 24 squares. Bake until golden brown and crisp, 25-30 minutes. Cool on a wire rack 1 hour or before serving.

1 piece: 294 cal., 21g fat (6g sat. fat), 20mg chol., 145mg sod., 26g carb. (13g sugars, 2g fiber), 5g pro.

HUMMINGBIRD CUPCAKES

Turn the traditional hummingbird cake—flavored with pineapple, bananas and walnuts—into a bite-sized treat with these incredible cupcakes.
—Jessie Oleson, Santa Fe, NM

Prep: 40 min. • **Bake:** 20 min. + cooling
Makes: 2 dozen

- 1 cup butter, softened
- 2 cups sugar
- 3 large eggs, room temperature
- 2 tsp. vanilla extract
- 2 cups mashed ripe bananas
- ½ cup drained canned crushed pineapple
- 3 cups all-purpose flour
- 1 tsp. baking soda
- 1 tsp. ground cinnamon
- ½ tsp. salt
- 1 cup sweetened shredded coconut
- 1 cup chopped walnuts

CREAM CHEESE FROSTING
- 1 pkg. (8 oz.) cream cheese, softened
- ½ cup butter, softened
- 3¾ cups confectioners' sugar
- 1 tsp. vanilla extract

1. In a large bowl, cream butter and sugar until light and fluffy, 5-7 minutes. Add eggs, 1 at a time, beating well after each addition. Beat in vanilla. In a small bowl, combine bananas and pineapple.
2. Combine the flour, baking soda, cinnamon and salt; add to the creamed mixture alternately with banana mixture, beating well after each addition. Fold in coconut and walnuts.
3. Fill 24 paper-lined muffin cups about two-thirds full. Bake at 350° until a toothpick inserted in the center comes out clean, 20-25 minutes. Cool the cupcakes for 10 minutes before removing from pans to wire racks to cool completely.
4. In a small bowl, beat the cream cheese and butter until fluffy. Add confectioners' sugar and vanilla extract; beat until smooth. Frost cupcakes.

1 cupcake: 410 cal., 20g fat (11g sat. fat), 67mg chol., 230mg sod., 56g carb. (39g sugars, 2g fiber), 4g pro.

CINNAMON PECAN BARS

I'm a special ed teacher and we bake these bars in my life skills class. It is an easy recipe that my students have fun preparing.
—Jennifer Peters, Adams Center, NY

- -

Prep: 10 min. • **Bake:** 25 min.
Makes: 2 dozen

1 **pkg. butter pecan cake mix (regular size)**
½ **cup packed dark brown sugar**
2 **large eggs, room temperature**
½ **cup butter, melted**
½ **cup chopped pecans**
½ **cup cinnamon baking chips**

1. Preheat oven to 350°. In a large bowl, combine cake mix and brown sugar. Add eggs and melted butter; mix well. Stir in pecans and baking chips. Spread into a greased 13x9-in. baking pan.
2. Bake until golden brown, 25-30 minutes. Cool in pan on a wire rack. Cut into bars.
1 bar: 185 cal., 9g fat (4g sat. fat), 26mg chol., 190mg sod., 25g carb. (17g sugars, 0 fiber), 2g pro.

BRING IT
Plastic putty knives (about $1 each) from the hardware store make super serving utensils for 13x9 desserts. The plastic edges won't scratch your pans, and the cheap price means you won't be heartbroken if you lose one.

WINNIE'S MINI RHUBARB & STRAWBERRY PIES

Every spring, we had strawberries and rhubarb on our farm outside Seattle. These fruity hand pies remind me of those times and of Grandma Winnie's baking.
—Shawn Carleton, San Diego, CA

- -

Prep: 25 min. + chilling
Bake: 15 min. + cooling • **Makes:** 18 mini pies

3 **Tbsp. quick-cooking tapioca**
4 **cups sliced fresh strawberries**
2 **cups sliced fresh rhubarb**
¾ **cup sugar**
1 **tsp. grated orange zest**
1 **tsp. vanilla extract**
¼ **tsp. salt**
¼ **tsp. ground cinnamon**
3 **drops red food coloring, optional**
Pastry for double-crust pie (9 in.)
Sweetened whipped cream, optional

1. Preheat oven to 425°. Place tapioca in a small food processor or spice grinder; process until finely ground.
2. In a large saucepan, combine the strawberries, rhubarb, sugar, orange zest, vanilla, salt, cinnamon, tapioca and, if desired, food coloring; bring to a boil. Reduce heat; simmer, covered, until strawberries are tender, 15-20 minutes, or stirring occasionally. Transfer to a large bowl; cover and refrigerate overnight.
3. On a lightly floured surface, roll half of dough to an 18-in. circle. Cut 12 circles with a 4-in. biscuit cutter, rerolling scraps as necessary; press crust onto bottom and up sides of ungreased muffin cups. Cut 6 more circles with remaining crust. Spoon strawberry mixture into muffin cups.
4. Bake until filling is bubbly and crust golden brown, 12-15 minutes. Cool in pan 5 minutes; remove to wire racks to cool. If desired, serve with whipped cream.
1 mini pie: 207 cal., 10g fat (6g sat. fat), 27mg chol., 171mg sod., 27g carb. (11g sugars, 1g fiber), 2g pro.

BUTTER PECAN CHEESECAKE

Fall always makes me yearn for this pecan cheesecake, but it's delicious any time of year. You'll want to put it on your list of holiday desserts.
—Laura Sylvester, Mechanicsville, VA

Prep: 30 min. • **Bake:** 70 min. + chilling
Makes: 16 servings

- 1½ cups graham cracker crumbs
- ½ cup finely chopped pecans
- ⅓ cup sugar
- ⅓ cup butter, melted

FILLING
- 3 pkg. (8 oz. each) cream cheese, softened
- 1½ cups sugar
- 2 cups sour cream
- 1 tsp. vanilla extract
- ½ tsp. butter flavoring
- 3 large eggs, room temperature, lightly beaten
- 1 cup finely chopped pecans

1. In a large bowl, combine the cracker crumbs, pecans, sugar and butter; set aside ⅓ cup for topping. Press remaining crumb mixture onto the bottom and 1 in. up the sides of a greased 9-in. springform pan.
2. Place springform pan on a double thickness of heavy-duty foil (about 18 in. square). Securely wrap foil around pan.
3. In a large bowl, beat cream cheese and sugar until smooth. Beat in the sour cream, vanilla and butter flavoring. Add eggs; beat on low speed just until combined. Fold in chopped pecans. Pour into crust; sprinkle with the reserved crumb mixture. Place springform pan in a large baking pan; add 1 in. of hot water to larger pan.
4. Bake at 325° until center is almost set, 70-80 minutes. Remove springform pan from water bath. Cool on a wire rack for 10 minutes. Carefully run a knife around edge of pan to loosen; cool 1 hour longer. Refrigerate overnight, covering when completely cooled. Remove sides of pan.

1 slice: 456 cal., 33g fat (16g sat. fat), 116mg chol., 224mg sod., 33g carb. (27g sugars, 1g fiber), 7g pro.

CARAMEL WHISKEY COOKIES

A bit of yogurt replaces part of the butter here, but you would never know. I get a lot of requests for these and can't make a cookie tray without them.
—Priscilla Yee, Concord, CA

Prep: 30 min. • **Bake:** 10 min./batch
Makes: 4 dozen

- ½ cup butter, softened
- ½ cup sugar
- ½ cup packed brown sugar
- ¼ cup plain Greek yogurt
- 2 Tbsp. canola oil
- 1 tsp. vanilla extract
- 2½ cups all-purpose flour
- 2 tsp. baking powder
- 1 tsp. baking soda
- ¼ tsp. salt

TOPPING
- 24 caramels
- 1 Tbsp. whiskey
- 3 oz. semisweet chocolate, melted
- ½ tsp. kosher salt, optional

1. Preheat oven to 350°. In a large bowl, beat butter and sugars until crumbly. Beat in yogurt, oil and vanilla. In another bowl, whisk flour, baking powder, baking soda and salt; gradually beat into sugar mixture.
2. Shape into 1-in. balls; place 2 in. apart on ungreased baking sheets. Flatten with bottom of a glass dipped in flour. Bake for 7-9 minutes or until edges are light brown. Cool on pans 2 minutes. Remove to wire racks to cool completely.
3. In a microwave, melt caramels with whiskey; stir until smooth. Spread over cookies. Drizzle with chocolate; sprinkle with salt if desired. Let stand until set. Store in an airtight container.

1 cookie: 93 cal., 4g fat (2g sat. fat), 6mg chol., 83mg sod., 14g carb. (9g sugars, 0 fiber), 1g pro.

3. For topping, dissolve gelatin in boiling water in a large bowl. Stir in sweetened strawberries; chill until partially set. Carefully spoon over filling. Chill until firm, 4-6 hours. Cut into squares; if desired, serve with additional whipped topping and pretzels.

1 piece: 295 calories, 15g fat (10g saturated fat), 39mg cholesterol, 305mg sodium, 38g carbohydrate (27g sugars, 1g fiber), 3g protein.

EASY CINNAMON THINS

When a co-worker's husband came home from serving in Iraq, we had a potluck for him. These spicy-sweet cookies with coarse red sugar matched our patriotic theme.
—Janet Whittington, Heath, OH

Prep: 20 min. + standing • **Makes:** 2½ dozen

- 12 oz. white candy coating, chopped
- 1 tsp. cinnamon extract
- 30 Ritz crackers
- 12 finely crushed cinnamon hard candies
  Red colored sugar

1. In a microwave, melt candy coating; stir until smooth. Stir in extract.
2. Dip crackers in candy coating mixture; allow excess to drip off. Place on waxed paper. Decorate with candies and colored sugar as desired. Let stand until set.

1 cookie: 75 cal., 4g fat (3g sat. fat), 0 chol., 36mg sod., 10g carb. (8g sugars, 0 fiber), 0 pro.

STRAWBERRY PRETZEL DESSERT

A salty pretzel crust nicely contrasts with the cream cheese and gelatin layers.
—Aldene Belch, Flint, MI

Prep: 20min. • **Bake:** 10min. + chilling
Makes: 16 servings

- 2 cups crushed pretzels (about 8 ounces)
- ¾ cup butter, melted
- 3 tablespoons sugar

FILLING
- 2 cups whipped topping
- 1 package (8 ounces) cream cheese, softened
- 1 cup sugar

TOPPING:
- 2 packages (3 ounces each) strawberry gelatin
- 2 cups boiling water
- 2 packages (16 ounces each) frozen sweetened sliced strawberries, thawed
  Optional: Additional whipped topping and pretzels

1. In a bowl, combine the pretzels, butter and sugar. Press into an ungreased 13x9-in. baking dish. Bake at 350° for 10 minutes. Cool on a wire rack.
2. For filling, in a small bowl, beat the whipped topping, cream cheese and sugar until smooth. Spread over pretzel crust. Refrigerate until chilled.

CHOCOLATE GUINNESS CAKE

One bite and everyone will propose a toast to this silky-smooth chocolate cake. The cream cheese frosting reminds us of the foamy head on a perfectly poured pint of Guinness.
—Marjorie Hennig, Seymour, IN

Prep: 25 • **Bake:** 45 min. + cooling
Makes: 12 servings

- 1 cup Guinness (dark beer)
- ½ cup butter, cubed
- 2 cups sugar
- ¾ cup baking cocoa
- 2 large eggs, beaten, room temperature
- ⅔ cup sour cream
- 3 tsp. vanilla extract
- 2 cups all-purpose flour
- 1½ tsp. baking soda

TOPPING
- 1 pkg. (8 oz.) cream cheese, softened
- 1½ cups confectioners' sugar
- ½ cup heavy whipping cream

1. Preheat oven to 350°. Grease a 9-in. springform pan and line the bottom with parchment paper; set aside.
2. In a small saucepan, heat beer and butter until butter is melted. Remove from the heat; whisk in sugar and baking cocoa until blended. Combine the eggs, sour cream and vanilla; whisk into the beer mixture. Combine flour and baking soda; whisk into beer mixture until smooth. Pour batter into prepared pan.
3. Bake until a toothpick inserted in the center comes out clean, 45-50 minutes. Cool completely in pan on a wire rack. Remove cake from the pan and place on a platter or cake stand.
4. In a large bowl, beat cream cheese until fluffy. Add confectioners' sugar and cream; beat until smooth (do not overbeat). Frost top of cake. Refrigerate leftovers.
1 slice: 494 cal., 22g fat (13g sat. fat), 99mg chol., 288mg sod., 69g carb. (49g sugars, 2g fiber), 6g pro.

HOMEMADE LEMON BARS

My husband remembers these sweet bars from his childhood. Today, special meals with the family just aren't complete without them.
—Denise Baumert, Dalhart, TX

Prep: 25 min. • **Bake:** 25 min. + cooling
Makes: 9 servings

- 1 cup all-purpose flour
- ⅓ cup butter, softened
- ¼ cup confectioners' sugar

TOPPING
- 2 large eggs, room temperature
- 1 cup sugar
- 2 Tbsp. all-purpose flour
- 2 Tbsp. lemon juice
- ¾ tsp. lemon extract
- ½ tsp. baking powder
- ¼ tsp. salt
  Confectioners' sugar

1. Preheat oven to 350°. In a large bowl, beat flour, butter and confectioners' sugar until blended. Press onto bottom of an ungreased 8-in. square baking dish. Bake 15-20 minutes or until lightly browned.
2. For topping, in a large bowl, beat eggs, sugar, flour, lemon juice, extract, baking powder and salt until frothy; pour over hot crust.
3. Bake 10-15 minutes longer or until light golden brown. Cool completely in dish on a wire rack. Dust with confectioners' sugar.
1 piece: 235 cal., 8g fat (5g sat. fat), 65mg chol., 171mg sod., 38g carb. (25g sugars, 0 fiber), 3g pro.

DUTCH APPLE PIE TARTLETS

These adorable mini apple pie pastries make a delightful addition to a dessert buffet or snack tray. The recipe calls for convenient frozen phyllo shells, so they're surprisingly easy to make. The lemon curd filling adds a unique twist.
—Mary Ann Lee, Clifton Park, NY

Prep: 15 min. • **Bake:** 20 min.
Makes: 2½ dozen

- 1 **cup finely chopped peeled apple**
- ¼ **cup lemon curd**
- 2 **pkg. (1.9 oz. each) frozen miniature phyllo tart shells**

TOPPING
- ½ **cup all-purpose flour**
- 3 **Tbsp. sugar**
- ½ **tsp. ground cinnamon**
- ¼ **cup cold butter**
  Confectioners' sugar

1. In a small bowl, combine apples and lemon curd. Spoon into tart shells.
2. In another bowl, combine the flour, sugar and cinnamon; cut in butter until mixture resembles fine crumbs. Spoon over apple mixture. Place on an ungreased baking sheet.
3. Bake at 350° for 18-20 minutes or until golden brown. Cool on wire racks for 5 minutes. Dust with confectioners' sugar. Serve warm or at room temperature. Refrigerate leftovers.
1 tartlet: 57 cal., 3g fat (1g sat. fat), 6mg chol., 22mg sod., 7g carb. (3g sugars, 0 fiber), 1g pro. **Diabetic exchanges:** ½ starch, ½ fat.

FROSTED FUDGE BROWNIES

A neighbor brought over a pan of these rich brownies when I came home from the hospital with our baby daughter. I asked her how to make brownies like that, and I've made them ever since for family occasions, potlucks and parties at work. They're great!
—Sue Soderlund, Elgin, IL

- -

Prep: 10 min. + cooling
Bake: 25 min. + cooling • **Makes:** 2 dozen

- 1 **cup plus 3 Tbsp. butter, cubed**
- ¾ **cup baking cocoa**
- 4 **large eggs, room temperature**
- 2 **cups sugar**
- 1½ **cups all-purpose flour**
- 1 **tsp. baking powder**
- 1 **tsp. salt**
- 1 **tsp. vanilla extract**

FROSTING

- 6 **Tbsp. butter, softened**
- 2⅔ **cups confectioners' sugar**
- ½ **cup baking cocoa**
- 1 **tsp. vanilla extract**
- ¼ **to ⅓ cup 2% milk**

1. In a saucepan, melt butter. Remove from the heat. Stir in cocoa; cool. In a large bowl, beat eggs and sugar until blended. Combine flour, baking powder and salt; gradually add to egg mixture. Stir in vanilla and the cooled chocolate mixture until well blended.

2. Spread into a greased 13x9-in. baking pan. Bake at 350° until a toothpick inserted in center comes out clean, 25-28 minutes (do not overbake). Cool on a wire rack.

3. For frosting, in a large bowl, cream butter and confectioners' sugar until light and fluffy, 5-7 minutes. Beat in cocoa and vanilla. Add enough milk for the frosting to achieve spreading consistency. Spread over brownies. Cut into bars.

1 brownie: 277 cal., 13g fat (8g sat. fat), 68mg chol., 248mg sod., 39g carb. (29g sugars, 1g fiber), 3g pro.

GINGERBREAD COOKIES WITH LEMON FROSTING

When I spread these spicy gingerbread rounds with my lemony cream cheese frosting, I knew I had a hit. Cardamom and allspice add a hint of chai tea flavor.
—Aysha Schurman, Ammon, ID

Prep: 25 min.
Bake: 10 min./batch + cooling
Makes: about 4 dozen

- ½ cup butter, softened
- ¾ cup packed brown sugar
- 2 large eggs, room temperature
- ¼ cup molasses
- 3 cups all-purpose flour
- 1 Tbsp. ground ginger
- 2 tsp. baking soda
- 1 tsp. ground allspice
- 1 tsp. ground cardamom
- 1 tsp. ground cinnamon
- 1 tsp. grated lemon zest
- ½ tsp. salt

FROSTING
- 4 oz. cream cheese, softened
- 2½ cups confectioners' sugar
- 1 Tbsp. grated lemon zest
- 2 Tbsp. lemon juice
- 1 tsp. vanilla extract

1. Preheat oven to 350°. Cream butter and brown sugar until light and fluffy, 5-7 minutes. Beat in eggs and molasses. In another bowl, whisk the next 8 ingredients; gradually beat into creamed mixture.
2. Shape into 1-in. balls; place 2 in. apart on ungreased baking sheets. Bake until tops are cracked, 8-10 minutes. Cool 2 minutes before removing from pans to wire racks to cool completely.
3. For frosting, beat cream cheese until fluffy. Add remaining ingredients; beat until smooth. Frost cookies. Refrigerate in an airtight container.
1 cookie with 1 tsp. frosting: 100 cal., 3g fat (2g sat. fat), 15mg chol., 105mg sod., 17g carb. (11g sugars, 0 fiber), 1g pro.

FROZEN KEY LIME DELIGHT

In the middle of summer, nothing hits the spot quite like this sublime Key lime dessert. Cold, creamy and tart, it looks like sunshine.
—Melissa Millwood, Lyman, SC

Prep: 1 hour + freezing **Makes:** 8 servings

- 1 cup all-purpose flour
- ½ cup salted cashews, chopped
- ½ cup sweetened shredded coconut
- ¼ cup packed light brown sugar
- ½ cup butter, melted
- 2 cups heavy whipping cream
- 1½ cups sweetened condensed milk
- 1 cup Key lime juice
- 3 tsp. grated Key lime zest
- 1 tsp. vanilla extract
  Optional: Whipped cream and Key lime slices

1. Preheat oven to 350°. In a small bowl, combine flour, cashews, coconut and brown sugar. Stir in butter. Sprinkle into a greased 15x10x1-in. baking pan. Bake for 20-25 minutes or until golden brown, stirring once. Cool on a wire rack.
2. Meanwhile, in a large bowl, combine cream, milk, lime juice, zest and vanilla. Refrigerate until chilled.
3. Fill cylinder of an ice cream freezer two-thirds full; freeze according to the manufacturer's directions.
4. Sprinkle half of the cashew mixture into an ungreased 11x7-in. dish. Spread ice cream over top; sprinkle with remaining cashew mixture. Cover and freeze 4 hours or until firm. Garnish servings with whipped cream and lime slices if desired.
1 piece: 672 cal., 46g fat (27g sat. fat), 131mg chol., 258mg sod., 60g carb. (42g sugars, 1g fiber), 9g pro.

CHOCOLATE-HAZELNUT CHEESECAKE PIE

I first prepared an Italian-style cheese pie years ago. When I added a chocolate-hazelnut topping, it proved so popular that I had to give out copies of the recipe.
—Steve Meredith, Streamwood, IL

- -

Prep: 25 min. • **Bake:** 30 min. + chilling
Makes: 8 servings

2   pkg. (8 oz. each) cream cheese, softened
½   cup sugar
½   cup mascarpone cheese
¼   cup sour cream
1   tsp. lime juice
1   tsp. vanilla extract
2   large eggs, room temperature, lightly beaten
1   chocolate crumb crust (9 in.)

TOPPING
½   cup semisweet chocolate chips
⅓   cup heavy whipping cream
½   tsp. vanilla extract
    Whole or chopped hazelnuts, toasted

1. Preheat oven to 350°. In a large bowl, beat cream cheese and sugar until smooth. Beat in mascarpone cheese, sour cream, lime juice and vanilla. Add eggs; beat on low speed just until blended. Pour into crust. Place on a baking sheet.

2. Bake 30-35 minutes or until center is almost set. Cool 1 hour on a wire rack.

3. Meanwhile, for topping, place chocolate chips in a small bowl. In a small saucepan, bring cream just to a boil. Pour over chips; stir with a whisk until smooth. Stir in the vanilla. Cool to room temperature or until mixture thickens to a spreading consistency, stirring occasionally.

4. Spread chocolate mixture over pie; refrigerate overnight. Just before serving, top with hazelnuts.

1 piece: 590 cal., 47g fat (25g sat. fat), 152mg chol., 319mg sod., 38g carb. (28g sugars, 1g fiber), 9g pro.

LEMON LAYER CAKE

This citrusy cake with a luscious cream cheese frosting will garner plenty of applause. The flavor, a duet of sweet and tangy notes, really sings.
—Summer Goddard, Springfield, VA

Prep: 35 min. • **Bake:** 25 min. + cooling
Makes: 12 servings

- 1 cup butter, softened
- 1½ cups sugar
- 2 large eggs, room temperature
- 3 large egg yolks, room temperature
- 1 Tbsp. grated lemon zest
- 2 Tbsp. lemon juice
- ¾ cup sour cream
- ¼ cup 2% milk
- 2½ cups all-purpose flour
- 1 tsp. salt
- 1 tsp. baking powder
- ½ tsp. baking soda

SYRUP
- ½ cup sugar
- ½ cup lemon juice

FROSTING
- 2 pkg. (8 oz. each) cream cheese, softened
- 1 cup butter, softened
- 4 cups confectioners' sugar
- 1½ tsp. lemon juice
- ⅛ tsp. salt
  Optional: Lemon slices or edible flowers

1. Preheat oven to 350°. Line bottoms of 2 greased 9-in. round baking pans with parchment; grease parchment.

2. Cream butter and sugar until light and fluffy, 5-7 minutes. Add eggs and egg yolks, 1 at a time, beating well after each addition. Beat in lemon zest and juice. In a small bowl, mix sour cream and milk. In another bowl, whisk together flour, salt, baking powder and baking soda; add to creamed mixture alternately with sour cream mixture.

3. Transfer to prepared pans. Bake until a toothpick inserted in center comes out clean, 24-28 minutes. Cool in pans for 10 minutes before removing to wire racks; remove parchment. Cool slightly.

4. For syrup, in a small saucepan, combine the sugar and lemon juice. Bring to a boil; cook until liquid is reduced by half. Cool completely.

5. For frosting, beat cream cheese and butter until smooth; beat in confectioners' sugar, lemon juice and salt until blended.

6. Using a long serrated knife, cut each cake horizontally in half. Brush layers with warm syrup; cool completely.

7. Place 1 cake layer on a serving plate; spread with 1 cup frosting. Repeat layers twice. Top with remaining cake layer. Frost top and sides with remaining frosting. If desired, top with lemon slices or edible flowers. Refrigerate leftovers.

1 slice: 841 cal., 48g fat (30g sat. fat), 219mg chol., 656mg sod., 96g carb. (72g sugars, 1g fiber), 8g pro.

CARROT CAKE SHORTBREAD

I really love carrot cake and wanted to make a cookie that had the same flavors, and these comforting cookies are are just the ticket! Cinnamon, maple and vanilla make them perfect for the holidays.
—Elisabeth Larsen, Pleasant Grove, UT

Prep: 35 min. + chilling
Bake: 15 min./batch + cooling
Makes: 4 dozen

- 1 cup butter, softened
- ½ cup packed brown sugar
- ¼ cup grated carrot
- 1 tsp. vanilla extract
- 2 cups all-purpose flour
- 1 tsp. ground cinnamon
- ¼ tsp. salt

ICING
- ½ cup confectioners' sugar
- ¼ cup maple syrup
- ½ cup finely chopped walnuts, toasted

1. In a large bowl, cream butter and brown sugar until light and fluffy, 5-7 minutes. Beat in carrot and vanilla. In another bowl, whisk flour, cinnamon and salt; gradually beat into creamed mixture.

2. Divide dough in half. Shape each into a disk; wrap in plastic. Refrigerate 1 hour or until firm enough to roll.

3. Preheat oven to 325°. On a lightly floured surface, roll each portion of dough to ¼-in. thickness. Cut with a floured 1¾-in. fluted round cookie cutter. Place 1 in. apart on greased baking sheets.

4. Bake 12-14 minutes or until edges are light brown. (For a crisper texture, bake cookies 13-15 minutes.) Remove from pans to wire racks to cool completely.

5. In a small bowl, mix confectioners' sugar and maple syrup until smooth; drizzle over cookies. Sprinkle with walnuts. Let stand until set.

1 cookie: 79 cal., 5g fat (3g sat. fat), 10mg chol., 44mg sod., 9g carb. (5g sugars, 0 fiber), 1g pro.

PATRIOTIC FROZEN DELIGHT

My husband and I pick lots of fruit at the berry farms in the area, then we freeze our harvest to enjoy all year long. This frozen dessert showcases blueberries and strawberries and has a refreshing lemon flavor.
—Bernice Russ, Bladenboro, NC

Prep: 10 min. + freezing • **Makes:** 12 servings

- 1 can (14 oz.) sweetened condensed milk
- ⅓ cup lemon juice
- 2 tsp. grated lemon zest
- 2 cups plain yogurt
- 2 cups miniature marshmallows
- ½ cup chopped pecans
- 1 cup sliced fresh strawberries
- 1 cup fresh blueberries

In a bowl, combine milk, lemon juice and zest. Stir in yogurt, marshmallows and pecans. Spread half into an ungreased 11x7-in. dish. Sprinkle with half of the strawberries and blueberries. Cover with the remaining yogurt mixture; top with remaining berries. Cover and freeze until firm. Remove from freezer 15-20 minutes before serving.

1 piece: 185 cal., 4g fat (0 sat. fat), 3mg chol., 71mg sod., 34g carb. (0 sugars, 0 fiber), 6g pro. **Diabetic exchanges:** 1 starch, 1 fruit, 1 fat.

CLASSIC LEMON MERINGUE PIE

Love lemon meringue pie? This is the only recipe you'll ever need. The flaky, tender, made-from-scratch crust is worth the effort.

—Lee Bremson, Kansas City, MO

Prep: 30 min. • **Bake:** 25 min. + chilling
Makes: 8 servings

1⅓ cups all-purpose flour
½ tsp. salt
½ cup shortening
1 to 3 Tbsp. cold water

FILLING
1¼ cups sugar
¼ cup cornstarch
3 Tbsp. all-purpose flour
¼ tsp. salt
1½ cups water
3 large egg yolks, lightly beaten
2 Tbsp. butter
1½ tsp. grated lemon zest
⅓ cup lemon juice
MERINGUE
½ cup sugar, divided
1 Tbsp. cornstarch
½ cup cold water
4 large egg whites
¾ tsp. vanilla extract

1. In a small bowl, combine flour and salt; cut in shortening until crumbly. Gradually add 3 Tbsp. cold water, tossing with a fork until dough forms a ball.

2. Roll out pastry to fit a 9-in. pie plate. Transfer pastry to pie plate. Trim to ½ in. beyond edge of plate; flute edges. Bake at 425° for 12-15 minutes or until lightly browned.

3. Place egg whites in a large bowl; let stand at room temperature for 30 minutes. Meanwhile, in a large saucepan, combine the sugar, cornstarch, flour and salt. Gradually stir in water until smooth. Cook and stir over medium-high heat until thickened and bubbly. Reduce heat; cook and stir 2 minutes longer.

4. Remove from the heat. Stir a small amount of hot filling into egg yolks; return all to the pan, stirring constantly. Bring to a gentle boil; cook and stir 2 minutes longer. Remove from the heat. Gently stir in butter and lemon zest. Gradually stir in lemon juice just until combined. Pour into the crust.

5. For meringue, in a saucepan, combine 2 Tbsp. sugar and cornstarch. Gradually stir in cold water. Cook and stir over medium heat until mixture is clear. Transfer to a bowl; cool.

6. Beat egg whites and vanilla until soft peaks form. Gradually beat in the remaining sugar, 1 Tbsp. at a time. Beat in cornstarch mixture on high until stiff glossy peaks form and sugar is dissolved. Spread evenly over hot filling, sealing edges to crust.

7. Bake at 350° for 25 minutes or until the meringue is golden brown. Cool on a wire rack for 1 hour. Refrigerate for at least 3 hours before serving.

1 piece: 444 cal., 17g fat (5g sat. fat), 87mg chol., 282mg sod., 68g carb. (43g sugars, 1g fiber), 5g pro.

PINK VELVET CUPCAKES

My daughter loves all things pink, so this recipe was just right for her birthday. Even my teenage son (not a fan of pink) ate his share, too.
—Paulette Smith, Winston-Salem, NC

Prep: 30 min. + chilling
Bake: 25 min. + cooling • **Makes:** 2 dozen

- 1 **cup butter, softened**
- 1¼ **cups sugar**
- ⅛ **tsp. pink paste food coloring**
- 3 **large eggs, room temperature**
- 1 **tsp. vanilla extract**
- 2½ **cups all-purpose flour**
- 1½ **tsp. baking powder**
- ¼ **tsp. baking soda**
- ¼ **tsp. salt**
- 1 **cup buttermilk**

WHITE CHOCOLATE GANACHE

- 2 **cups white baking chips**
- ½ **cup heavy whipping cream**
- 1 **Tbsp. butter**
  Pink coarse sugar and sugar pearls

1. In a large bowl, cream the butter, sugar and food coloring until light and fluffy, 5-7 minutes. Add eggs, 1 at a time, beating well after each addition. Beat in vanilla. Combine the flour, baking powder, baking soda and salt; add to creamed mixture alternately with buttermilk, beating well after each addition.

2. Fill 24 paper-lined muffin cups two-thirds full. Bake at 350° for 23-27 minutes or until a toothpick inserted in the center comes out clean. Cool for 10 minutes before removing from pans to wire racks to cool completely.

3. Meanwhile, place white chips in a small bowl. In a small saucepan, bring cream just to a boil. Pour over chips; whisk until smooth. Stir in butter. Transfer to a large bowl. Chill for 30 minutes, stirring once.

4. Beat on high speed for 2-3 minutes or until soft peaks form and frosting is light and fluffy. Frost cupcakes. Top cupcakes with coarse sugar and sugar pearls. Store in the refrigerator.

1 cupcake: 266 cal., 15g fat (9g sat. fat), 57mg chol., 154mg sod., 29g carb. (20g sugars, 0 fiber), 3g pro.

RASPBERRY MOSCOW MULE CAKE

This Moscow mule cake is my favorite one to make from scratch. It's so moist and flavorful, and it reminds me of my favorite cocktail.
—Becky Hardin, St. Peters, MO

Prep: 25 min. • **Bake:** 70 min. + cooling
Makes: 16 servings

- 1½ cups unsalted butter, softened
- 2¾ cups sugar
- 5 large eggs, room temperature
- 1 Tbsp. vanilla extract
- 3 cups cake flour
- ½ tsp. salt
- 1 cup alcoholic raspberry ginger beer or nonalcoholic plain ginger beer
- 2 cups fresh raspberries

SYRUP
- ½ cup alcoholic raspberry ginger beer or nonalcoholic plain ginger beer
- ½ cup sugar
- ¼ cup lime juice

GLAZE
- 1½ cups confectioners' sugar
- 2 to 3 Tbsp. lime juice

1. Preheat oven to 325°. Grease and flour a 10-in. fluted tube pan.
2. In a large bowl, cream butter and sugar until light and fluffy, 5-7 minutes. Add eggs, 1 at a time, beating well after each addition. Beat in vanilla. In another bowl, whisk cake flour and salt; add to creamed mixture alternately with ginger beer, beating well after each addition (mixture may appear curdled).
3. Gently fold raspberries into batter; pour into prepared pan. Bake until a toothpick inserted in center comes out clean, 70-80 minutes. Meanwhile, in a small saucepan, bring syrup ingredients to a boil. Reduce heat; simmer 10 minutes. Cool slightly.
4. Poke holes in warm cake using a fork or wooden skewer. Slowly spoon syrup over cake. Cool 15 minutes before removing from pan to a wire rack; cool completely.
5. For glaze, in a small bowl, mix the confectioners' sugar and enough lime juice to reach desired consistency; pour over cake. Let stand until set. If desired, top with additional fresh raspberries.
Note: For testing, we used Crabbie's Raspberry Alcoholic Ginger Beer.
1 slice: 488 cal., 19g fat (11g sat. fat), 104mg chol., 100mg sod., 75g carb. (53g sugars, 1g fiber), 5g pro.

MAKE AHEAD
BLACKBERRY NECTARINE PIE

Blackberries are a big crop in my area, so I've made this pretty double-fruit pie many times. I can always tell when my husband wants me to make it because he brings home berries that he picked behind his office.
—Linda Chinn, Enumclaw, WA

Prep: 25 min. + chilling • **Makes:** 8 servings

- ¼ cup cornstarch
- 1 can (12 oz.) frozen apple juice concentrate, thawed
- 2 cups fresh blackberries, divided
- 5 medium nectarines, peeled and coarsely chopped
- 1 reduced-fat graham cracker crust (8 in.)
  Reduced-fat whipped topping, optional

1. In a small saucepan, mix cornstarch and apple juice concentrate until smooth. Bring to a boil. Add ½ cup blackberries; cook and stir 2 minutes or until thickened. Remove from heat.
2. In a large bowl, toss nectarines with remaining blackberries; transfer to crust. Pour apple juice mixture over fruit (crust will be full). Refrigerate, covered, 8 hours or overnight. If desired, serve pie with whipped topping.
1 piece: 240 cal., 4g fat (1g sat. fat), 0 chol., 106mg sod., 50g carb. (32g sugars, 4g fiber), 3g pro.

MALTED MILK COOKIES

My family loves anything made with malted milk, so these are a favorite!
—Nancy Foust, Stoneboro, PA

Prep: 40 min.
Bake: 10 min./batch + cooling
Makes: 4 dozen

- 1 cup butter, softened
- 2 cups packed brown sugar
- 2 large eggs, room temperature
- ⅓ cup sour cream
- 2 tsp. vanilla extract
- 4¾ cups all-purpose flour
- ¾ cup malted milk powder
- 2 tsp. baking powder
- ½ tsp. baking soda
- ½ tsp. salt

FROSTING
- 3 cups confectioners' sugar
- ½ cup malted milk powder
- ⅓ cup butter, softened
- 1½ tsp. vanilla extract
- 3 to 4 Tbsp. 2% milk
- 2 cups coarsely chopped malted milk balls

1. Preheat oven to 350°. In a large bowl, cream butter and brown sugar until light and fluffy, 5-7 minutes. Beat in eggs, sour cream and vanilla. In another bowl, whisk flour, milk powder, baking powder, baking soda and salt; gradually beat into the creamed mixture.
2. Divide dough into 3 portions. On a lightly floured surface, roll each to ¼-in. thickness. Cut with a floured 2½-in. round cookie cutter. Place 2 in. apart on parchment-lined baking sheets.
3. Bake until edges are light brown, 10-12 minutes. Remove from pans to wire racks to cool completely.
4. For frosting, beat confectioners' sugar, malted milk powder, butter, vanilla and enough milk for spreading consistency. Frost cookies. Sprinkle with candies.
1 cookie: 189 cal., 6g fat (4g sat. fat), 22mg chol., 131mg sod., 31g carb. (20g sugars, 0 fiber), 2g pro.

TRIPLE FUDGE BROWNIES

When you're in a hurry to make dessert, here's a mix of mixes that's convenient and quick. The result is a big pan of very rich, fudgy brownies. Friends who ask for the recipe are amazed that it's so easy.
—Denise Nebel, Wayland, IA

Prep: 10 min. • **Bake:** 30 min.
Makes: 4 dozen

- 1 pkg. (3.9 oz.) instant chocolate pudding mix
- 1 pkg. chocolate cake mix (regular size)
- 2 cups semisweet chocolate chips
  Confectioners' sugar
  Vanilla ice cream, optional

1. Prepare pudding according to package directions. Whisk in dry cake mix. Stir in chocolate chips.
2. Pour into a greased 15x10x1-in. baking pan. Bake at 350° until the top springs back when lightly touched, 30-35 minutes.
3. Dust with confectioners' sugar. Serve with ice cream if desired.
1 brownie: 91 cal., 3g fat (2g sat. fat), 1mg chol., 86mg sod., 15g carb. (10g sugars, 1g fiber), 1g pro.

BRING IT
These frosting-free brownies are a shoo-in for their simplicity. To dress 'em up for the kids, tote along their favorite sundae toppings, like whipped cream in a can, ice cream, maraschino cherries, sprinkles and sauces. Good times!

MACAROON BARS

Guests will never recognize the crescent dough that goes into these bars. You can make these treats in no time.
—Carolyn Kyzer, Alexander, AR

Prep: 10 min. • **Bake:** 30 min. + cooling
Makes: 3 dozen

3¼ cups sweetened shredded coconut, divided
1 can (14 oz.) sweetened condensed milk
1 tsp. almond extract
1 tube (8 oz.) refrigerated crescent rolls

1. Sprinkle 1½ cups coconut into a well-greased 13x9-in. baking pan. Combine milk and extract; drizzle half over the coconut. Unroll crescent dough into 1 long rectangle; seal seams and perforations. Place in pan. Drizzle with remaining milk mixture; sprinkle with remaining coconut.
2. Bake at 350° for 30-35 minutes or until golden brown. Cool completely on a wire rack before cutting. Refrigerate leftovers.
1 bar: 103 cal., 5g fat (4g sat. fat), 4mg chol., 85mg sod., 12g carb. (9g sugars, 0 fiber), 2g pro.

★ ★ ★ ★ ★ **READER REVIEW**

"I poured the sweetened condensed milk into a measuring glass for mixing in the almond extract—then it was easy to dispense half per layer. I also sprinkled almond slices on top before baking. It looked and tasted delicious!"

MRS. COWAN TASTEOFHOME.COM

CHOCOLATE CROISSANT BREAD PUDDING

I didn't start off as a big fan of bread puddings, but one time I found myself with a large surplus of croissants and decided to get fancy with them. This dark chocolate croissant bread pudding became special to me the minute I tasted it.
—Jenn Tidwell, Fair Oaks, CA

Prep: 20 min. + standing • **Bake:** 40 min.
Makes: 9 servings

4 large eggs, lightly beaten
1½ cups 2% milk
½ cup sugar
½ cup orange juice
1 Tbsp. grated orange zest
1 tsp. ground cinnamon
1 tsp. vanilla extract
¼ tsp. ground nutmeg
Dash salt
½ cup dark chocolate chips
4 croissants, cut into 1-in. pieces

1. Preheat oven to 350°. In a large bowl, whisk the first 9 ingredients until blended. Stir in chocolate chips. Gently stir in the croissants; let stand until bread is softened, about 15 minutes.
2. Transfer to a greased 8-in. square baking dish. Bake until puffed and golden, and a knife inserted near the center comes out clean, 40-45 minutes. Serve warm.
1 serving: 270 cal., 12g fat (7g sat. fat), 103mg chol., 190mg sod., 35g carb. (24g sugars, 2g fiber), 7g pro.

ORANGE BAVARIAN
This refreshing treat is perfect after a hearty meal.
—Adeline Piscitelli, Sayreville, NJ

- -

Prep: 15 min. + chilling
Makes: 14 servings

- 3 pkg. (3 oz. each) orange gelatin
- 2¼ cups boiling water
- 1 cup sour cream
- 1 qt. orange sherbet, softened
- 1 can (11 oz.) mandarin oranges, drained and halved
  Red and green grapes, optional

Dissolve gelatin in water. Stir in sour cream until smooth. Mix in sherbet until melted. Chill until partially set. Fold in oranges. Pour into a 7-cup ring mold coated with cooking spray. Cover and chill 8 hours or overnight. Just before serving, unmold onto a platter; fill the center with grapes if desired.

1 piece: 126 cal., 4g fat (2g sat. fat), 13mg chol., 43mg sod., 22g carb. (20g sugars, 0 fiber), 2g pro.

STRAWBERRY POKE CAKE
Strawberry shortcake takes on a wonderful new twist with this super simple recipe. Strawberries liven up each pretty slice.
—Mary Jo Griggs, West Bend, WI

- -

Prep: 25 min. • **Bake:** 25 min. + chilling
Makes: 12 servings

- 1 pkg. white cake mix (regular size)
- 1¼ cups water
- 2 large eggs, room temperature
- ¼ cup canola oil
- 2 pkg. (10 oz. each) frozen sweetened sliced strawberries, thawed
- 2 pkg. (3 oz. each) strawberry gelatin
- 1 carton (12 oz.) frozen whipped topping, thawed, divided
  Fresh strawberries, optional

1. In a large bowl, combine the cake mix, water, eggs and oil; beat on low speed for 30 seconds. Beat on medium for 2 minutes.
2. Pour into 2 greased and floured 9-in. round baking pans. Bake at 350° until a toothpick inserted in the center comes out clean, 25-35 minutes. Cool for 10 minutes; remove from pans to wire racks to cool completely.
3. Using a serrated knife, level tops of cakes if necessary. Return layers, top side up, to 2 clean 9-in. round baking pans. Pierce cakes with a meat fork or wooden skewer at ½-in. intervals.
4. Drain juice from strawberries into a 2-cup measuring cup; refrigerate berries. Add water to juice to measure 2 cups; pour into a small saucepan. Bring to a boil; stir in gelatin until dissolved. Chill for 30 minutes. Gently spoon over each cake layer. Chill for 2-3 hours.
5. Dip bottom of 1 pan into warm water for 10 seconds. Invert cake onto a serving platter. Top with chilled strawberries and 1 cup whipped topping. Place second cake layer over topping.
6. Frost cake with the remaining whipped topping. Chill for at least 1 hour. Serve with fresh berries if desired.

1 piece: 376 cal., 14g fat (7g sat. fat), 35mg chol., 301mg sod., 56g carb. (37g sugars, 1g fiber), 4g pro.

LAYERED CHOCOLATE-RASPBERRY TRIANGLES

My chocolaty triangles layered with raspberry jam are a must during the holiday season. The cakelike bars look festive, and one batch goes a long way.
—Mary Ann Lee, Clifton Park, NY

Prep: 45 min. • **Bake:** 15 min. + standing
Makes: 4 dozen

> 6   **large eggs, separated**
> 1½ **cups butter, softened**
> 1½ **cups sugar**
> 2   **tsp. vanilla extract**
> 2½ **cups all-purpose flour**
> 3   **oz. unsweetened chocolate, melted and cooled slightly**
> 3   **oz. white baking chocolate, melted and cooled slightly**
> ¼ **cup seedless raspberry jam**
> 1   **cup (6 oz.) semisweet chocolate chips, melted**
>   **White baking chocolate shavings**

1. Place egg whites in a large bowl; let stand at room temperature 30 minutes. Preheat oven to 350°. Line bottoms of 2 greased matching 13x9-in. baking pans with parchment; grease papers.
2. In a large bowl, cream butter and sugar until light and fluffy, 5-7 minutes.
3. Add egg yolks, 1 at a time, beating well after each addition. Add vanilla. Stir in flour.
4. With clean beaters, beat egg whites on medium speed until stiff peaks form. Fold into batter. Transfer half of the batter to another bowl. Fold melted unsweetened chocolate into 1 bowl; spread into a prepared pan. Fold melted white chocolate into remaining batter; spread into second prepared pan.
5. Bake 12-16 minutes or until a toothpick inserted in center comes out clean. Cool 5 minutes. Invert onto wire racks. Remove parchment; cool completely.

6. Transfer chocolate layer to a baking sheet lined with a large piece of plastic wrap. Spread jam over top; place white chocolate layer over jam. Wrap securely with plastic wrap. Set a cutting board or heavy baking pan over top to flatten layers. Let stand at room temperature 3-4 hours (Or, refrigerate overnight and return to room temperature before continuing.)
7. Unwrap cake; place on a cutting board. Spread top with melted chocolate chips. Top with white chocolate shavings. Let stand until set. Trim edges with a knife. Cut into 24 squares; cut squares diagonally in half.
1 triangle: 158 cal., 9g fat (5g sat. fat), 42mg chol., 55mg sod., 18g carb. (11g sugars, 1g fiber), 2g pro.

BUTTERY LEMON SANDWICH COOKIES

My grandson approves of these lemony sandwich cookies made with crackers and prepared frosting. Decorate with whatever sprinkles you like.
—Nancy Foust, Stoneboro, PA

Prep: 20 min. + standing • **Makes:** 2½ dozen

> ¾ **cup lemon frosting**
> 60 **Ritz crackers**
> 24 **oz. white candy coating, melted**
>   **Nonpareils, jimmies or sprinkles, optional**

Spread frosting on bottoms of half of the crackers; cover with remaining crackers. Dip sandwiches in melted candy coating; allow excess to drip off. Place on waxed paper; decorate as desired. Let stand until set. Store in an airtight container in the refrigerator.
1 sandwich cookie: 171 cal., 9g fat (6g sat. fat), 0 chol., 70mg sod., 23g carb. (19g sugars, 0 fiber), 0 pro.

PEANUT BUTTER BUNDT CAKE

This peanut butter cake with frosting is heavenly to me. I use smooth peanut butter, but crunchy would work, too.
—Karen Holt, Rock Hill, SC

Prep: 15 min. • **Bake:** 75 min. + cooling
Makes: 16 servings

1	cup butter, softened
½	cup creamy peanut butter
1	cup sugar
1	cup packed brown sugar
5	large eggs, room temperature
3	tsp. vanilla extract
3	cups all-purpose flour
½	tsp. salt
½	tsp. baking powder
¼	tsp. baking soda
1	cup 2% milk

FROSTING

¼	cup butter, softened
2	Tbsp. creamy peanut butter
2	cups confectioners' sugar
1	to 3 Tbsp. 2% milk

1. Preheat oven to 325°. Grease and flour a 10-in. fluted tube pan.

2. In a large bowl, cream butter, peanut butter and sugars until light and fluffy, 5-7 minutes. Add eggs, 1 at a time, beating well after each addition. Beat in vanilla. In another bowl, whisk flour, salt, baking powder and baking soda; add to creamed mixture alternately with milk, beating after each addition just until combined. Transfer to prepared pan.

3. Bake until a toothpick inserted in center comes out clean, 65-75 minutes. Cool in pan 5 minutes before removing to a wire rack to cool completely.

4. For the frosting, in a large bowl, beat butter, peanut butter, sugar and salt. Beat in enough of the milk to achieve desired consistency. Spread over top of cake.

1 piece: 465 cal., 22g fat (11g sat. fat), 98mg chol., 300mg sod., 62g carb. (43g sugars, 1g fiber), 7g pro.

CHERRY CHEWBILEES

This is a good dish to carry to potlucks and parties. It's a hit at home, too—my husband rates it as one of his favorites.
—Debbi Smith, Crossett, AR

Prep: 25 min. • **Bake:** 30 min. +chilling
Makes: 20 servings

1¼	cups all-purpose flour
½	cup packed brown sugar
½	cup butter-flavored shortening
1	cup chopped walnuts, divided
½	cup sweetened shredded coconut

FILLING

2	pkg. (8 oz. each) cream cheese, softened
⅔	cup sugar
2	large eggs, room temperature
2	tsp. vanilla extract
2	cans (21 oz. each) cherry pie filling

1. Preheat oven to 350°. Line a 13x9-in. baking pan with foil, letting ends extend up sides; grease foil.

2. Combine flour and brown sugar; cut in shortening until fine crumbs form. Stir in ½ cup nuts and coconut. Set aside ½ cup crumb mixture for topping. Press remaining mixture into prepared pan. Bake until lightly browned, 12-15 minutes.

3. Meanwhile, for filling, beat cream cheese, sugar, eggs and vanilla until smooth. Spread over hot crust. Bake 15 minutes. Spread pie filling on top. Combine remaining nuts and reserved crumbs; sprinkle over cherries. Bake 15 minutes more. Cool completely on a wire rack. Refrigerate until chilled. Lifting with foil, remove mixture from pan. Cut into bars.

1 piece: 251 cal., 14g fat (5g sat. fat), 34mg chol., 54mg sod., 29g carb. (20g sugars, 1g fiber), 4g pro.

Brownie Batter Dip
page 250

No-Cook Recipe Rescue

When you're in a hurry, sometimes you need an easy recipe that doesn't require any cooking at all. Here you'll find more than two dozen dishes that require just a quick stir or a little dicing or slicing.

NO-BAKE COOKIE BUTTER BLOSSOMS

Chewy and sweet, these easy treats mix Rice Krispies, cookie spread and chocolate in an unforgettable spin on an old favorite.
—Jessie Sarrazin, Livingston, MT

- -

Prep: 25 min. + standing
Makes: about 2½ dozen

1	cup Biscoff creamy cookie spread
½	cup corn syrup
3	cups Rice Krispies
32	milk chocolate kisses

In a large saucepan, combine cookie spread and corn syrup. Cook and stir over low heat until blended. Remove from heat; stir in the Rice Krispies until coated. Shape level tablespoons of mixture into balls; place onto waxed paper. Immediately press a kiss into the center of each cookie. Let stand until set.

1 cookie: 93 cal., 4g fat (1g sat. fat), 1mg chol., 22mg sod., 14g carb. (10g sugars, 0 fiber), 1g pro.

BRING IT
The kisses make these cute and fun, but if you're really pressed for time, just press the mixture into an 11x7-in. pan instead. Let stand until firm, then cut into bars. Voila! You're on your way, with one easy-to-carry pan.

LEMON CURD TARTLETS

This has been in my party recipe collection for over 30 years and never fails to satisfy my guests. I can always rely on these fancy treats to please even the fussiest in the crowd.
—Jessica Feist, Brookfield, WI

- -

Prep: 35 min. + chilling • **Makes:** 15 tartlets

3	large eggs
1	cup sugar
½	cup lemon juice
1	Tbsp. grated lemon zest
¼	cup butter, cubed
1	pkg. (1.9 oz.) frozen miniature phyllo tart shells, thawed
	Fresh raspberries, mint leaves and/or sweetened whipped cream, optional

1. In a small heavy saucepan over medium heat, whisk the eggs, sugar, lemon juice and zest until blended. Add butter; cook, whisking constantly, until mixture is thickened and coats the back of a metal spoon. Transfer to a small bowl; cool for 10 minutes. Cover and refrigerate until chilled.

2. Just before serving, spoon lemon curd into tart shells. Garnish with raspberries, mint and/or whipped cream if desired. Refrigerate leftovers.

1 tartlet: 115 cal., 5g fat (2g sat. fat), 50mg chol., 45mg sod., 16g carb. (14g sugars, 0 fiber), 2g pro. **Diabetic exchanges:** 1 starch, 1 fat.

MOCK CHAMPAGNE PUNCH

Of all the punch recipes I've tried, I keep coming back to this pretty, fizzy one that's nonalcoholic.
—Betty Claycomb, Alverton, PA

Takes: 10 min.
Makes: 16 servings

- 1 qt. white grape juice, chilled
- 1 qt. ginger ale, chilled
  Strawberries or raspberries

Combine white grape juice and ginger ale; pour into a punch bowl or glasses. Garnish with berries.
½ cup: 58 cal., 0 fat (0 sat. fat), 0 chol., 8mg sod., 14g carb. (14g sugars, 0 fiber), 0 pro.

10-MINUTE TACO DIP

I've made this recipe more times than I can count! The colorful dip looks very appealing on a party table, and the taste never disappoints.
—Rhonda Biancardi, Blaine, MN

Takes: 10 min. • **Makes:** 12 servings

- 1 pkg. (8 oz.) cream cheese, softened
- 1 cup sour cream
- 1 carton (8 oz.) French onion dip
- 1 envelope taco seasoning
- 4 cups shredded lettuce
- 2 cups shredded cheddar cheese
- 1½ cups chopped tomatoes
  Tortilla chips

In a large bowl, beat the cream cheese, sour cream, onion dip and taco seasoning until blended. Spread onto a 12-in. round serving platter. Top with lettuce, shredded cheese and tomatoes. Serve with chips.
1 serving: 226 cal., 18g fat (12g sat. fat), 54mg chol., 578mg sod., 7g carb. (2g sugars, 1g fiber), 7g pro.

DREAMY FRUIT DIP

Everyone will love this thick cream cheese fruit dip. Serve it alongside apple wedges, pineapple chunks, strawberries and seedless grapes.
—Anna Beiler, Strasburg, PA

Takes: 10 min. • **Makes:** about 4 cups

- 1 pkg. (8 oz.) cream cheese, softened
- ½ cup butter, softened
- ½ cup marshmallow creme
- 1 carton (8 oz.) frozen whipped topping, thawed
  Assorted fresh fruit

In a small bowl, beat cream cheese and butter until smooth. Beat in marshmallow creme. Fold in whipped topping. Serve with fruit. Store in the refrigerator.
2 Tbsp.: 75 cal., 6g fat (5g sat. fat), 15mg chol., 51mg sod., 3g carb. (2g sugars, 0 fiber), 1g pro.

HOW TO CUT PINEAPPLE
Cut off crown of fruit. Stand pineapple upright, and cut off the rind using a sharp knife. Cut off base. Stand pineapple upright, and cut off fruit next to, but not through, the core. Slice or cube as desired.

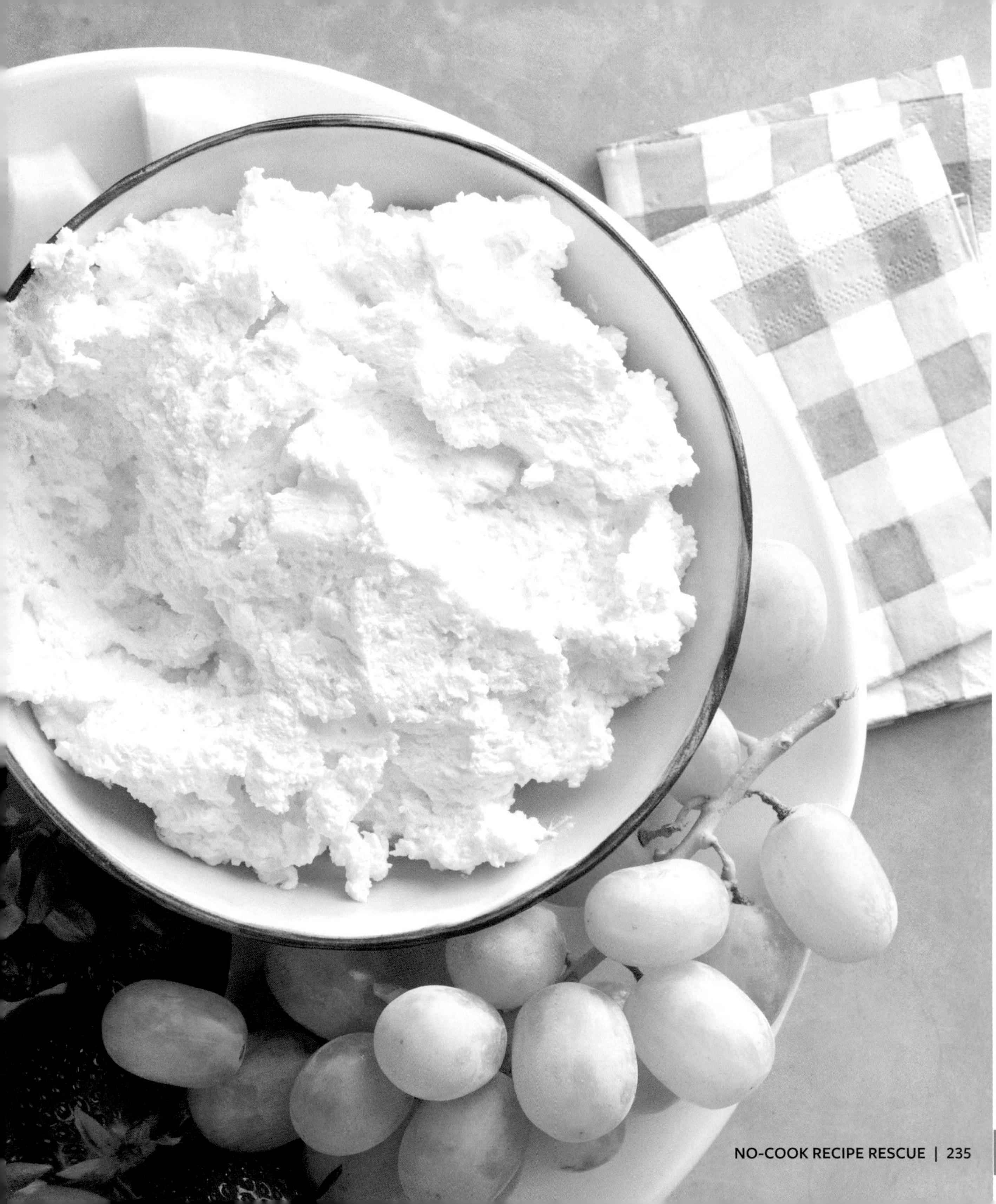

CHOCOLATE CHIP DIP

Is there a kid alive (or a kid at heart) who wouldn't gobble up this creamy dip for graham crackers? You can also use apple wedges for dipping.
—Heather Koenig, Prairie du Chien, WI

Takes: 15 min. • **Makes:** 2 cups

- 1 pkg. (8 oz.) cream cheese, softened
- ½ cup butter, softened
- ¾ cup confectioners' sugar
- 2 Tbsp. brown sugar
- 1 tsp. vanilla extract
- 1 cup miniature semisweet chocolate chips
  Graham cracker sticks

In a small bowl, beat cream cheese and butter until light and fluffy. Beat in sugars and vanilla until smooth. Stir in chocolate chips. Serve with graham cracker sticks.
2 Tbsp.: 180 cal., 14g fat (9g sat. fat), 31mg chol., 84mg sod., 14g carb. (13g sugars, 1g fiber), 2g pro.

APRICOT-RICOTTA CELERY

This filling also doubles as a dip for sliced apples. I often make it ahead so kids can help themselves to an after-school snack.
—Dorothy Reinhold, Malibu, CA

Takes: 15 min. • **Makes:** about 2 dozen

- 3 dried apricots
- ½ cup part-skim ricotta cheese
- 2 tsp. brown sugar
- ¼ tsp. grated orange zest
- ⅛ tsp. salt
- 5 celery ribs, cut into 1½-in. pieces

Place apricots in a food processor. Cover and process until finely chopped. Add the ricotta cheese, brown sugar, orange zest and salt; cover and process until blended. Stuff or pipe into celery. Chill until serving.
1 piece: 12 cal., 0 fat (0 sat. fat), 2mg chol., 25mg sod., 1g carb. (1g sugars, 0 fiber), 1g pro.

MAKE AHEAD
MAKE-AHEAD MARINATED SHRIMP

Dress up your holiday buffet table with this tasty shrimp recipe. You'll have plenty of time to enjoy your party—this elegant appetizer is that easy.
—Phyllis Schmalz, Kansas City, KS

Prep: 15 min. + marinating • **Makes:** 6 cups

- ¾ cup water
- ½ cup red wine vinegar
- ¼ cup olive oil
- ¾ tsp. salt
- ¾ tsp. minced fresh oregano or ¼ tsp. dried oregano
- ¾ tsp. minced fresh thyme or ¼ tsp. dried thyme
- 1 garlic clove, minced
- ¼ tsp. pepper
- 1½ lbs. peeled and deveined cooked shrimp (16-20 per lb.)
- 1 can (14 oz.) water-packed artichoke hearts, rinsed, drained and halved
- ½ lb. small fresh mushrooms, halved

In a large bowl, combine first 8 ingredients. Add shrimp, artichokes and mushrooms; turn to coat. Cover and refrigerate 8 hours or overnight, turning occasionally.
⅓ cup: 81 cal., 4g fat (0 sat. fat), 57mg chol., 210mg sod., 3g carb. (0 sugars, 0 fiber), 9g pro. **Diabetic exchanges:** 1 lean meat, ½ fat.

FROZEN BERRY PIE

This recipe makes two attractive pies using store-bought chocolate crumb crust. I work full time, so I like the fact that this yummy pie can be made ahead. I serve each slice with a dollop of whipped cream, a strawberry and chocolate curls.
—Awynne Thurstenson
Siloam Springs, AR

- -

Prep: 25 min. + freezing
Makes: 2 pies (6 servings each)

- 1   pkg. (8 oz.) cream cheese, softened
- 1   cup sugar
- 1   tsp. vanilla extract
- 4   cups chopped fresh strawberries
- 1   carton (12 oz.) frozen whipped topping, thawed
- ½   cup chopped pecans, toasted
- 2   chocolate crumb crusts (9 in.)

1. In a large bowl, beat the cream cheese, sugar and vanilla until smooth. Stir in the strawberries. Fold in whipped topping and pecans. Pour into crusts.
2. Cover and freeze for 3-4 hours or until firm. Remove from freezer 15-20 minutes before serving.
1 slice: 398 cal., 21g fat (11g sat. fat), 21mg chol., 192mg sod., 47g carb. (31g sugars, 3g fiber), 4g pro.

★ ★ ★ ★ ★ **READER REVIEW**

"I reccomend that when you make the pie you do not freeze it, but just put it in the refrigerator. When I make it that way, I get rave reviews. I also make a version with blueberries and a shortbread crust."

RKANGEL52 TASTEOFHOME.COM

CRANBERRY-CHILE CHEESE SPREAD

Appetizers just don't get much easier than this ritzy-looking cheese spread with its refreshing hint of lime. I turn to this recipe whenever unexpected guests drop in.
—Laurie LaClair, North Richland Hills, TX

- -

Takes: 10 min. • **Makes:** 14 servings

- 2   pkg. (8 oz. each) cream cheese, softened
- 1   can (14 oz.) whole-berry cranberry sauce
- 1   can (4 oz.) chopped green chiles, drained
- 1   green onion, sliced
- 1   Tbsp. lime juice
- ½   tsp. garlic salt
- ½   tsp. cayenne pepper
- ½   tsp. chili powder
       Assorted crackers

Place cream cheese on a serving plate. In a small bowl, combine the cranberry sauce, green chiles, onion, lime juice and spices. Spoon over cream cheese. Serve with assorted crackers.
¼ cup: 157 cal., 11g fat (7g sat. fat), 36mg chol., 200mg sod., 12g carb. (7g sugars, 1g fiber), 3g pro.

BEER DIP

*Ranch dressing mix flavors this savory dip
packed with shredded cheese and made
to go with pretzels. Once you start eating
it, you can't stop!*
—Michelle Long, New Castle, CO

Takes: 5 min. • **Makes:** 3½ cups

- 2 **pkg. (8 oz. each) cream cheese,
  softened**
- ⅓ **cup beer or nonalcoholic beer**
- 1 **envelope ranch salad dressing mix**
- 2 **cups shredded cheddar cheese**
  Pretzels

In a large bowl, beat the cream cheese,
beer and dressing mix until smooth. Stir
in cheddar cheese. Serve with pretzels.
2 Tbsp.: 89 cal., 8g fat (5g sat. fat), 26mg
chol., 177mg sod., 1g carb. (0 sugars, 0 fiber),
3g pro.

MARINATED MOZZARELLA CUBES

Jars of these marinated cheese cubes make wonderful gifts any time of the year...if you can bear to part with them!
—Arline Roggenbuck, Shawano, WI

- -

Prep: 10 min. + marinating • **Makes:** 4 cups

1	lb. mozzarella cheese, cut into 1-in. cubes
1	jar (7 oz.) roasted red peppers, drained and cut into bite-sized pieces
6	fresh thyme sprigs
2	garlic cloves, minced
1¼	cups olive oil
2	Tbsp. minced fresh rosemary
2	tsp. Italian seasoning
¼	tsp. crushed red pepper flakes
	Bread or crackers

1. In a quart jar with a tight-fitting lid, layer a third of the cheese, peppers, thyme and garlic. Repeat layers twice.

2. In a small bowl, whisk the oil, rosemary, Italian seasoning and pepper flakes. Pour into jar; seal and turn upside down. Refrigerate overnight, turning several times. Serve with bread or crackers.

¼ cup: 121 cal., 10g fat (4g sat. fat), 22mg chol., 224mg sod., 1g carb. (1g sugars, 0 fiber), 6g pro.

GREEK DELI KABOBS

For an easy Mediterranean-style appetizer, marinate broccoli and mozzarella, then skewer with sweet red peppers and salami. Everybody loves food on a stick!
—Vikki Spengler, Ocala, FL

- -

Prep: 30 min. + marinating • **Makes:** 2 dozen

1 lb. part-skim mozzarella cheese, cut into 48 cubes
24 fresh broccoli florets (about 10 oz.)
½ cup Greek vinaigrette
24 slices hard salami
2 jars (7½ oz. each) roasted sweet red peppers, drained and cut into 24 strips

1. In a shallow dish, combine cheese, broccoli and vinaigrette. Turn to coat; cover and refrigerate 4 hours or overnight.
2. Drain cheese and broccoli, reserving vinaigrette. On 24 appetizer skewers, alternately thread cheese, salami, broccoli and peppers. Brush with reserved vinaigrette.

1 kabob: 109 cal., 7g fat (4g sat. fat), 19mg chol., 374mg sod., 2g carb. (1g sugars, 0 fiber), 8g pro.

CHRISTMAS CHEESE BALL

This rich cheese spread is delicious and wonderfully attractive.

—Esther Shank, Harrisonburg, VA

Prep: 15 min. + chilling
Makes: 2 cheese balls (1½ cups each)

- 2 pkg. (8 oz. each) cream cheese, softened
- 2 cups shredded sharp cheddar cheese
- 1 Tbsp. finely chopped onion
- 1 Tbsp. diced pimientos
- 1 Tbsp. diced green pepper
- 2 tsp. Worcestershire sauce
- 1 tsp. lemon juice
  Chopped pecans, toasted
  Assorted crackers

In a large bowl, combine first 7 ingredients. Shape into two balls; roll in pecans. Cover and chill. Remove from the refrigerator 15 minutes before serving. Serve with assorted crackers.

2 Tbsp.: 70 cal., 6g fat (4g sat. fat), 21mg chol., 94mg sod., 1g carb. (0 sugars, 0 fiber), 3g pro.

AVOCADO DIP

I created this creamy dip because I could never find a guacamole that appealed to me. My husband usually doesn't even like avocado dip, but we both really enjoy this one!

—Kay Dunham, Amity, MO

Takes: 15 min. • **Makes:** 2½ cups

- 2 medium ripe avocados, peeled and pitted
- 1 pkg. (8 oz.) fat-free cream cheese
- ⅓ cup plain yogurt
- ⅓ cup picante sauce
- 1 Tbsp. lime juice
- ½ tsp. salt
- ¼ tsp. garlic powder
  Tortilla chips

In a small bowl, mash avocados and cream cheese until smooth. Stir in the yogurt, picante sauce, lime juice, salt and garlic powder. Serve with chips. Refrigerate any leftovers.

¼ cup: 73 cal., 5g fat (1g sat. fat), 2mg chol., 258mg sod., 5g carb. (1g sugars, 2g fiber), 4g pro. **Diabetic exchanges:** 1 fat.

NUTTY RICE KRISPIE COOKIES

My mom and I used to make these treats for Christmas every year. Making them with just the microwave means they're super easy and fun to mix up with the kids.

—Savanna Chapdelaine, Orlando, FL

Takes: 15 min. • **Makes:** about 2 dozen

- 1 pkg. (10 to 12 oz.) white baking chips
- ¼ cup creamy peanut butter
- 1 cup miniature marshmallows
- 1 cup Rice Krispies
- 1 cup salted peanuts

1. In a large microwave-safe bowl, melt baking chips; stir until smooth. Stir in the peanut butter until blended. Add marshmallows, Rice Krispies and peanuts. Drop by heaping tablespoonfuls onto waxed paper-lined baking sheets. Cool completely. Store in an airtight container.

1 cookie: 127 cal., 8g fat (3g sat. fat), 2mg chol., 49mg sod., 11g carb. (9g sugars, 1g fiber), 3g pro.

GRASSHOPPER CHEESECAKE

What do you get when you combine a popular mint-chocolate drink with a cheesecake? Pure delight! Garnish the top with piped whipped cream and cookie crumbs.
—Marie Rizzio, Interlochen, MI

Prep: 25 min. + chilling • **Makes:** 12 servings

- 35 chocolate wafers, finely crushed (about 1⅔ cups)
- ¼ cup butter, melted
- 1 Tbsp. plus ¾ cup sugar, divided
- 1 envelope unflavored gelatin
- ½ cup cold water
- 1 pkg. (8 oz.) cream cheese, softened
- ⅓ cup green creme de menthe
- 2 cups heavy whipping cream, whipped

1. In a small bowl, combine the cookie crumbs, butter and 1 Tbsp. sugar. Press half of mixture onto the bottom of a greased 9-in. springform pan. Refrigerate crust until chilled.

2. In a small saucepan, sprinkle gelatin over cold water; let stand for 1 minute. Heat over low heat, stirring until gelatin is completely dissolved. Cool.

3. In a large bowl, beat cream cheese and remaining sugar until fluffy. Gradually beat in gelatin mixture. Stir in creme de menthe. Set aside ½ cup whipped cream for garnish. Fold remaining whipped cream into cream cheese mixture.

4. Pour half of the filling over crust. Top with remaining crumb mixture, reserving 2 Tbsp. for garnish. Pour remaining filling into pan; garnish with reserved whipped cream. Sprinkle with reserved crumbs. Chill until set. Remove sides of pan before slicing.

Make ahead: Cheesecake may be made a few days in advance. Cover and refrigerate.

1 slice: 394 cal., 27g fat (16g sat. fat), 75mg chol., 204mg sod., 32g carb. (25g sugars, 1g fiber), 4g pro.

DELI BEEF HERO SUBS

Marinated artichokes, roasted peppers and green olives add loads of flavor to these crusty roast beef sandwiches. They're also good with pastrami or corned beef.
—Cameron Byrne, Riverton, WY

Prep: 35 min. • **Makes:** 12 servings

- 6 oz. cream cheese, softened
- ¾ cup ricotta cheese
- ¾ cup pimiento-stuffed olives
- 2 garlic cloves, peeled
- 2 French bread baguettes (10½ oz. each), split
- 1 lb. sliced deli roast beef
- 2 jars (7½ oz. each) roasted sweet red peppers, drained and julienned
- 2 jars (7½ oz. each) marinated quartered artichoke hearts, drained and chopped

1. Place the cream cheese, ricotta cheese, olives and garlic in a food processor. Cover and process until blended. Spread over cut sides of baguettes.

2. Layer bread bottoms with roast beef, peppers and artichokes; replace tops. Cut each into 6 slices.

1 serving: 426 cal., 21g fat (7g sat. fat), 43mg chol., 1000mg sod., 45g carb. (3g sugars, 3g fiber), 15g pro.

SOUTH DAKOTA FRITO TREATS

Yep, they're made with corn chips! These salty sweets were a staple after meetings at the quilt guild I belonged to when I lived in South Dakota.
—Carol Tramp, Wynot, NE

Prep: 15 min. + standing • **Makes:** 2 dozen

- 2 pkg. (9¾ oz. each) corn chips, divided
- 2 cups semisweet chocolate chips, divided
- 1 cup sugar
- 1 cup light corn syrup
- 1 cup creamy peanut butter

1. Spread 1 package of corn chips on the bottom of a greased 13x9-in. baking pan; sprinkle with 1 cup chocolate chips.

2. In a large heavy saucepan, combine sugar and corn syrup. Bring to a boil; cook and stir 1 minute. Remove from heat; stir in peanut butter. Pour half of the peanut butter mixture over chip mixture. Top with remaining corn chips and chocolate chips; drizzle with remaining peanut butter mixture. Let stand until set. Cut into bars.

1 bar: 337 cal., 18g fat (5g sat. fat), 0 chol., 196mg sod., 43g carb. (29g sugars, 2g fiber), 5g pro.

SHRIMP TARTLETS

Mini tart shells are filled with a cream cheese mixture, then topped with cocktail sauce and shrimp for this picture-perfect appetizer. You could also serve several as a quick, light meal.
—Gina Hutchison, Smithville, MO

Takes: 20 min. • **Makes:** 2½ dozen

1	pkg. (8 oz.) cream cheese, softened
1½	tsp. Worcestershire sauce
1	to 2 tsp. grated onion
1	tsp. garlic salt
⅛	tsp. lemon juice
2	pkg. (1.9 oz. each) frozen miniature phyllo tart shells
½	cup seafood cocktail sauce
30	peeled and deveined cooked shrimp (31-40 per lb.), tails removed

Optional: Minced fresh parsley and lemon wedges

1. Beat the first 5 ingredients until blended. Place tart shells on a serving plate. Fill with cream cheese mixture; top with cocktail sauce and shrimp.

2. Refrigerate until serving. If desired, sprinkle with parsley and serve with lemon wedges.

1 tartlet: 61 cal., 4g fat (2g sat. fat), 23mg chol., 143mg sod., 4g carb. (1g sugars, 0 fiber), 3g pro.

REFRIGERATOR LIME CHEESECAKE

I made this for a Father's Day party, and it was a hit! I guarantee compliments when you serve this fantastic dessert.
—Cher Anjema, Kleinburg, ON

Prep: 30 min. + chilling • **Makes:** 12 servings

- 32 soft ladyfingers, split
- 1 envelope unflavored gelatin
- ¼ cup lime juice, chilled
- 2 pkg. (8 oz. each) cream cheese, softened
- 1 cup sugar
- 6 oz. white baking chocolate, melted and cooled
- 2 tsp. grated lime zest
- 1 cup heavy whipping cream, whipped
  Fresh strawberry and lime slices, optional

1. Arrange 20 ladyfingers around the edges and 12 ladyfingers on the bottom of an ungreased 8-in. springform pan; set aside. In a small saucepan, sprinkle gelatin over cold lime juice; let stand for 1 minute. Heat over low heat, stirring until the gelatin is completely dissolved; cool.
2. Meanwhile, beat cream cheese and sugar until smooth. Gradually beat in melted chocolate, lime zest and gelatin mixture. Fold in whipped cream. Pour into prepared pan. Cover and refrigerate until set, about 3 hours. Remove sides of pan. If desired, garnish with strawberry and lime slices.
1 slice: 408 cal., 25g fat (16g sat. fat), 100mg chol., 267mg sod., 42g carb. (35g sugars, 0 fiber), 6g pro.

S'MORES NO-BAKE COOKIES

There's no easier way to get that s'mores goodness in your kitchen. Mix these cookies together and refrigerate until you're ready to share.
—*Taste of Home* Test Kitchen

Prep: 15 min. + chilling • **Makes:** 2½ dozen

- 1⅔ cups milk chocolate chips
- 2 Tbsp. canola oil
- 3 cups Golden Grahams
- 2 cups miniature marshmallows

1. In a large microwave-safe bowl, microwave chocolate chips and oil, uncovered, at 50% power until the chocolate is melted, stirring every 30 seconds, 1-1½ minutes. Stir in cereal until blended; fold in marshmallows.
2. Drop mixture by rounded tablespoonfuls onto waxed paper-lined baking sheets. Refrigerate until firm, about 15 minutes.
1 cookie: 79 cal., 4g fat (2g sat. fat), 2mg chol., 39mg sod., 11g carb. (8g sugars, 1g fiber), 1g pro.

ANTIPASTO APPETIZER SALAD

Use a slotted spoon to serve this as an appetizer with baguette toasts, or ladle it over romaine lettuce to enjoy as a salad.
—Tamra Duncan, Lincoln, AR

Prep: 10 min. + chilling • **Makes:** 6 cups

1 jar (16 oz.) roasted sweet red pepper strips, drained
½ lb. part-skim mozzarella cheese, cubed
1 cup grape tomatoes
1 jar (7½ oz.) marinated quartered artichoke hearts, undrained
1 jar (7 oz.) pimiento-stuffed olives, drained
1 can (6 oz.) pitted ripe olives, drained
1 tsp. dried basil
1 tsp. dried parsley flakes
   Pepper to taste
   Toasted baguette slices or romaine lettuce, torn

1. In a large bowl, combine the first 9 ingredients; toss to coat. Cover and refrigerate at least 4 hours before serving.
2. Serve with baguette slices or over romaine lettuce.

½ cup: 132 cal., 11g fat (3g sat. fat), 15mg chol., 651mg sod., 6g carb. (2g sugars, 1g fiber), 4g pro.

PEAR WALDORF PITAS

Here's a guaranteed table brightener for a shower, luncheon or party. Just stand back and watch these sandwiches vanish. For an eye-catching presentation, I tuck each one into a colorful folded napkin.
—Roxann Parker, Dover, DE

Prep: 20 min. + chilling
Makes: 20 mini pitas halves

- 2 medium ripe pears, diced
- ½ cup thinly sliced celery
- ½ cup halved seedless red grapes
- 2 Tbsp. finely chopped walnuts
- 2 Tbsp. lemon yogurt
- 2 Tbsp. mayonnaise
- ⅛ tsp. poppy seeds
- 20 miniature pita pocket halves
  Lettuce leaves

1. In a large bowl, combine pears, celery, grapes and walnuts. In another bowl, whisk yogurt, mayonnaise and poppy seeds. Add to pear mixture; toss to coat. Refrigerate 1 hour or overnight.

2. Line pita halves with lettuce; fill each with 2 Tbsp. pear mixture.

1 pita half: 67 cal., 2g fat (0 sat. fat), 0 chol., 86mg sod., 12g carb. (3g sugars, 1g fiber), 2g pro. **Diabetic exchanges:** 1 starch.

BROWNIE BATTER DIP

I'm all about the sweeter side of dips, and this brownie batter one pretty much fits in with my life's philosophy: Chocolate makes anything better. Grab some fruit, cookies or salty snacks and start dunking.
—Mel Gunnell, Boise, ID

Takes: 10 min. • **Makes:** 2½ cups

- 1   pkg. (8 oz.) cream cheese, softened
- ¼   cup butter, softened
- 2   cups confectioners' sugar
- ⅓   cup baking cocoa
- ¼   cup 2% milk
- 2   Tbsp. brown sugar
- 1   tsp. vanilla extract
    M&M's minis, optional
    Animal crackers, pretzels and/or sliced apples

In a large bowl, beat cream cheese and butter until smooth. Beat in confectioners' sugar, cocoa, milk, brown sugar and vanilla extract until smooth. If desired, sprinkle with M&M's minis. Serve with dippers of your choice.

2 Tbsp.: 117 cal., 6g fat (4g sat. fat), 19mg chol., 62mg sod., 15g carb. (14g sugars, 0 fiber), 1g pro.

CUCUMBER PARTY SANDWICHES

This is one of my favorite appetizers. We have lots of pig roasts here in Kentucky, and these small sandwiches are perfect to serve while the pig is cooking.
—Rebecca Rose, Mount Washington, KY

Prep: 20 min. + standing • **Makes:** 2½ dozen

- 1 pkg. (8 oz.) cream cheese, softened
- 2 Tbsp. mayonnaise
- 2 tsp. Italian salad dressing mix
- 30 slices cocktail rye or pumpernickel bread
- 60 thin cucumber slices
  Optional: Fresh dill sprigs and slivered red pearl onions

1. Beat cream cheese, mayonnaise and dressing mix until blended; let stand for 30 minutes.

2. Spread cream cheese mixture on bread. Top each with 2 cucumber slices and, if desired, dill sprigs and red onion slivers. Refrigerate, covered, until serving.

1 open-faced sandwich: 53 cal., 4g fat (2g sat. fat), 8mg chol., 92mg sod., 4g carb. (1g sugars, 1g fiber), 1g pro.

FOCACCIA SANDWICHES

Slices of this pretty sandwich make any casual get-together more speical. Add or change ingredients to your taste.
—Peggy Woodward, Shullsburg, WI

Takes: 15 min. • **Makes:** 2 dozen

⅓ cup mayonnaise
1 can (4¼ oz.) chopped ripe olives, drained
1 focaccia bread (about 12 oz.), split
4 romaine leaves
¼ lb. shaved deli ham
1 medium sweet red pepper, thinly sliced into rings
¼ lb. shaved deli turkey
1 large tomato, thinly sliced
¼ lb. thinly sliced hard salami
1 jar (7 oz.) roasted sweet red peppers, drained
4 to 6 slices provolone cheese

In a small bowl, combine mayonnaise and olives; spread over the bottom half of bread. Layer with remaining ingredients; replace bread top. Cut into 24 wedges; secure with toothpicks.

1 piece: 113 cal., 6g fat (2g sat. fat), 13mg chol., 405mg sod., 9g carb. (1g sugars, 1g fiber), 5g pro.

TEST KITCHEN TIP
A rectangular-shaped focaccia bread, measuring about 12x8 in., works best for this sandwich.

PARTY CHEESE BALLS

These tangy cheese balls are guaranteed to spread cheer at your next gathering. The ingredients create a colorful presentation and a savory combination of flavors. As a grandmother who loves to cook, I send many pantry presents off to college.
—Shirley Hoerman, Nekoosa, WI

Prep: 20 min. + chilling
Makes: 2 cheese balls (1¾ cups each)

1 pkg. (8 oz.) cream cheese, softened
2 cups shredded cheddar cheese
1 jar (5 oz.) sharp American cheese spread
1 jar (5 oz.) pimiento cheese spread
3 Tbsp. finely chopped onion
1 Tbsp. lemon juice
1 tsp. Worcestershire sauce
Dash garlic salt
½ cup chopped pecans, toasted
½ cup minced fresh parsley
Assorted crackers

1. In a large bowl, beat first 8 ingredients until blended. Cover and refrigerate until easily handled, about 45 minutes.
2. Shape into 2 balls; roll in parsley and pecans. Cover and refrigerate. Remove from the refrigerator 15 minutes before serving with crackers.

2 Tbsp.: 99 cal., 9g fat (5g sat. fat), 25mg chol., 188mg sod., 2g carb. (1g sugars, 0 fiber), 4g pro.

Recipe Index